SPIRIT

Amazon Spirit

Daily Meditations for Lesbians in Recovery

Eleanor Nealy

A PERIGEE BOOK

A PERIGEE BOOK
Published by The Berkley Publishing Group
200 Madison Avenue
New York, NY 10016

Copyright © 1995 by Eleanor Nealy.

Book design by Stanley S. Drate/Folio Graphics Co., Inc.

Cover design by James R. Harris
Cover illustration by James Barkley

All rights reserved This book, or parts thereof,
may not be reproduced in any form without permission.

First edition: June 1995

Published simultaneously in Canada.

Library of Congress Cataloging-in-Publication Data

Nealy, Eleanor.
    Amazon spirit : daily meditations for lesbians in recovery /
Eleanor Nealy.
      p. cm.
    "A Perigee book."
    Includes index.
    ISBN 0-399-51940-8 (pbk.)
    1. Lesbians—Alcohol use. 2. Lesbians—Psychology. 3. Lesbians—
Religious life. 4. Recovering alcoholics—Psychology. 5. Self-
esteem in women. 6. Alcoholism—Religious aspects—Meditations.
7. Homosexuality—Religious aspects—Meditations.
8. Homophobia—Religious aspects—Meditations. 9. Devotional
calendars.
  I. Title.
HV5139.N43   1995
616.86'10651'086643—dc20
                                                                                94-39337
                                                                                    CIP

Printed in the United States of America

10 9 8 7 6 5 4 3 2 1

This book is printed on acid-free paper.

The author gratefully acknowledges permission to reprint material from the following:

Lucille Clifton. Excerpt from: "i am running into a new year," copyright © 1987 by Lucille Clifton. Reprinted from *Good Woman: Poems and a Memoir 1969–1980*, by Lucille Clifton, with permission of BOA Editions, Inc., 92 Park Ave., Brockport, NY 14420.

Joy Harjo, excerpt from "Eagle Poem" from *In Mad Love & War*, copyright © 1990 by Joy Harjo, Wesleyan University Press, by permission of the University Press of New England.

"Dream Deferred" by Langston Hughes, from *The Panther and the Lash* by Langston Hughes, copyright 1951 by Langston Hughes, by permission of Alfred A. Knopf, Inc.

Prologue from "Legacy" by Pat Parker, from *Jonestown & Other Madness*, copyright © 1985 by Pat Parker, Firebrand Books, Ithaca, New York. Used by permission of the publisher.

"the drum beats" by Victoria Lena Manyarrows, from *Piece of My Heart: A Lesbian of Colour Anthology*, copyright © 1991, SisterVision Press. Used by permission of the author.

"On Not Being Able to Imagine the Future" by Robin Becker, from *Backtalk*, copyright © 1982 by Robin Becker, Alice James Press, Cambridge, MA. Used by permission of the author.

"Stations" by Audre Lorde, from *Our Dead Behind Us*, copyright © 1986 Audre Lorde, W. W. Norton and Co., Inc. Used by permission of the publisher.

"The seven of pentacles" by Marge Piercy, from *Circles on the Water*, copyright © 1982 by Marge Piercy, by permission of Alfred A. Knopf, Inc.

"the words of a woman who breathes fire: one" by Kitty Tsui, from *Lesbian Poetry: An Anthology*, Persephone Press. Used by permission of the author.

Introduction

Most research indicates that the number of lesbians experiencing alcohol and other drug-related problems is two to three times higher than the number of heterosexual women experiencing those problems. In spite of these statistics, we remain largely invisible in mainstream substance-abuse treatment programs. Traditional recovery counseling rarely addresses either the parallel effects of our addictions and our oppression, or the particular concerns of our lives in recovery.

In treatment and in gay twelve-step meetings, we are often in the minority, with attendance and conversation dominated by men. While lesbian meetings exist in most metropolitan areas, many of us continue to struggle with isolation in recovery. Furthermore, the pervasive effects of heterosexism and homophobia force us to constantly translate what non-gay therapists, counselors, and sober peers tell us, or simply leave out significant aspects of our lives.

This book represents an attempt to fill this gap, providing a daily meditation book that speaks especially to us as lesbians and offering a recovery resource that explores the unique challenges of our sobriety. I wrote this book for myself, as much as for you. I, too, wanted a meditation book that included and celebrated my identity and pride. I, too, wanted a book that reflected the diversity of our experience as lesbians in recovery. I, too, wanted a spiritual, not religious, resource that valued and reflected my life concerns. In many ways, writing these meditations has been both a ninth- and twelfth-step exercise. It has been an opportunity for me to make amends and to "give back" some of the joys and insights I have gained in recovery. While it is written especially for lesbians in recovery from addictions, much of the material is applicable to all lesbians in our common recovery from the effects of growing up and living in a heterosexist and homophobic society.

While I was initially unsure about how to choose quotes, I quickly realized once again just how invisible we are—for every quote I found by a woman, there were hundreds by men. Finding enough quotes by visible and openly identified lesbians was even harder. In the end, I included a few quotes by men who were important to me, but drew the remainder from women's writings, using as many by lesbians as possible.

The primary effects of our addictions were self-hatred and shame, isolation and alienation. Until we learn to value and celebrate our identity as lesbians, we remain in danger of relapse. The support of a sober lesbian community is essential to healthy recovery. It is my hope that these meditations will be a resource for all of us working toward increased self-esteem, community, and affiliation. Discovering and nurturing our own "Amazon Spirit," as individuals and as a community, is the path to wholeness and integration in recovery.

While many folks have been supportive in the process of writing this book, I want to express particular gratitude to the following individuals: to Anne, Janine, Nancy, and Regina for nurturing my own recovery journey; to Jan and Leo for the beauty of "Top of the World" as a place for reflection and writing; to my colleagues at the Center and within the UFMCC for their ongoing support and encouragement; to our daughters for the joy and healing they have brought into my life; and special thanks to the woman who brings me flowers and formats my hard drive, my *compañera de vida*, Sandra, for innumerable hours of emotional support and technical assistance.

January 1

I am a new creation; action, vision, insight, and voice are mine. Creativity springs forth from my center, my energies give birth, my ideas bear fruit.
—THE REV. NANCY L. RADCLYFFE

During our addictions, we gradually lost touch with ourselves. Our ability to take action became limited. Our sense of vision and hope diminished. Our insight into ourselves and others became increasingly inaccurate. Our voice became anxious and muted. While drugs and alcohol may have sparked our energy and ideas during the early stages of our addiction, over time they numbed our creative selves, leaving us empty and powerless.

As we enter this new year in recovery, we are given a second chance at life. Each action we take fills us with new energy. Each time we speak out, our voice becomes more powerful. The hope of other sober lesbians rekindles our own vision. The experience and wisdom of others illuminates our insight and understanding.

As we stay sober over the coming year, we will become a new creation. As we allow our creativity to be rekindled, we will discover new ideas and fresh energy within us. Our continued recovery can be the source of new hope, creativity, and power for the whole lesbian community.

Today I will draw upon the energy I have found in recovery, allowing it to empower my own creative vision and voice.

January 2

> There are years that ask questions and years that answer.
> —ZORA NEALE HURSTON

None of us can predict what lies before us in this calendar year. We have at best a glimpse of the months ahead. What questions will we face? What challenges will we encounter? What relationships will end? What new ones will we begin? What new skills will we learn? What old patterns will we relinquish? What new doors will open? Will this be a year in which we ask questions, or a year of discovering answers?

Zora Neale Hurston reminds us that life is full of questions and answers. There is a rhythm to our lives, an ebb and flow of learning and growing. Questions and answers, joys and difficulties, celebrations and sorrows are a natural part of life. Accepting this rhythm allows us to move through our lives with grace and dignity. While we cannot predict the events of this year, we can choose to "go with the flow," to live gently amid the questions and the answers of our lives.

As I reflect on this new year, I will look with anticipation for the ways it will challenge and empower my recovery.

January 3

Although the connections are not always obvious, personal change is inseparable from social and political change.
—HARRIET LERNER

Our personal recovery is essential to the health of the whole lesbian community. Our personal change and growth is intimately connected to the social and political changes necessary for the empowerment of the larger lesbian community.

As we become healthy, our community becomes healthy. As we heal ourselves and one another, we heal the lesbian community. As we free ourselves from the debilitating effects of societal homophobia, we free the lesbian community. As we learn to think and feel clearly, the lesbian community becomes empowered to think and feel more fully. As we discover our strength and power, the lesbian community finds its strength and power for change.

The changes we make in our personal recovery are the foundation for changes in society. Each step we take toward health ensures the health of the whole community. A sober, healthy lesbian community is the only route to lasting social and political change.

Today I will affirm the ways my personal growth contributes to the goals of the larger lesbian community.

January 4

Women, let's not let the danger of the journey and the vastness of the territory scare us—let's look forward and open paths in these woods. —GLORIA ANZALDÚA

I have a tendency to let my mind run five hundred miles ahead of me. I get one glimpse of what might be down the road and I'm off and running, dreaming about the possibilities, thinking up new ideas, strategizing solutions, and speculating about the outcome. Sometimes this can be fun; we all need to envision the future. But other times this running ahead gets me in trouble.

It is easy to become anxious and overwhelmed when we look too far down the road. That's why there is so much emphasis in twelve-step programs on living one day at a time. Today's challenges and rewards are enough.

Recovery is a wide open journey before us. Sometimes we get glimpses of how much work there is to do, how many changes we need to make, how far we have to go . . . in spite of how far we have already come. The challenge is to imagine and acknowledge the future but focus on and live in today. The road in front of us may be uncharted wilderness, but one step at a time, we can make a path that leads to wholeness and sobriety.

Today I will let go of my fear of the unknown and strive to stay in the moment.

January 5

You cannot shake hands with a clenched fist.
—INDIRA GANDHI

Life is too short to spend it wrapped up in resentment. While anger has the potential to empower us and move us into action, resentment paralyzes us. It strangles our energies and immobilizes our emotional and spiritual resources. Resentment builds walls around our soul; it locks us in, and locks others out. Resentment takes energy; over time it siphons off our ability to love, care for, or value anything and anyone. Resentment unresolved festers away inside of us, eating at the very core of our being.

Moving beyond our resentments involves taking the focus off others and beginning to examine ourselves. We don't need to do this out of goodwill toward another; we can do it simply because letting go of our resentments is healthy for us. Refusing to let go of our resentments is refusing to grow. Moving beyond our resentments releases our energies and opens our hearts to new experiences of healing and love.

In recovery I am learning that though they may be directed at others, resentments most hurt my own spiritual growth.

January 6

What you do matters. All you need is to do it.
—JUDY GRAHN

Finding a sense of purpose in our lives is an important aspect of continued recovery. All of us have moments when we wonder why we are here and what it is we are meant to accomplish. When things are not going exactly as we anticipated or we haven't made as much progress as we had hoped for, it is easy to begin wondering whether or not our efforts are "worth it."

Lesbian writer Judy Grahn forcefully reminds us that what we do does matter. We may not always immediately see the effects of our actions, but they do have an impact. Rather than getting bogged down in pondering the meaning in our lives, sometimes we just need to take the actions and put in the effort, trusting that it will all work out in the end. Trying to find the meaning of the process while we are in the middle of it may be a bit like an artist attempting to predict exactly what her painting will look like before she's begun it. Sometimes we have to get to the end of a task before its meaning is apparent.

Today I will trust that my actions have an impact even when this is not apparent in the moment.

January 7

In some of our families . . . this love and acceptance often has a significant and devastating requirement that we not voice or live the reality of our sexuality.
—THE REV. SANDRA L. ROBINSON

Many times family, friends, or coworkers offer us limited acceptance. They tolerate us if we "keep quiet." They may socialize with us, and even with our lovers, as long as we don't talk about being lesbians or share too much of our day-to-day lives. They are willing to accept us, as long as we don't "flaunt it." We can come to family dinners or workplace parties, but they'd rather we didn't hold hands, kiss each other, or mention yesterday's lesbian softball game.

This kind of qualified acceptance forces us to deny the wholeness of our lives. It insists that we cut off parts of ourselves and leave them outside when we socialize. It reinforces societal myths and lies that tell us there is something wrong with us. And, whether we acknowledge it or not, it eats away at our self-esteem.

In recovery we can learn to insist on recognition and acceptance. We may not experience it overnight, but we can choose visibility and respect rather than qualified acceptance.

I deserve to be visible; I deserve unqualified acceptance and love. I do not need to settle for less.

January 8

> Where you used to be, there is a hole in the world, which I find myself constantly walking around in the daytime, and falling into at night. I miss you like hell.
> —EDNA ST. VINCENT MILLAY

All of us have times in our lives when we experience the profound emptiness and loneliness that comes with missing someone we love. It may happen when we spend time away from our lover, or when a relationship breaks up, or when someone we care about dies. Whatever the cause, the emptiness gnaws away at us, making it almost impossible to go through the motions of our day-to-day lives.

When we are in the midst of these feelings, we need to be gentle with ourselves. Pushing ourselves to "get over it" will only make things worse. We need to slow down and sit with our feelings before they can pass. We need to surround ourselves with other sober lesbians who can nurture and support us, perhaps even "carry" us when it seems too much to keep going forward. We may need their reminders that drinking and drugging won't make things better.

Missing someone is a painful feeling that won't go away by pretending it doesn't exist. But if we take care of ourselves gently, over time, we will begin to heal.

Even in the midst of my loneliness and pain, I will remind myself that healing is possible.

January 9

There is nowhere you can go and only be with people who are like you. Give it up.
—BERNICE JOHNSON REAGON

Learning how to live with, value, and celebrate our diversity is an important part of our collective recovery. Growing up in an oppressed group means that we all internalize an "us vs. them" lens through which we view the world. This lens keeps us separate from and afraid of one another. This lens convinces us that our needs are the most important. It lies, and leads us to believe that there is not enough to go around and thus allows the dominant group to pit us against one another in our struggles for liberation.

In recovery we are learning the importance of valuing one another's stories, of respecting one another's needs, of listening to one another's dreams and visions. We are learning that each person's contribution is important. We are discovering that the challenge of seeing beyond ourselves and our needs stretches and enriches us. Being with people who are completely like us may seem easier in the moment, but it will surely limit our growth and wholeness in the long run.

◊

Recovery challenges me to look beyond myself and learn to respect our differences and value our diversity.

January 10

Complacency is a far more dangerous attitude than outrage.
—NAOMI LITTLEBEAR

Once in a while I get complacent. I think this isn't so bad. I haven't thought about a drink for some time. Maybe I can relax. Maybe I don't have to work so hard. Maybe I'm cured.

A friend's recent relapse after years of sobriety jolted me into reality. Her experiences led me to a fresh awareness of the fragility of our recovery. What we have achieved thus far is not guaranteed. There is no point in recovery after which we can announce, "I've made it. I'm safe." Relapse is always a possibility.

Complacency can show up in two ways: taking our sobriety for granted or becoming comfortable with the way things are. Either way, complacency is always dangerous. On a daily basis, I need to reflect on what I have as a result of being in recovery. No, things aren't perfect yet, but I am sober. I have sober people in my life who care about me and like me. I am increasingly able to take responsibility for myself and thus have a renewed sense of self-esteem and respect. My ability to identify and express my true feelings is continually growing. I am learning to value my unique abilities and contributions. Having identified the gifts of recovery, I then need to reach forward for the next step. Healthy recovery is full of gratitude and growth.

◊

Am I grateful for what I have been given and achieved in recovery? Am I willing to reach forward to keep changing and growing?

January 11

> Dear children, you must try to say
> Something when you are in need.
> Don't confuse hunger with greed;
> And don't wait until you are dead.
>
> —RUTH STONE

Many of us have difficulty being direct about what we want and need in our relationships. We tend to beat around the bush, trying to communicate what we want without actually coming out and saying it. We drop hints, hoping our friends and lovers will pick up on them. On occasion we just expect them to "read our minds."

The problem with beating around the bush is twofold. First, it isn't fair to others. No one—no matter how much they love us—can read our minds. If our requests are not clear, others are cheated out of an opportunity to share with us, either because they are not sure what we want or because they don't have the slightest idea that there is something they could do. Second, being indirect isn't fair to us. The less direct we are, the less chance we have of actually getting what we want. And being indirect often sets us up to feel ignored and angry.

An important part of building healthy relationships with family, friends, and lovers involves learning how to be honest and direct in our requests. There is nothing wrong with asking for something. The challenge lies in how we do the asking.

Are there ways my communication is indirect? How can I become more clear about my requests?

January 12

> To those leaning on the sustaining infinite, today is big with blessings. —MARY BAKER EDDY

Can we imagine starting each day with excitement? Can we imagine envisioning the day ahead of us as "big with blessings"? If we are truly learning and growing and celebrating our recovery, we are developing the capacity to begin each day with anticipation.

"Leaning on the sustaining infinite" may have as many definitions as there are lesbians reading today's meditation. It may be the strength we have found in recovery. It may be the healing energy at work in our twelve-step group. It may be our own understanding of the divine within or around us. It may be the creative energy of the universe. However we define it, this sense of a power beyond ourselves is part of what enables us to find anticipation and joy in our recovery. This energy sustains us and connects us to ourselves and others. These relationships nurture us, and in turn, we learn to nurture and care for ourselves.

Trusting this process as sober lesbians can bring us joy. Trusting this process can enable us to approach each day with anticipation of its blessings.

How can I approach this day in excitement and anticipation? What blessings are in store for me as I continue in recovery?

January 13

I wanted a perfect ending . . . Now I've learned, the hard way, that some poems don't rhyme, and some stories don't have a clear beginning, middle, and end. Life is about not knowing, having to change, taking the moment and making the best of it. –GILDA RADNER

I'm the kind of person who really falls for the perfect, storybook ending. I like movies with a clear plot. I hate it when a story ends without getting all the loose ends wrapped up, and you're left wondering what happened to some of the characters. But like Gilda Radner, in recovery I am learning that real life isn't always nice and neat.

During our addictions, we spent a lot of time and energy trying to arrange life on our terms—trying to make people do what we wanted them to do, trying to fix situations so they would turn out exactly the way we wanted them to be.

Once in recovery, we discover that in order to have serenity, we must accept life the way it actually is, not the way we wish it could be. That doesn't mean we can't work toward change. But it does mean we have to start with an accurate view of how things are, and an acceptance that we can't always prearrange the outcome. What we can be sure of is the present. Our challenge, as Radner notes, is to grasp this moment and "make the best of it."

◊

Today I will try to accept life on life's terms, with all of its changes. I will try to seize this day and make the best of it.

January 14

Alcohol is an allergy of the body and an obsession of the mind.
—RITA MAE BROWN

For a long time, I did not understand why alcohol affected me the way it did. I did not understand why I got drunk, why I blacked out, or why there was nothing social about my drinking. Having come from a teetotaling Baptist family, I thought maybe it was because I hadn't "learned" how to drink properly. I decided if I just practiced hard enough, I could get this drinking thing down right.

Now I realize that I have an allergy to alcohol and other addictive substances. My body reacts to alcohol differently from the way the body of a social drinker does. This allergy includes both a mental obsession and a physical compulsion. As with any other allergy, I can avoid triggering it off simply by avoiding the allergic substances.

These basic truths of addiction are essential to my ongoing recovery. I am not like everybody else. I cannot drink safely. I am in danger of relapse the minute I begin to forget that I have an allergy.

Today I will remember that my alcoholism is both a mental obsession and a physical allergy.

January 15

Lesbianism is a recognition, an awakening, a reawakening of our passion for each (woman) other (woman) and for same (woman).
—CHERYL CLARKE

There are many parallels between entering recovery and recognizing our sexual orientation. Both involve a period of conflict and confusion. During this time we have difficulty acknowledging the truth about ourselves and our lives.

As we move out of this period, we experience an awakening of our spiritual, mental, emotional, physical, and sexual selves. Both sobriety and acceptance of our lesbian selves involve a recognition of our passion for life and our compassion for ourselves and others. Both remind us of our connectedness to those around us.

Today we can celebrate these awakenings. We can share the joy of recognizing ourselves sober. We can revel in the passion of loving this woman, other women, all women. We can celebrate the ways we have come to recognize our sober lesbian self in the lives of other sober dykes.

Today I am grateful for the awakenings and reawakenings I have experienced in recovery.

January 16

> **Some women wait for something
> to change and nothing
> does change
> so they change
> themselves.**
>
> —AUDRE LORDE

We spend a lot of our lives waiting for other people and other things in our lives to change. We wait for others to accept us as lesbians. We wait for our families to approve of us. We wait for society to grant us basic civil rights. We wait for lovers to become faithful. We wait for coworkers to treat us with respect. We wait for things to get easier before we tackle a new project. We wait for life to settle down before we get sober.

Audre Lorde offers an alternative. Waiting for change that never happens wears us down. Waiting for change that never happens leaves us disappointed and discouraged.

Perhaps instead of waiting for others, we can change. Changing ourselves often creates a ripple effect. Our changes affect those around us. At the very least, changing ourselves shifts our expectations. We cannot control the rate at which others change, but in recovery we can choose to change ourselves.

**Today I will focus on changing my attitudes
and behaviors, rather than waiting
for others to change.**

January 17

To this day I wonder why it [coming out] is not called "coming home" ... It was the most natural thing in the world. I wondered where I had been all my life.
—SARAH LUCIA HOAGLAND

For many of us, coming out did indeed feel like coming home. We spent years wondering why we seemed different, why we didn't fit in, struggling to piece together what was wrong with us. We kept trying to act like other people, striving to live up to what we thought society expected of us. What a relief to discover that there was nothing wrong with us. What a relief to come home.

Coming home means we can relax and let down our guard. Coming home means we can let go of everyone's expectations and simply be ourselves. Coming home means we can settle in and enjoy our identity as lesbians.

Sobriety is another "coming home" experience. Sobriety allows us to truly be ourselves. Sobriety teaches us how to be ourselves. Sobriety is giving us back our pride.

Today I will be grateful for the ways I am coming out and coming home to myself and others.

January 18

Almost every recent day my mind tongue tasted the bitter heat of scotch. I salivated. It seemed real again. That getting drunk would make everything better. All the world issues and ordinary life problems would fade to oblivion. Nothing would hurt. —VICKI SEARS

All of us experience moments in recovery similar to the one described by Vicki Sears. Our "euphoric recall" kicks in and we remember how "good" it felt to drink or drug. We get tired of living life on life's terms. We don't want to feel; we want out. We begin to convince ourselves that getting drunk or high would fix things. At least, we think, it would stop the pain.

As sober lesbians, we need to pay attention to these illusions. We need to step back and examine our discomfort. What are we trying to escape?

We must confront our euphoric recall for what it is—an illusion. In our hearts, we know that drinking and drugging will not make anything better. In our hearts, we know that oblivion would be short-lived. In our hearts, we know that our pain would be multiplied, not diminished. We need to listen to our sober hearts, not our addictive fantasies.

Today I will be aware of my tendency toward euphoric recall, recognizing that it can quickly lead me back to my addiction.

January 19

Faith and doubt are both needed—not as antagonists, but working side by side—to take us around the unknown curve.
—LILIAN SMITH

Doubt is not always bad. It has its purpose in our lives. Doubt, working together with our faith, can strengthen us and enable us to safely navigate difficult situations. Doubt and faith together are a bit like working the accelerator and the clutch as you shift into reverse gear. The accelerator moves the car forward while the clutch modulates the movement.

Doubt slows us down, makes us question what we think is true, makes us stop and pay closer attention to what is going on around us. Doubt alerts us to impending danger, leads us to take precaution, keeps us from charging full speed into the possible chaos ahead.

Then when the time is right, when we have thought things through and prepared ourselves for action, faith moves us forward. Faith allows us to weigh our doubts, determining which need heeding and which can be pushed aside, or pushed through, to new ways of being.

Today I will honor both my doubts and my faith as valuable tools for my journey.

January 20

If I had to wear high heels and a dress, I would be a mental case.
—K. D. LANG

k.d. lang burst onto the country music scene in the 1980s to a flurry of controversy. When you watch early concert performances, it is clear that while people loved her energy and talent, they were not quite sure what to make of her. She did not fit easily into traditional categories. Lang had difficulty getting airtime on pop radio stations because her music was too country. She faced challenges from country stations because her music was too rowdy and because she did not look the part of a female country music singer. Throughout it all, lang refused to acquiesce to the expectations of others and insisted on being herself. She would wear the clothes that fit her; she would look the way she wanted to look; she would sing music the way she wanted to sing it.

What difficulties am I facing today as a result of the expectations of those around me? Are there ways in which I have sacrificed my own mental health by allowing others to determine what is right for me? Am I turning over my power? Do I allow others to tell me what to wear? Whom I can love? How I should look? What kind of work is appropriate?

Today I will refuse to allow others to make me a mental case by telling me how to live my life.

January 21

Afraid is a country where they issue us passports at birth and hope we never seek citizenship in any other country.
—AUDRE LORDE

As lesbians, most of us know what it is like to live in fear. Fear of being different, fear of being found out, left out, or rejected, fear of not being able to be our whole selves. Fear of losing our jobs, losing our children, losing our families' love and affection. So we "straighten" up the house, or change the pronouns in a conversation about what we did over the weekend. We are afraid of what others might think of us or how they will react. Sometimes, we are afraid for our very lives and physical safety.

Many of us still live in fear even in recovery. We wish we didn't, but we do. Even those of us who consider ourselves "out of the closet" still experience moments of anxiety when we are faced, once again, with the need or possibility of coming out.

The challenge is to sort out when our fears are realistic—when we are on the street and someone is yelling "dyke" at us—and when our fears come from within—from our needs for love, approval, and acceptance. In recovery, we don't have to stay locked up in our fears.

Today, I will focus on accepting myself for who I am and let go of my fears about how others see me.

January 22

For over half my life I thought my task was to struggle and then one day I would enjoy the fruits of my labor.
—ADA MARÍA ISASI-DIAZ

Sometimes we think that we ought to be farther along in our personal growth than we are. We wonder why we have to keep revisiting the same issues over and over again. We somehow imagine that after a certain point everything should be smooth sailing; the hard part should be over by now, shouldn't it?

In an essay entitled "A Hispanic Garden in a Foreign Land," Isasi-Diaz writes about her discovery that *"la vida es la lucha"*—the struggle is life. Feminist theologian Nelle Morton refers to the same concept in her book entitled *The Journey Is Home*.

Recovery is an ongoing process. There is no fixed end point, no point of arrival when we can say to ourselves, "Well, that's it. I've made it. I can stop working now." As sober lesbians, we learn that recovery is the journey; the journey is home; *la vida es la lucha*.

Today I will remember that struggle and growth are a natural part of my journey. Recovery never ends.

January 23

Humility is not the acceptance of humiliation, allowing others to humiliate us or indulging in self-humiliation. Humility has its source in the word *humus*, of the earth, grounded.
— JUDITH MCDANIEL

During our addictions, we often used drugs or alcohol to ground us. They gave us a sense of ourselves. Early on, they helped us feel connected to ourselves and others. Chemicals made us feel a part of things. They made us feel connected to this planet.

In recovery we need to find healthy ways to feel grounded. Judith McDaniel's insight into the word humility offers a new twist on an often misunderstood concept. True humility is about being grounded—not in drugs or alcohol, not in our successes or failures, not in other people—but grounded in ourselves. True humility is about knowing and loving ourselves as sober lesbians. It is about acknowledging our strengths and weaknesses, and valuing the ways they make us who we are. True humility is about being rooted in *this* life, rooted in *our* lives. It is about knowing ourselves, and loving ourselves, and living *our* life on life's terms.

Today I will remember that true humility is being rooted and grounded in my sense of myself.

January 24

Perfectionist standards do not allow for failure. They do not even allow for life, and certainly not for death.
—MARION WOODMAN

Most of us struggle with perfectionism. We expect ourselves to be the best, to get sober faster, to be more recovered than we are by now, to be the most together lesbian in recovery. We may not dare to voice these standards aloud, but they live within us nonetheless.

This expectation of perfection has a paradoxical effect. We think it motivates us, pushes us to do better. Instead, it tends to paralyze us. Expecting perfection hems us in. It sets us up for failure from the very beginning. After all, how often do we actually achieve perfection?

Expecting perfection makes us afraid to try new things. It limits us. Expecting perfection sabotages our recovery. Sobriety is about life. It is about life to its fullest. And as Marion Woodman notes, perfection does not allow for life. Real life is too imperfect.

How does my desire for perfection limit me? Can I begin to set more realistic standards for myself?

January 25

Character builds slowly, but it can be torn down with incredible swiftness. —FAITH BALDWIN

As addicts in recovery, we know how difficult it is to rebuild character. Many of us struggled long and hard to make amends and clear away the wreckage of our addictive pasts. We have learned the hard way that reestablishing our reputations cannot be accomplished overnight.

As we continue in recovery, these lessons from our own journey help us in our interactions with others. Sometimes in our anger, we are hasty in judging others. Without knowing the whole story, we may demean their choices and malign their motives. Without thinking, we may criticize them publicly and create consequences that range far beyond what we initially intended.

Just as we needed a fresh start in recovery, others deserve the chance to tell their side of the story before being judged. Negative comments about someone's character can be difficult to retract. Learning to think before we speak is important to our new sober life.

Today I will reflect upon what I have to say about others before speaking, remembering that character and reputation are valuable.

January 26

We have to dare to be ourselves, however frightening or strange that self may prove to be. —MAY SARTON

Sometimes we get caught up in wishing we were different. It's like we have a bad case of the "If only's": If only we had her gifts or looks; if only we had her ability to make friends; if only our relationship hadn't ended that way; if only the boss had given us a second chance; if only we had gotten sober sooner . . .

The "if only's" keep us spinning our wheels, running in place. They hold us fixed in an in-between place, unable to move forward toward healing and growth.

The truth is, we are all we have. What we are today is really all that can be counted upon for sure. What we do with ourselves today is how we create a new tomorrow. Daring to truly be ourselves, proud and unafraid, is the essence of recovery.

Today I will risk being myself, saying and doing the things that reflect the new and sober lesbian emerging from within me.

January 27

Dwelling on the negative simply contributes to its power.
—SHIRLEY MACLAINE

During our addiction, most of our thoughts were negative. We expected things to go wrong; we expected to fail; we expected others to disappoint or reject us. Often these predictions turned out to be true.

Continuing this pattern of negative thinking into recovery sabotages our growth and interferes with our serenity. When we expect the negative, it often happens. When we expect the negative, we limit our ability to envision other alternatives. When we expect the negative, we short-circuit our power to effect change in our lives and in the world around us.

Healthy recovery demands imagining the positive. It challenges us to move beyond our addiction to pessimism. It calls us to let go of our fear and anxiety, allowing them to be replaced with anticipation and excitement. Envisioning positive change and growth creates a space for it to become reality.

Today I will focus on positive possibilities, rather than dwelling on negative expectations.

January 28

No one can make you feel inferior without your consent. —ELEANOR ROOSEVELT

Too often we allow others to have power over us. We allow them to define our world and tell us what is good or bad. We allow them to get inside our souls and tell us what to feel. Sometimes it is easier to blame them for making us feel bad, hurt, rejected, or oppressed than it is to take responsibility for creating our own feelings. In reality, how we feel is our responsibility, not theirs.

As lesbians, we often let other people define our sexuality, our relationships, and our lives. We give them the power to control who and how we love. And we give them the power to shape our feelings about ourselves.

Part of recovery is about taking back this power. Part of recovery is about saying to ourselves and others, "I am a lesbian and I am proud to be who I am. What I am is good, who I love is right, and I will not allow you to make me feel otherwise."

Today I will refuse to allow others to make me inferior. I will claim my right to celebrate who I am and who I love.

January 29

We are not born all at once, but by bits. The body first, and the spirit later. —MARY ANTIN

Mary Antin's insight accurately describes the process of our recovery. In sobriety, we are reborn, bit by bit. First our bodies recover. We detox physically, literally sweating the drugs and alcohol out of our systems. Slowly, as the first weeks go by, our bodies begin to be reborn; we begin to eat and sleep like normal human beings.

After a time, we discover that our minds have begun to clear up. We begin to remember things we had forgotten. We learn to read again. Our ability to focus and concentrate returns. Gradually our emotions are awakened. We begin to feel things that we can't even recognize. Sometimes it is as if we are literally flooded with emotions.

Bit by bit, this process called recovery is bringing us back to life; first the body, then the mind, then our emotions, then our spirit. It never happens all at once; it would be too overwhelming if it did. Step by step, slowly but surely, as we stay sober, we are reborn.

Today I will remember that recovery is a process. I will not get better overnight, but I will get better.

January 30

The conviction of being loved and lovable, valued and valuable ... is the beginning of the most fundamental kind of self-esteem.　　　—GLORIA STEINEM

Very few of us enter recovery with a sense of ourselves as loved and valued. Even fewer believe we are inherently lovable or valuable. Many of us failed to experience these qualities even years before our addictions began. For some of us, they may be complete unknowns.

Staying in recovery demands that we begin to develop this kind of self-esteem. After all, recovery is about being good to ourselves, and it is impossible to be good to ourselves if we don't think we are worth it.

Developing these convictions as adults begins with a choice. If we wait until we feel this way, it will never happen. We have to begin by choosing to believe and act as if we are loved and lovable and valued and valuable. Believing, and then acting on, this choice will eventually bring us to the point of conviction.

Today I will be responsible for my recovery by choosing to act as if I am both loved and lovable, valued and valuable.

January 31

For in our human, sexual, sensual selves, lives the breath of a spirit which connects and leads us to love, to our divine selves. My life had been an endless contradiction of faith until I affirmed the rightness of myself as a lesbian. —THE REV. JUDY DAHL

Discovering the breath of the spirit within us is possible only as we come to affirm the wholeness of our identity. Recognizing the divine in us occurs only as we come to accept the fullness of who we are. Denying ourselves is a denial of the God/dess within us. Splitting off and compartmentalizing those aspects of ourselves that we perceive as unacceptable alienates us from ourselves, from others, and from our understanding of the spirit.

Finding a sense of self-esteem in recovery requires coming to know the goodness of our sexual, sensual selves. As long as we persist in old beliefs about our sexuality as dirty, we cannot experience the joys of recovery. As long as we continue to internalize the myth that tells us being a sexually and sensually alive lesbian is wrong, our spiritual lives will remain an endless maze of contradictions. Affirming the rightness of ourselves as sober lesbians and learning to celebrate the joys of our sexual and sensual selves places us on the path to self-discovery and spiritual awakening.

Are there ways I continue to fragment my sexual and spiritual selves? How can I further affirm the wholeness of my sober lesbian identity?

February 1

**What happens to a dream deferred? Does it dry up/
like a raisin in the sun?**　　　　　　　—LANGSTON HUGHES

During our addictions, we often had lots of dreams. We were experts at grandiosity, filled with plans and schemes for making it big, getting it right, always sure that this time it would be different. As our addictions progressed, we became less and less capable of making those dreams become reality. We reached the point where we could barely make it through the day, let alone make it to the "big time." Seeing our hopes and dreams dissolve often left us frustrated, hopeless, and bitter.

Recovery offers us a second chance, a new beginning. Often we discover that the dreams deferred by our addictions have not disappeared. They are still within us and, with sobriety, are within our reach. They may need to be altered. They may need to be adjusted to match our true gifts and abilities. But we don't need to give them up. Recovery offers us the opportunity to take those dreams that have long lived within us and make them a reality.

What dreams have I carried within me? What hopes have been too much to even speak aloud? Can I begin to envision them becoming real in recovery?

February 2

It is never too late to be what you might have been.
—GEORGE ELIOT

During our addictions we often felt locked into situations and events. Whatever fate had dished out to us, we were stuck with it. Whatever feelings we awoke with were ours for the rest of the day. If things were going badly, we often just threw in the towel and gave up, even if the day was only halfway through.

One of the great comforts of twelve-step programs is the assurance that we can always start our day over again. No matter what has transpired thus far, no matter how poorly the day has gone, we can always make the choice to step back and start afresh. We may not be able to reverse what has occurred, but we can choose, for our part, to start over again.

If we wish we could carry less shame about being a lesbian, it is not too late to begin. If we wish we had made different career choices, we can explore our options now. If we wish it was easier to build healthy relationships with lovers and friends, we can start learning and practicing the necessary skills today. Recovery offers a second chance at life. It is never too late to start over again.

Today I will remember that regardless of what happens, it is never too late to begin over again.

February 3

Work is where you get paid to learn about your character defects. —ANONYMOUS

What does it mean to be sober at work? What does emotional sobriety look like on our jobs? How does our recovery challenge and change our relationship to careers and employment? How does recovery affect our relationships with employers and coworkers?

Applying the principles of recovery at work is an ongoing process. Many of us have difficulty with authority and supervision. We may struggle with workaholism, placing the needs of others before our sobriety. Our need to be right may interfere with relationships with coworkers. Our desire for approval and acceptance may make us vulnerable to criticism.

The twelfth step of Alcoholics Anonymous suggests that we practice the principles of recovery in all our affairs. As sober lesbians, our places of employment become one more opportunity for self-awareness and growth in recovery.

Today I will strive to allow my recovery to inform my attitudes and actions at work.

February 4

How long will it take before I walk to the other side and believe in your love? —MILAGROS PAREDES

Most psychologists believe that the development of basic trust is an essential task for infants and young children. Without this trust, people go through life distrusting others, unable to form healthy relationships with those they love.

This poses a certain dilemma for us as lesbians. Growing up lesbian in this society creates a certain distrust. We know that we can't be open with everyone. We know that there are lots of people who would like to see us dead, or at the very least not have to see us at all. We know that other people's love and acceptance is often contingent upon our willingness to be quiet about our sexual orientation.

Rebuilding trust is an essential part of everyone's recovery. It is an even more critical task for us as lesbians. If we want to enjoy the safety and nurture of healthy relationships, we must learn whom to trust and how to begin trusting them.

How can I begin to believe those who care about me and love me? What small steps can I take today to begin to trust their love?

February 5

When we yield to discouragement it is usually because we give too much thought to the past and to the future.
—ST. THERESE OF LISIEUX

All of us struggle with discouragement. Even the optimists among us are not immune to its appearance in our lives. We all have moments of feeling worn out by the challenges of work, relationships, and community. We get tired of listening to homophobic coworkers, tired of acting assertive with families who would rather pretend our lover doesn't exist, tired of being the ones who have to "explain lesbianism" to the straight world.

St. Therese's perception is accurate. When discouragement really gets to us, it is generally because we are caught up in either the past or the future. Either we are focused on a long list of stategies that haven't worked, or we are miles ahead of ourselves, assuming nothing we do will have an impact on the way things are now.

Moving beyond our discouragement requires focusing on the present. It means we have to stop thinking about what hasn't worked in the past. And it means we have to quit looking ahead, trying to predict what might or might not work tomorrow. Staying in the moment is the only way to replace discouragement with fresh hope.

◇

Today when I feel discouraged, I will ask myself where my attention is focused—on the past, the future, or the present?

February 6

A bad review is like baking a cake with all the best ingredients and having someone sit on it.
—DANIELLE STEEL

Learning to deal with criticism is never easy. Most of us take it personally. Someone criticizes the way we look or the way we've completed a project at work, and we think they don't like us. We jump from one small piece of negative feedback to assuming everything we did was wrong. Our parents make one comment about our lover and we assume they can't stand her. Now, they may in fact dislike her, but that doesn't change our need to respond differently to criticism in recovery.

Criticism will always be a part of life. Sometimes it will be constructive and legitimate. Other times it will be unsolicited and inappropriate. Our challenge is to learn to listen to what others say and to evaluate its relevance to our lives. Is what they have to say accurate? If so, we can take their feedback and use it to make changes. If not, we need to let go of their criticism and move on. Other people's criticism does not define us. We need not allow someone else's negativity to make or break our day or our lives.

◊

Today I will be open to constructive feedback, but will refuse to allow another's negativity to diminish my self-esteem.

February 7

There is no "supposed to be" in bodies. The question is not size or shape or years of age, or even two of everything, for some do not.

—CLARISSA PINKOLA ESTÉS

Beginning when we are children, we receive a lot of negative messages about our bodies. They're too tall, too short, too thin, too fat, too weak, too old, too flabby. You name it, and somebody probably thinks it's not quite right.

Self-acceptance in recovery means learning to let go of the old messages we were taught, as well as rejecting the ones we continue to be bombarded with through the media. We are who we are. Our bodies look the way our bodies look. There is no one way that all bodies are supposed to be. Creation is too infinitely varied for there ever to be a one right way for anything! Learning to accept ourselves means rejecting the myth of a perfect standard by which we all are judged.

Estés goes on to say that the most important question is whether a body can feel, whether it can share love and experience joy. These are the qualities that matter.

Today I will accept my body as it is, recognizing that this is an important part of learning to accept myself.

February 8

The approval we crave as social animals has finally to be outgrown so that we can take charge of our lives. . . . If we have any sense at all, we learn to make and keep our own promises to ourselves and become accepting rather than accepted people. —JANE RULE

Wanting the approval and acceptance of others is a normal human need and desire. It is especially apparent in young children. When you watch them interact with nurturing adults, you can almost see them soaking up love and approval like a sponge. Few of us received enough unconditional acceptance and approval as children. And what we did receive was often withdrawn once we began piecing together the truth of our identity as lesbians.

Consequently, many of us are starved for the acceptance and approval of others, and this can leave us dependent on others for emotional strength. In the long run, this void within us can only be filled as we learn to accept and embrace ourselves. We must give ourselves the love and approval we so desperately need.

Jane Rule suggests that we begin taking charge of our lives by making and keeping our promises to ourselves. She challenges us to focus less on our need to be accepted and more on our increasing ability to be "accepting people" toward ourselves and those around us.

What actions can I take to accept myself and give myself the love and approval needed for my continuing recovery?

February 9

The truth about our childhood is stored up in our body, and although we can repress it, we can never alter it ... someday the body will present its bill.

—ALICE MILLER

Many of us recognize the accuracy of Alice Miller's words. We have had experiences in recovery when our bodies have presented their bills; they have demanded that we reckon with the truth of our childhood.

It may be the truth of experiences of abuse or neglect. It may be the truth of physical illness or other difficulties. It may be the truth of being forced to deny our sexuality. Whatever the source, once the memories and feelings surface, they can never be pushed aside and repressed in quite the same way. Whether we like it or not, whether we feel prepared or not, we are pushed into grappling with the truth of our childhood.

During these times in our recovery, it is important to reach out to our sober support system and ask for help. We cannot, and should not, try to face and work through these emotions in isolation. We need the wisdom and experience of those who have gone before us. We deserve all the support and compassion we can find. As difficult and painful as these times may be, once we have navigated them, our bodies, minds, and emotions will be set free.

◊

Today I will try to accept the ways that working through the pieces of my past is a part of my ongoing healing and recovery.

February 10

I did not understand that wanting doesn't always lead to action.
— JUDY CHICAGO

Years ago someone told me that our life is not determined by what we want, but by the choices we make. Though I was too young to fully understand this, the principle rang true within me.

There are things we want that we never manage to obtain. There are tasks we want to accomplish that we never complete. There are old patterns we talk about wanting to change that somehow never disappear.

Wanting is not enough. Wanting to accomplish something, wanting to make changes, wanting to be different, has to be followed by choices and action. Many of us wanted to be sober, or at least feel better, long before it happened. We did not enter recovery until we began making choices and taking actions that led us into sobriety.

What is it that I want today? What actions do I need to take to make this happen?

February 11

The old woman I shall become will be quite different from the woman I am now. Another I is beginning.
—GEORGE SAND

Who is the older lesbian that you would like to become? What does she look like? What does she value? Who are her friends and companions? How does she feel about her life's work? What does she still long to accomplish?

George Sand reminds us that this older lesbian is already beginning. In the midst of our present selves, this new lesbian has begun to emerge. We know the truth of this process from our experiences in recovery. The sober lesbians we have become are radically different from the women we were during our addictions. The minute we chose sobriety, a new lesbian began to emerge. With each sober choice we made, she grew and developed, making us the women we are today.

If there are aspects of ourselves with which we are not entirely happy, we can take hope—this new sober lesbian is constantly changing and growing. We can also reflect on what we would like to see her become as we age. And we can take steps to enable her to be as different as we would like her to be.

Today I will celebrate the new me that is emerging, nurturing her growth and wholeness.

February 12

When you live alone, you can be sure that the person who squeezed the toothpaste tube in the middle wasn't committing a hostile act. —ELLEN GOODMAN

Ellen Goodman humorously reminds us of some of the joys of being single. It may or may not be what we want today, but it does have its virtues. Being single means I don't have to act cheerful when I wake up; I can go where I want to without checking it out with anybody else; I can spend my money without having to make compromises; I can eat all the things my ex-lovers hated . . . every night, if I want to.

Being single can be healthy for our recovery. It allows us to focus on ourselves in a way that is different from living with someone else. It can help us get the focus off taking care of others and, instead, learn to care for ourselves. Being single can force us to learn to live with ourselves, to get to know ourselves better, to figure out what it is we like and don't like in life.

Singleness may not be what we want all the time, but when we find ourselves alone, it is best to take the opportunity and learn from it. Who knows, we might even come to enjoy finding things the way we left them!

Whether I am single or in a relationship, caring for myself must be a priority in my recovery.

February 13

Grab the broom of anger and drive off the beast of fear.
—ZORA NEALE HURSTON

Fear is a paralyzing emotion. When it takes root within us, we are left powerless and immobilized. By contrast, anger is energizing. Anger can motivate and activate our minds and our bodies. Consequently, anger can be a useful tool for combating and working through our fears.

Instead of living in fear about what others might think, we can allow our anger at their judgments to move us through our fear. Instead of letting their ideas about what is right and wrong rule our lives, we can channel our anger into constructive social change. Instead of closeting ourselves off in fear, we can utilize our anger to propel us out into the open. Anger is a powerful emotion and a valuable tool for our recovery process.

Today I will value my ability to get angry and use my anger to move me through my fears.

February 14

The love expressed between women is particular and powerful, because we have had to love in order to live; love has been our survival. —AUDRE LORDE

I believe that we have something special and unique to share with our world. I believe that our experiences have meaning for others beyond the lesbian and gay communities. I believe our love has much to say to a broken and often loveless world.

First, our relationships highlight the incredible diversity of love. Our intimate relationships are different from traditional "storybook" couples. There is no "he" and "she." Historically prescribed roles do not work for us. We represent the many powerful lovers that do not "fit the mold."

Second, our intimate relationships illuminate the enduring power of love. Despite society's attempts to silence and destroy us, lesbians continue to fall in and out of love. Despite society's efforts to make us invisible, lesbians continue to find one another and live out their lives together.

Our lives prove that love cannot be confined. It cannot be silenced. It cannot be eradicated. Our lives prove that love can be, and is, our survival.

Today I will reflect on the ways I am sustained and empowered by my love for women.

February 15

When one kicks over a tea table and smashes everything on it but the sugar bowl, one may as well pick that up and drop it on the bricks, don't you think?
—MARGERY ALLINGHAM

We all struggle with the periodic urge to sabotage our success. It generally occurs when we have experienced a lot of change in our recovery process. We become fearful and uncomfortable. We're not sure we can handle all this growth. Suddenly, we feel compelled to do something to make things feel familiar. Acting out, finding a way to sabotage our progress, seems the perfect solution. The danger, as Margery humorously points out, is that once we have done the first deed, the second is always easier. It is amazing how quickly we can shift into a pattern of destructive or self-destructive acts.

Wanting to act out and sabotage our success is a signal we must pay attention to in recovery. We need to learn to recognize this impulse and then find other ways to address our discomfort and fear. Maybe we need to slow down. Maybe we need to talk about what is going on. Acting out runs the risk of sabotaging not only our current progress, but our recovery itself. After all, once we've kicked over the tea table, why not go all the way and smash the sugar bowl too?

◇

Today I will be conscious of the danger of giving in to my impulse to sabotage my growth and look for more constructive ways to respond to my fear and discomfort.

February 16

Growing up I felt that I was an alien from another planet dropped on my mother's lap. But for what purpose?
—GLORIA ANZALDÚA

When I was a young adolescent, some friends and I cooked up a story that we were beings from another planet sent here to research human life on Earth. We spent hours together creating accounts of life on this fictional planet and elaborating on the purposes of our work here. We even completed school assignments based on these identities. Looking back, I suspect this fantasy provided a sense of belonging and purpose. It bonded us together and, at the same time, gave us a sense of being different from others and, thus, special.

Learning how to find this sense of belonging and purpose as sober adult lesbians is an important aspect of our recovery. We spent too much time feeling out of place and separate from the rest of the world. We have wandered through much of our lives believing that we were somehow alien and that our lesbianism made us unique and different. Recovery allows us to rejoin the human race. Recovery is the starting point for discovering our true selves and beginning to identify a sense of purpose in our lives.

◇

Today I am recognizing that my sense of not belonging comes from my addiction and from growing up in a heterosexist society.

February 17

I had learned that I could be either a lesbian or a mother of my children, either in the wilderness or on holy ground, but not both. —MINNIE BRUCE PRATT

As lesbians, many of us have been forced to make unwanted and unfair choices. Society's homophobia has sometimes forced us to choose between being lesbians and being mothers, being lesbians and being part of our families, being lesbians and being employed, being lesbians and being happy. We were told—sometimes overtly, sometimes subtly—that we could not have it both ways.

Unlearning these lessons is a critical part of our recovery. Redefining these choices is a struggle we all face in sobriety. As sober lesbians, we have the ability and power to reframe our choices. We no longer need to accept someone else's definition of our reality. We can work together as a sober community to create the space we need to be all of who we are. As we empower one another in recovery, we will find the courage to integrate our choices and celebrate the wholeness of our being.

Today I am learning to make new choices in recovery, rejecting the false dichotomies forced on me by the homophobia of others.

February 18

I was determined to achieve the total freedom that our history lessons taught us we were entitled to, no matter what the sacrifice. —ROSA PARKS

Rosa Parks's refusal to sit in the back of the bus during the Civil Rights Movement of the 1960s illustrates her commitment to freedom. Her determination to enjoy the constitutional rights she was entitled to resulted in new freedom for her and her community. She is a powerful example for us of not settling for less—in our sobriety and in our lives.

We deserve basic respect from others. We deserve the right to be who we are as lesbians. We deserve the freedom that sobriety offers. We deserve the fullness of recovery.

Are we determined to attain these rights? Are we willing to take the risks necessary to achieve what we deserve? Are we determined to attain the full promises of recovery? Or will we settle for less?

Today I will remember that I have the right to be who I am and to enjoy the fullness of recovery.

February 19

I am not afraid of talking back to those who presume to know who I am and telling me that what I do is not natural.
—KITTY TSUI

These lines from Kitty Tsui's poem, "the words of a woman who breathes fire: one," highlight two of the joys of recovery. The first is recognizing when to be afraid and when to act courageously. The second involves identifying what things we should rightly fear and those we need no longer fear. As a consequence of these discoveries, we find the courage to talk back to those who would silence us.

Recalling the pain of our active addiction is essential to our continuing recovery. Similarly, remembering the oppression of our people is critical to our ability to live freely and courageously today. If we do not remember the past, we may take the freedom of our recovery and our sexual identity for granted.

◊

Today I am finding new courage to talk back to those who would define my world or silence my people.

February 20

These feelings were new and different because prior to this I rarely felt. I had no time for feelings, because survival claimed my time. —JOANNA KADI

Learning to live with our feelings is one of the greatest challenges in recovery. During our active addictions, we had little time for feelings. We did not own, and often barely recognized, our feelings. We were awash in denial, caught up in rationalizations, and out of touch with what we really cared about or felt. Feelings made us vulnerable and took up needed energies. Simply getting through each day exhausted us.

Once in recovery, we begin to get our feelings back. We begin to come alive again, or maybe come alive for the very first time. Sometimes it is overwhelming to find ourselves experiencing all these new and different feelings. Yet sitting with them and staying present for the feelings is essential if we are to maintain our recovery. We don't have to experience our feelings all at once; we can take them slowly, one feeling at a time. And we can remind ourselves that rediscovering our feelings is a normal, healthy part of our recovery.

Today I will be patient with myself as I learn to live in and with my feelings.

February 21

We cannot alter history by ignoring it nor the contradictions who we are.
—AUDRE LORDE

Our story is our story. We cannot change the place of our birth, it's timing, the composition of the families into which we were born, or our racial/ethnic heritage. We cannot rewrite history to alter its course of events. We cannot eliminate those things we wished had not occurred to us, or those things we wish we had not said or done. Whether we are happy with it or not, these pieces are a part of what makes up our story. And they are a part of what makes us who we are today.

Continued growth in recovery demands that we grapple with our past. We cannot ignore it or pretend it did not happen that way. As lesbians in recovery, we need to face our histories, struggling to sort out that for which we are responsible, individually or corporately. We need to examine our stories and make peace with our lives as they have been, not as we perhaps would wish them to have been. Only in acknowledging and accepting the truth of our lives can we begin to build a freely chosen future.

Today I will acknowledge and accept the ways my history makes me who I am in this moment.

February 22

If I had to characterize one quality as the genius of feminist thought, culture, and action, it would be the *connectivity*.
—ROBIN MORGAN

Feminist scholars and therapists at the Stone Center in Wellesley, Massachusetts, speak of addiction as a "contraction of connection" and of recovery as an "expansion of connection."

During our addictions, our worlds became smaller and smaller. Even if we continued to interact with people, our conversations revealed little of what was really going on inside. Many of us gradually gave up even that superficial interaction with the world around us. We withdrew within ourselves, becoming more and more isolated and depressed. As this occurred, we also became increasingly disconnected from ourselves, from our beliefs, values, thoughts, and feelings.

In recovery we have to expand our circle of sober relationships and learn how to reach out to and be present with others. In recovery we have to rediscover what is important to us, what it is we hope for and dream of. We have to discover what makes us feel good, what makes us excited, what makes us sad, what makes us angry. True integration and wholeness begin to happen only as we expand our sense of connectedness to ourselves, to others, and to the world.

◊

Is my sense of connection expanding or contracting? How can I nurture an expanding sense of connection today?

February 23

She had lost her way in a labyrinth of conjecture.
—EDITH WHARTON

I once heard someone in recovery say that their mind was like a refrigerator: it ran twenty-four hours a day. People in recovery often remind us that it was "our best thinking that got us into trouble." They suggest that instead of trying to figure everything out on our own, we need to be open to the wisdom and experience of those who have been sober longer than us.

While there are times when we need to think clearly and think for ourselves, there are also times when our thinking gets us into trouble. There are times when we think too much, when we get lost in our own imagination. In our anxiety or stress, we go round and round the possibilities, unable to find a way through the fog in our own heads. We analyze endlessly. Eventually, we are either so confused or exhausted that action is impossible.

During these times, we need to learn to stop the endless stream of analysis. We need to remember that sometimes we have to act, not think, our way into growth. We need to reach out to others and draw upon their strength and experience. We need to ask for help in finding our way out of the "labyrinth of conjecture" we have created.

Today I will focus on discerning when to think, when to ask for help, and when to act.

February 24

Each being is sacred—meaning that each has inherent value that cannot be ranked in a hierarchy or compared to the value of another being. —STARHAWK

One aspect of our emerging spiritual awakening is the ability to recognize ourselves as sacred. Have we reclaimed the goodness of our lives as lesbians? Do we truly believe, in the depths of our souls, that who we are is inherently good and valuable? Can we envision all of the particularities of our identity as blessed and sacred?

Recognizing our inherent worth means we stop comparing ourselves to others. Coming to believe in our own value means we are set free from the need to measure ourselves against others.

Recognizing the sacredness of ourselves and others means acknowledging that while there is much we share in common, we each have our own gifts and abilities. We each have strengths and limitations. Acknowledging our sacredness means accepting that even our limitations are not "bad"; they simply are part of who we are.

Today I will affirm my inherent value and celebrate the wholeness of my identity, without comparing myself to those around me.

February 25

Be bold. If you're going to make an error, make a doozy, and don't be afraid to hit the ball.
—BILLIE JEAN KING

I can remember my eight- or nine-year-old baby butch self, baseball bat in hand, waiting for the pitcher to throw the ball, praying that I wouldn't strike out. Many of us grew up absolutely terrified of making a mistake. The environment was filled with anger and blame. There was little room for the trial and error that is part of learning. Perfection was a constant expectation. Some of us grew up in homes where there were no "mistakes"; anything someone did "wrong" was viewed as deliberate or maliciously intended.

Without room for mistakes, there is little room to be ourselves. Without room for imperfection, we become paralyzed and unable to take risks. We monitor our every action and reaction, so terrified of "doing it wrong" that we often do nothing at all.

Today we are discovering that mistakes are normal. Being imperfect and making mistakes is part of being human. Nothing new, nothing significant, happens unless we are willing to risk making mistakes.

Today I will give myself permission to experiment, recognizing that mistakes are part of learning.

February 26

To die for the revolution is a one-shot deal; to live for the revolution means taking on the more difficult commitment of changing our day-to-day life patterns.
—FRANCES M. BEAL

During our addiction, our lesbian bravado often made us willing to do the heroic. We could pull off anything once! But disciplining ourselves to follow through with the day-to-day, nitty-gritty work was virtually impossible.

In recovery these patterns are changing. We are beginning to "show up" for our lives. We are learning to accept our need for change, and learning to do the work needed to achieve our goals. Staying sober requires commitment, and we are learning to take that skill and apply it to other areas of our lives as well.

Dying for the revolution—whether the one within us or the one around us—is easy; we probably could have pulled that off while we were drunk. But the real revolution, personal or political, takes constant and persistent effort. Changing the day-to-day patterns of our lives requires passion and commitment. This we can only achieve through recovery.

Today I will remember that real change, within and around me, occurs through sober commitment and persistence.

February 27

The very common "lover" sometimes implies an impermanence or predominant physicality which is not appropriate. "Partner" sounds financial, and "mate" conjures up images zoological.
—SANDY RAPP

Sandy Rapp writes about the difficulties we experience in giving voice to our relationships with those we love. Society has names for heterosexual lovers—girlfriend, fiancée, wife—but there are few names for our relationships. We struggle to define ourselves and our lovers. While we have come up with a variety of names, Rapp's observation is accurate: none are adequate.

This lack of an adequate name has a greater impact on us than we often recognize. Not having an adequate name robs us of the depth and strength of our commitments. Not having an adequate name subtly says that whom we love is not important, not fully legitimate, not to be valued in this society. Not having an adequate name inhibits our ability to celebrate our identity and the identity of those we love.

Feminist theologian Mary Daly writes about the ways in which we as women and lesbians have had the "power of naming" stolen from us. It is time to take that power back. Society will not find us an adequate name. We will have to name ourselves.

Today I am learning to speak the truth about myself and those I love. I am finding new names that value my relationships.

February 28

> "Wearing too many hats" or the "Circle of Confusion Syndrome"—as I call it—is something that both feminists and artists of color are familiar with.
>
> —MIDI ONODERA

Midi Onodera makes this comment at the close of a fictitious story about the chaos that ensued when an exhausted politically active lesbian gave the wrong speech at a political rally, delivering one that had actually been written for a very different political context. She goes on to talk about the frustrations of tokenism, as well as the difficulties of being all things to all people.

Learning to take care of ourselves in recovery is not easy. Those of us who are addicts do not find balance naturally. We tend to do things in the extreme, often long into recovery. Even good things—doing service, being politically active, getting active in social and cultural groups—can wear us out if we try and tackle too much at one time. Healthy recovery involves learning to listen to our bodies and our minds so we can pace our activities. Refusal to take time out to care for ourselves is guaranteed to lead to disaster sooner or later.

Am I taking on too much? Am I wearing too many hats at one time? Where do I need to slow down and pay attention to my needs?

February 29

The mere sense of living is joy enough.
—EMILY DICKINSON

In looking at the day ahead of us, people in recovery sometimes say, "a good day would be nice, but a sober day will be enough." Learning to accept sobriety as enough is an important tool for our serenity in recovery.

It might be nice if we get along well with our lover today, but staying sober is enough. It might be nice if our family makes great strides toward affirming our identity today, but staying sober is enough. It might be nice if we can accomplish everything that is on our agenda for the day, but staying sober will be enough.

Developing this kind of attitude enables us to celebrate our recovery regardless of the particular events of each day. Learning to accept sobriety as enough grounds our priorities. It reminds us that the mere sense of being alive is more than we ever had during our addiction. It reminds us that whatever else happens today, living sober is joy enough.

Today I will celebrate the truth that living sober is joy enough.

March 1

I have thought the cancer was in my control. If I decide she will recover, it will go away....
—HONOR MOORE

Recently I sat with someone as she talked about her lover's upcoming surgery and shared the fear and anxiety with which they both were struggling. We shared together the pain of not being able to make her lover feel better, of not being able to magically make their anxiety go away, essentially of not being able to "fix it." As I listened, I was reminded again of how difficult it is for us to accept our powerlessness over the lives of others, especially those to whom we are closest.

In reality, we have very little control over what happens to those around us. We can't often make things go the way we want them to. We can't protect our children, friends or lovers from getting sick, losing a job, or being slighted by their family. We can't shield them from feeling disappointed, rejected, or hurt. While we can be supportive and nurturing, we can't even make them feel good—about being successful, about accomplishing something, or about being who they are.

Accepting this reality is about learning to live life on life's terms. Accepting this reality is essential to our serenity and well-being. Accepting this reality is an ongoing part of our recovery.

Today I will be present for those I love, accepting my powerlessness and allowing them to live their own lives.

March 2

What is your religion? I mean—not what you know about religion but the belief that helps you most?
—GEORGE ELIOT

Regardless of what we believe about institutional religion, George Eliot's question is worth pondering. What is the belief that helps you most? What is the thing that gets you through each day? What is it that gives your life a sense of meaning and purpose? What is the belief that empowers and sustains you?

Our responses to these questions may be fairly consistent, or may vary with the changing circumstances of our lives. There are no right or wrong answers to these questions; there are only our responses. The answers we were taught at earlier points in our lives, and perhaps believed in at the time, may no longer be appropriate for us as healthy, sober lesbians. Beginning to search out the beliefs that are important to us—be they about ourselves, others, the world, or the divine—may be useful in our current quest for a working sense of spirituality in recovery.

Today I will reflect on the beliefs that help me most—not those I was taught or expected to hold—but the ones I find helpful in my recovery.

March 3

When one is a stranger to oneself then one is estranged from others. If one is out of touch with oneself, then one cannot touch others.
—ANNE MORROW LINDBERGH

During our addiction, we were strangers to ourselves. Drugs and alcohol functioned to hide ourselves from ourselves. We lost touch with our likes and dislikes, our thoughts and emotions, and even those things that mattered most to us. This estrangement from ourselves alienated us from others. When we lose the ability to recognize who we are, we are unable to share ourselves with others.

In recovery we begin to reconnect with ourselves. Getting sober, in and of itself, removes much of the fog that clouded our ability to see ourselves. As we stay sober, we increasingly recover our capacity to think, feel, touch, and be present for ourselves and others. Regaining a sense of ourselves enables us to repair our relationships with others. Taking responsibility for ourselves enables us to allow others to be themselves. As we come to know ourselves and our story more accurately and fully, we are empowered to share our strength and experience with others in a way that nurtures and empowers them.

As I continue learning about myself in recovery, I am more fully able to reach out and be present with others.

March 4

You gain strength, courage, and confidence by every experience in which you really stop to look fear in the face.
—ELEANOR ROOSEVELT

Courage is not the absence of fear. True courage is the ability to act in the face of fear. Being strong and confident does not mean we have conquered our fears. In reality, it means that we have learned to live with our fears.

Fear is an emotion that is a basic part of life for all human beings. Fear is unavoidable. In our addictions, we ran from our fears. We drank and drugged them away. We immersed ourselves in other people to deny them. We did whatever we could to hide from the possibility of having to face our fears.

Running from our fears is like running away from an angry dog; it invariably comes after us. Recovery is about learning to stand still and face our fears. It is about acknowledging our fears and then learning to act in spite of these fears. Only in facing our fears can we truly learn to live with them and move through them.

What fears have I been avoiding? Is there a way I can begin to face them?

March 5

> We left, as we have left all our lovers, as all lovers leave all lovers, much too soon to get the real loving done.
> —JUDY GRAHN

Learning when and how to maintain our commitments is a challenge we all encounter in recovery. During our addictions, we often made commitments that were unrealistic. We promised eternity to one another when we could not deliver today. We promised to be honest and faithful with another when we could not be these things with ourselves. When our commitment faltered or the other disappointed us, we were out the door, gone without good-byes, frantically running away from our vulnerability and pain.

It wasn't that we intended to break our commitments. It was more a case of not knowing how to maintain them. When things became difficult, we lacked the inner knowledge and resources necessary to see it through. After all, nobody ever really sat us down and taught us what it takes to make a relationship work. In recovery we have the opportunity to learn and practice those skills. In recovery there is a chance that we might not always have to leave our lovers before the real loving is done.

What makes it difficult for me to make a commitment? What skills do I still need in order to maintain my commitments?

March 6

All of us must feel free to decide whether or not to use our abilities to raise children, and society must open up to let us make honest, clear decisions.
—LINDA J. HOLTZMAN

In an article on Jewish lesbian parenting, Linda Holtzman notes the difficulty of making and celebrating our decisions in an environment where our choices are limited. When we are unable to choose freely, we experience limited options. When we are unable to choose freely, our ability to celebrate our decisions is curtailed. In the face of external constraints, some of us even moderate our desires—for example, deciding early on that we do not want children, rather than wanting them and not being able to have them.

Healthy decisions in recovery—whether about raising children or other issues—require the ability to make choices, and to make them as freely as possible. While we cannot change society overnight, we must work together to create enough space for all of us to make our choices freely, honestly, and openly. As sober lesbians, we must create the space needed for celebrating our decisions.

In what ways have my life choices been curtailed? How can I begin to create the space needed to affirm my choices in recovery?

March 7

> Feeling is the basic bodily ingredient that mediates our connectedness to the world. When we cannot feel, literally, we lose our connection to the world.
> —BEVERLY WILDUNG HARRISON

In our addictions we often felt lost. We thought everyone else knew how to make this thing called life work except us. We often felt confused about what happened and powerless to effect changes in our lives. Quite literally, we felt disconnected from ourselves, from those around us, and from our world.

This sense of disconnection was the result of being out of touch with our feelings. Our feelings were buried under our addiction—stifled, diminished, distorted, sometimes completely shut down. Without an accurate connection to our feelings, it was impossible for us to feel connected to our world. Feelings provide feedback about our interactions with others. They help us pay attention to ourselves. They keep us in touch with our bodies and what is going on inside us. Feelings help us navigate life.

In recovery we begin to reconnect with, and learn to interpret, our feelings. While this process is not always comfortable, it is essential.

Today I will value my feelings as the instrument of my connection in this world.

March 8

A voice is a gift; it should be cherished and used, to utter fully human speech if possible. Powerlessness and silence go together. —MARGARET ATWOOD

Some of us are afraid to speak. We are afraid to speak out to our parents, afraid to speak back to our lovers, afraid to speak up in support groups. We are afraid because we worry about how we will sound, what we should say, or what others will think. In our fear, we remain silent and powerless. Sometimes the fear is so paralyzing, it is almost as if we have lost our voice.

Finding that voice, finding our voice, is part of recovery. Atwood is right: our voice is a gift. It is one of the gifts of sobriety, and it deserves to be celebrated and cherished and shouted out loud. If we don't speak up, no one will benefit from our experience, strength, and hope. If we don't speak back, our lovers will never know what we want. If we don't speak out, our parents will go on ignoring us at family gatherings. Learning to use our voice clearly and appropriately is one way to reclaim our power in recovery.

Where have I been afraid to speak? How can I begin to exercise the gift of my voice?

March 9

Three failures denote uncommon strength. A weakling has not enough grit to fail thrice.
—MINNA THOMAS ANTRIM

Most of us have difficulty responding to failure. We tend to quickly jump from failing at something to being a failure. . . . Nobody shows up for the new lesbian singles group we started and we think it is our fault; our new date doesn't like the restaurant we picked out and we beat ourselves up for blowing the relationship; we say something we later regret to one of our children and immediately we feel like a terrible mother.

Minna Antrim invites us to rethink failure. She invites us to take our failures and transform them into an indication of courage and strength. After all, if we have failed at something, that means we tried something. Every failure means that we took action, and taking action requires willingness to risk; it takes grit and courage.

The next time we are tempted to berate ourselves for not getting it right, perhaps we can pause and remember that at least we had the courage to try. And if we get it wrong two or three times, we can still be patient with ourselves. After all, three failures is a sign of "uncommon strength."

Today I will be patient with myself; what counts the most is my willingness to take action regardless of the results.

March 10

> If you don't like the way the world is, you change it. You have an obligation to change it. You just do it one step at a time.
> —MARION WRIGHT EDELMAN

Often our frustration and anger results from forgetting how slowly change occurs. Real change, fundamental change, does not happen overnight. It happens one action, one task, one step at a time. This is true whether the change that we are working for is within ourselves or in the world around us.

As addicts, we have a tendency to look for immediate gratification. We also live in a society that fosters this sense of immediacy with its emphasis on instant food, easy-access cash, and overnight success stories. In the midst of all this, we easily forget that these quick fixes are an illusion.

The hard truth of recovery is that substantive change occurs slowly. Accepting the nature of this process lessens our impatience and frustration. Acceptance slows us down and allows us to move in concert with the change process. Acceptance facilitates persistence and serenity.

Today I will be patient with myself, acknowledging that real change takes time.

March 11

Genuine forgiveness does not deny anger but faces it head-on.
—ALICE MILLER

Denying our anger makes genuine forgiveness impossible. Refusing to acknowledge our anger sends it underground. There it festers untouched, guaranteed to slowly eat away at us or erupt in violence at some later time.

Refusing to acknowledge our anger denies the injustice that was committed. It suppresses the truth and forces us into a denial of the past. And that denial keeps us locked in the past, unable to move forward in our recovery.

The very existence of our anger is generally a reflection of our relationship with someone or something. We get angry about the things that matter to us. Thus, refusing to acknowledge our anger cuts us off from the source of our passion and our compassion.

Real forgiveness does not demand that we swear off our anger. Real forgiveness acknowledges the offense and speaks the truth about what has happened. Real forgiveness is possible only when there is room for both our honesty and our anger.

Today I will acknowledge my anger, recognizing that refusing to do so locks me into the injustices of my past.

March 12

I think it pisses God off if you walk by the color purple in a field somewhere and don't notice it.
—ALICE WALKER

This poignant comment by Shug in Alice Walker's novel *The Color Purple* reminds us that noticing and appreciating the little things in life is important. During our addiction, we were usually so wrapped up in what was going on inside us that we failed to notice much of the world around us. From Shug's perspective, we probably pissed God off a lot—perhaps less for what we did and more for what we failed to appreciate about the gift of our life.

One of the signs of our emerging spirituality in recovery is the ability to begin appreciating the little things. It is one of the signs of our spiritual awakening—literally a waking up of our spirits. It may be noticing how good it feels to be in a room full of sober lesbians. It may be paying attention to the less obvious ways newcomers in recovery are changing. It may be learning to appreciate the little things our girlfriend does that we value. Whatever it is, learning to notice and appreciate these small events is a sign that we are coming alive, a sign that we are coming back to ourselves and to one another.

What little things in my life have I been ignoring lately? How can I develop a greater sense of appreciation?

March 13

It's gonna hurt, now. Anything dead coming back to life hurts.
—TONI MORRISON

These words from Toni Morrison's novel *Beloved* remind us how painful the recovery process can be. Getting sober is not easy, and learning to live sober is one of the most difficult things we will ever do for ourselves.

One of the reasons recovery can be so painful is because it literally is a "coming back to life." When we have spent years deadening our pain, coming back to life can hurt. When we have spent years pushing aside our fears, coming back to life can be terrifying. When we have spent years ignoring our shame and self-hatred, coming back to life can be overwhelming.

When we are in these painful places, we need to remember that there is a difference between the pain we experienced in our addictions and the pain of recovery. There is a difference between the pain of isolation and alienation and the pain of coming back to life. This time our pain is a sign of new birth. This time we are coming back to life.

Today I will remember that my pain in recovery is a sign of new birth and new life in sobriety.

March 14

Money is only money, beans tonight and steak tomorrow. So long as you can look yourself in the eye.

—MERIDEL LE SUEUR

Le Sueur's comments remind us that money, in and of itself, has no meaning; it is neither good nor bad. Its importance emerges out of the beliefs and values we attach to it.

How did your family-of-origin handle money? Did your parents talk openly about finances, or was it one of those never-mentioned topics? Did you grow up in an economy of scarcity or abundance? Was your family worried about making ends meet, or was there an attitude that said, "We may not have a lot, but there will be enough"? Did people plan ahead or did they live from crisis to crisis? Were you allowed to ask for what you needed or wanted? Did you learn how to handle money from your parents, or was that something you were expected to magically know once you were an adult? Who handled the money? Did that person have more power because they were in charge of the finances?

All of these questions can help us reflect on the meanings we have attached to the money in our present lives. Beginning to sort through the messages we received about money while growing up may help us understand some of our present difficulties or patterns.

What difficulties am I presently experiencing in recovery that involve finances? How are they related to past attitudes and beliefs about money?

March 15

In either case, passing as "straight" or passing for white, the "passing" person must accept the twin albatross of silence and invisibility. —CHERYL CLARKE

Passing exacts a high price in our lives. It demands that we surrender a part of who we are. It renders us invisible and thus, isolated. It robs us of a sense of pride in our identities. Passing can be chosen (though rarely freely) as the easier way to navigate a potentially dangerous situation, or passing can be imposed upon us, such as when others refuse to acknowledge our presence no matter how blatant we may be.

As lesbians, most of us have experienced the strain of passing—finding our lover uninvited to a family dinner, pretending to be straight so we can continue raising our children, leaving our lover's pictures at home rather than on our desk at work, realizing that our brother never asks about our lover. All of these experiences take their toll on us. They wear us down and wear us out. Maintaining silence is hard work.

In this essay, "Saying the Least Said, Telling the Least Told: The Voices of Black Lesbian Writers," Cheryl Clarke calls us, as women, as lesbians, as women of color, to visibility and vigilance. May we have the courage to accept this struggle.

Where is the impact of silence and invisibility draining my energies for life? Can I choose instead to be visible?

March 16

We tend to think of the erotic as an easy, tantalizing sexual arousal. I speak of the erotic as the deepest life force, a force which moves us toward living in a fundamental way.
—AUDRE LORDE

Fundamentalist religious folks sometimes talk about lesbians with the phrase "Hate the sin, love the sinner," as if to say that they could care about us as human beings, while simultaneously hating the way we live our lives. Most of us recognize the impossibility of this belief.

In Audre Lorde's definition of the erotic, our sexuality is not something that can be separated from the rest of our lives. Being a lesbian may not be all of who we are, it may not define all of how we view ourselves, but our sexuality is at the core of our being. It does inform and permeate all of who we are.

During our active addictions, we had difficulty seeing our positive qualities and celebrating our identity. Many of us separated ourselves from our sexuality—physically, mentally, and emotionally. In recovery we are learning to value our identity. We are learning to reclaim and celebrate our sexual selves. We are learning that the erotic within us is something to be cherished and nurtured.

In recognizing the wholeness of my life, I am reclaiming my sexuality as an integral aspect of my identity.

March 17

This has been a wonderful evening. Gertrude has said things tonight it'll take her ten years to understand.
—ALICE B. TOKLAS

Recovery brings much new information. In recovery, we begin learning that we are loved and lovable. We uncover gifts and abilities that we thought were buried under our addictions. We uncover new talents and try out new ways of doing things. Recovery brings new relationships and healthier patterns of connecting with ourselves and others. We learn that we do not always have to have all the answers, that it is perfectly all right, and even good for us, to ask for help and allow others into our lives.

It takes us a long time to truly internalize these truths. We may hear them and begin to take them in intellectually, but it often takes a long time to really absorb them emotionally. We may have a whole series of "light bulb" experiences in which we suddenly realize that a piece of information truly applies to us. Still, we can often share this wisdom with others years before we have fully accepted it and put it into practice in our own lives. Coming to truly own these new truths is a lifelong journey.

Today I recognize that absorbing and applying new information takes time. My growth in recovery will not happen overnight.

March 18

Usually in the telling of what we have hidden we discover that others have had experiences similar to our own, that we are not alone ... That discovery is part of the healing, part of the recovery.
—JUDITH MCDANIEL

Steps four and five in twelve-step programs ask us to take an inventory of ourselves and our lives and then share this with our higher power and with another human being. Some of us struggle with these steps. They may sound too religious, perhaps like going to confession. For others, the struggle is about how difficult it is to trust; our past experiences of self-disclosure have not been easy, and we are reluctant to try again.

The importance of step five, regardless of how formally or informally we choose to complete it, lies in the discovery that we are not alone. The ultimate effect of our addiction was isolation. We were alienated from ourselves and those around us. We were alone in our fear and our shame. This sense of separation needs to be healed if we are going to experience the joys of recovery. Sharing ourselves and our lives with another human being marks the beginning of our healing. When we discover that other sober lesbians share similar experiences of fear and shame, our burdens are lessened; our fear and our shame become lighter and hold less power to rule our lives.

Today I will remember that sharing my fear and shame with others opens me to the healing power of recovery.

March 19

The battle to keep up appearances unnecessarily, the mask—whatever name you give creeping perfectionism—robs us of our energies. —ROBIN WORTHINGTON

Keeping up appearances is exhausting. It may be the appearance of being straight. It may be looking good or looking happy. It may be needing to appear as if we always know what we are doing. It may be looking however we think other people expect us to look in the moment.

Whatever the mask, it robs us of creative energy, energy that could be used for healing ourselves and others. Wearing a mask separates us. It creates a barrier that precludes connection. Keeping up appearances prevents others from knowing who we really are. It keeps them at a distance and keeps us safe.

What we sometimes fail to realize is that this mask, worn long enough, separates us from ourselves as well. Eventually we lose the ability to tell the difference between our masked self and our real self. We are so worn out with keeping up with appearances, we lose touch with who we really are. We forget what is underneath our mask.

Today I will remember that the masks I use to protect myself also separate me from myself and others.

March 20

Turning it over is not an act of giving up or an act of alienation; it is, rather, a recognition that creating ourselves—and creating a world our selves would want to live in—is a life-long process.
—JUDITH MCDANIEL

Turning it over is a difficult concept. It may seem as if this means becoming passive observers. It may seem as if we are being asked to give up our power. Judith McDaniel describes turning it over as the act of committing ourselves to the struggle. It means making the choice, over and over again, to be a part of our recovery, to do the work that healing demands.

As lesbians, we have had enough of feeling alienated. We have had enough of living in a world where we felt unwanted and invisible. We have had enough of giving up our power and allowing others to define us. As sober lesbians, turning it over means committing ourselves to this journey called recovery. It means committing ourselves to do the work necessary to healing ourselves and becoming participants in the healing of the entire lesbian community. It means finding our power, and taking back our power, so that we can all live in a world where no one is powerless or alone again.

Today I will remember that turning it over is not about giving up; it is about committing myself to the journey.

March 21

It took me seven years of getting drunk and one of sobriety to finally be able to say out loud and clear, "Yes, I am a Cochona, a Maricona, a Nicaraguan dyke."
—GINA ANDERSON

We often carry a lot of baggage from our active addiction. We berate ourselves for what we think we failed to accomplish. We carry guilt about the things we did, as well as the things we believe we should have done. We wallow in self-pity, wondering why we didn't get sober sooner and imagining how different our lives might have been if we had.

Gina Anderson reminds us that the time spent in our addictions is not necessarily a waste. She doesn't say it took one year of sobriety to claim and celebrate her lesbian identity; she says it took seven years of getting drunk *and* one year of sobriety.

We are being too hard on ourselves when we write off the past as nothing but wasted time. The lessons learned during our active addictions contribute to the growth we experience in recovery. We may not be happy with all the choices we made during our addiction, but continuing to berate ourselves contributes nothing to our ongoing healing and recovery. Staying sober promises to alleviate our regrets. The longer we are in recovery, the easier it is to see the wholeness of our lives.

◇

Today I will strive to accept that it takes however long it takes for me to make changes. I cannot get there faster by beating up on myself.

March 22

Watching a woman kill herself by inches of a bottle is not a revolutionary act.
—CATHERINE RISINGFLAME MOIRAI

The real revolutionary act is living a clean and sober life despite the insanity of the racist, sexist, and homophobic world in which we live.

When I first came out, entering a women's bar was an incredible act of bravery. I was absolutely terrified of stepping over the line that had been drawn by those around me, the line that separated normal from abnormal, healthy from sick, moral from perverted. Swaggering (so as to camouflage my fear) up to the bar and ordering a beer was, I thought, a revolutionary act. Dancing, bottle in hand, with hundreds of other lesbians was a political statement. Going to bed with another woman, even if I had to be drunk, was radical.

What I didn't understand then was that my courage to be "revolutionary" came from a bottle. Alcohol took away my fears about what others might think. It blotted out the guilt and shame I carried within me. And eventually, that same bottle began to kill me.

Today in recovery, I know that the real revolutionary acts happen when we are able to stand together, clean and sober, and face up to our terror, root out the shame, and move through the fears instilled by our homophobic culture. Learning to live as proud, sober lesbians *is* a revolutionary act.

Today I will affirm and celebrate the true courage I am finding in recovery.

March 23

God is inside you and inside everybody else. You come into the world with God. But only them that search for it inside find it.   —ALICE WALKER

Healthy spirituality is all about a healthy connection and engagement with God (however you define her) and others. As lesbians, finding this healthy sense of God may be one of the hardest tasks we face in recovery. God was often, and may still be, a tool of our oppression—someone to be feared, someone who was used against us, someone who was willing and ready to condemn us for our sexuality.

What was your childhood image of God? What were the characteristics of this God? How did this God affect your growth and development as a child, an adolescent, a young adult?

Most of us in recovery find that we have to let go of old ideas about God. We have to find new ways of imaging this power greater than ourselves. We have to move beyond the messages we grew up with and learn new truths about ourselves in relationship to our Creator. We need to discover new language to describe our sense of the spirit at work within us.

As we discover the source of our life and strength, we find the power and the courage to reach out to those around us. As we connect with our own spirit, we are enabled to build healthy connections with others.

◊

Today I will be open to new images of the spirit at work in myself and others.

March 24

My private measure of success is daily. If this were to be the last day of my life would I be content with it? To live in a harmonious balance of commitments and pleasures is what I strive for. —JANE RULE

Each of us needs to find our own "private measure of success." Early on in recovery the formula may be simple: staying sober, sticking to our plan, or avoiding the crises of others. As we continue in recovery, these goals remain and others are added: learning a new skill, building healthy relationships, or changing behavior patterns that are no longer useful.

It can be helpful to spend time reflecting on each day's events and our participation in them. Were we able to meet our commitments? Have we done what we could to nurture and take care of ourselves? Have we been respectful and honest in our dealings with others? Were we able to give something back from the gifts of our recovery?

Taking this time to reflect on our day is not an excuse to "beat up" on ourselves. It is a healthy tool for reviewing our growth, examining our relationship with ourselves and others, and identifying where we may need to make adjustments tomorrow.

What is my "private measure of success"? What do I need to be or do to make each day count as a good day?

March 25

No person is your friend who demands your silence, or denies your right to grow. —ALICE WALKER

Addictive relationships force me to give up myself in order to be with you. In an addictive relationship, there isn't room for both of us as two separate, unique, and valued human beings. In an addictive relationship, I have to set aside my needs, I have to "be quiet," I have to constantly be careful not to "rock the boat" or cause a confrontation. Addictive relationships tell me that to be your lover or your friend I have to be like you . . . in other words, I have to give up me.

Healthy friendships and relationships celebrate and affirm our unique identities. They value our individual contributions. They grapple with, and learn to appreciate, our differences. They challenge and encourage our growth. Healthy friendships and relationships have enough room for us to be both separate and together. In a healthy relationship, I don't have to lose me in order to be with you.

Learning to value and take care of our own needs, while at the same time caring for others, is an important task of recovery. It is also a process that takes time.

Today I will reflect on my friendships, evaluating whether they support my recovery by offering me room to change and grow.

March 26

Words are more powerful than perhaps anyone suspects, and once deeply engraved in a child's mind, they are not easily eradicated. —MAY SARTON

Dyke, Butch, Bulldagger, Homo, Tomboy, Lezzie, Queer, Misfit, Pervert, Morally Depraved, Child Molester, Degenerate. These are the words many of us grew up with. Even if they were not hurled directly at us, we heard them used for others and, somewhere deep inside, knew these words were meant for us as well.

It is no wonder the use of drugs and alcohol among lesbians is three times higher than among heterosexual women. Words like these get inside of us when we're very young; words like these hurt and damage our sense of self-worth; words like these sabotage our success as adults and make it difficult to tolerate the vulnerability and intimacy necessary for healthy relationships.

Recovery involves rooting out these ugly words, myths, and stereotypes and discovering the truth about ourselves. It means recovering our true worth as sane and sober lesbians. Recovery empowers us to rename ourselves in ways that celebrate our identity.

As a lesbian in recovery, today I will affirm the names that bring me self-respect and dignity.

March 27

Another belief of mine: that everyone else my age is an adult, whereas I am merely in disguise.
—MARGARET ATWOOD

The "impostor syndrome" is a phenomenon common to most of us, as lesbians and as women. It is the belief that we are not who we appear to be, the sense that there is something fraudulent about our lives. It involves a gap between how we think others see us and how we feel about ourselves. Regardless of how sober and competent they think we are, we know the truth. And, if they knew—if they knew how anxious we are, if they knew how little we know, if they knew how irresponsible we are—they wouldn't think so highly of us.

This phenomenon happens most often when we are successful. Rather than absorb this reality and allow it to empower us, we write it off and discount our achievements. And if we cannot discount our achievements, we devalue ourselves: it was just a fluke; I was lucky; I sure fooled them this time.

In recovery we need to let the truth of our lives affect our self-esteem. In sobriety we really are learning how to be responsible. In sobriety we really are learning to show up for our lives. In sobriety we really are learning to care appropriately for others. It is time for our self-image to catch up with reality.

Is my self-esteem out of sync with the truth of my recovery? How can I begin to make changes in my self-image?

March 28

Solitude is one thing and loneliness is another.
—MAY SARTON

Learning the difference between loneliness and solitude is an important lesson in recovery. Most of us are familiar with loneliness. Whether we were isolators or "party people," we suffered from profound loneliness during our addictions. No matter how many people were with us, we felt isolated and alone.

Solitude is a new experience for us in recovery, and it puzzles us. Perhaps a good working definition is that solitude is the ability to be alone without being lonely. Enjoying an occasional time of solitude has a lot to do with our ability to be with ourselves. Being alone, without feeling lonely, means we are able to enjoy spending time with ourselves; it means we have to like ourselves.

In later writings, May Sarton suggests that loneliness is the "poverty of self," while solitude is the "richness of self." It is another way of saying that when we feel lonely, we feel empty; we feel like we are not enough. In contrast, solitude reflects our appreciation of ourselves and our ability to feel content even when we are alone.

◇

Am I able to spend time with myself without feeling lonely? Have I learned to like myself enough to value solitude?

March 29

And blessed be the women who get you through.
—ROBIN MORGAN

The above words form the opening and closing lines to a wonderful poem by Robin Morgan. In between these lines there is a litany of women—the woman who lets you stay in her apartment, the woman who cries with you, the woman who loans you a book, the woman who rings you up to see how it's going, the woman who makes you eat something, the woman who makes you laugh, the woman who feeds your cats when you're gone.

Each of us have women in our lives who have played important roles in our growth and development. They have nurtured us, listened to us, cared for us, worked with us, challenged us, and played with us. Some of them were essential to our survival. At the very least, our lives would be severely diminished had they not been a part of us. Their presence has truly enriched and blessed us.

Today I will compose my own litany of women who have nourished my survival and growth. Blessed be these women!

March 30

I am certain before I begin writing a piece that I will not be able to put sentences together, or worse, that all I have to say has been said before. —SUSAN GRIFFIN

Insecurity is a basic human emotion. We all experience it from time to time, especially just before we embark on something important to us. No matter how talented an artist is, there is a moment of insecurity just before she begins a new project. No matter how gifted a speaker is, there is a moment of insecurity just before she gives her presentation. No matter how many times we have come out, there is a moment of insecurity just before we break the news again. There may be even more than a moment of insecurity; sometimes it lingers until we have to figure out what is going on inside us and where the fears are rooted.

Moving beyond these fears requires that we acknowledge their humanness and be gentle with ourselves. Then when we are ready, there is no way out of them but through them. Moving beyond our insecurities eventually means that we have to face them and step into them. In other words, we have to begin the task in front of us. Most of the time our insecurities begin to dissolve once we are involved and working.

Today I will acknowledge my insecurities as a part of being human.

March 31

**A woman no longer afraid, a child no longer ascared,
I see fully now; no longer separated from my feelings.
I claim my power to create and relate; I stand up,
speak up, speak against—no longer severed from
myself.**
— THE REV. NANCY L. RADCLYFFE

Addiction separates us from ourselves. It alienates us from the very source of our being. In cutting us off from our feelings, the progression of our addiction cuts us off from our true power and strength.

The journey of recovery is about reclaiming our sense of ourselves—rediscovering who we are, redefining our identity as sober lesbians, recreating our ability to feel, reconnecting to the strength and power that are inherently ours.

Recovery means we no longer need to live in fear. Recovery means we no longer need to allow others to define and control our reality. As sober lesbians, recovery means we are set free to take back our power, standing up and speaking out for who we are because we are no longer separated from ourselves.

**Today I will celebrate the ways that I have been
set free to be myself.**

April 1

If we want the world to accept us, we must first accept ourselves. If we want the world to give us respect, not to look at us with shame, we must first be willing to give ourselves respect. We must be proud of who we are and we cannot do that while we hide.
—MARTINA NAVRATILOVA

These remarks, from a speech Martina Navratilova gave at the 1993 March on Washington, challenge us to examine our thoughts and beliefs about ourselves in order to be more effective in our work for social change. She reminds us that as long as we act as if there is something wrong with being a lesbian, others will treat us that way. As long as we act as if being a lesbian is something to hide, others will expect us to remain in the closet.

If we want things to be different, we must be different. It is not enough to work for social change, without addressing the changes needed within us and within our community. Accepting ourselves and being proud of who we are is the first step toward a society in which we are accepted and affirmed. It is the first step toward a society in which we are accorded dignity and respect. We cannot expect the world to change if we are unwilling to change ourselves.

Today I will focus on accepting myself and being proud of who I am, recognizing that this is the first step toward gaining what I want from others.

April 2

When the blood sugar is extremely low, the resulting irritability, nervous tension, and mental depression are such that a person can easily go berserk.
—ADELLE DAVIS

During our addictions, most of us failed to care for our physical selves. We ate irregularly, if at all, and certainly didn't worry about a "balanced diet," or the status of our blood sugar levels! We skipped doctor's appointments, avoided the dentist, and probably never saw a gynecologist. We ignored our aches and pains until they became overwhelming.

Today's quote reminds us of the connections between our physical and emotional well-being. Our physical health has an impact on how we think and feel about ourselves. In recovery we need to remember to eat on a regular basis. It is essential to our ability to think clearly and respond appropriately. We need to get enough sleep. We need to deal with pain when it occurs, and not procrastinate on calling the doctor until it is an emergency.

Dealing with our physical body-selves is an important aspect of our recovery. Learning to take care of our bodies is another way of caring for ourselves in sobriety.

Today I will try to pay attention to my physical well-being, remembering that it affects my mental and emotional health.

April 3

Steps eight and nine ensure that alcoholics can no longer consider themselves victims. In these steps we say, yes, we have been harmed by alcohol; but ultimately we are required to take responsibility for our actions.
—JUDITH MCDANIEL

In step eight we make a list of all persons we have harmed and become willing to make amends to them. In step nine we make direct amends to these persons except when to do so would injure them or others. These two steps allow us to examine our attitudes and behaviors during our addiction and then challenge us to take responsibility for the ways our choices may have affected others.

It is likely that all of us have been victims at some point in our lives, and we need to deal with these painful experiences. Steps eight and nine ensure that we see ourselves as more than victims. Yes, others have hurt us and let us down. Others have rejected, ostracized, alienated, and ridiculed us. However, we are not powerless victims. Our choices and behavior, especially during our addictions, sometimes created pain and disappointment for others. Steps eight and nine call us to account for these actions. Taking responsibility for ourselves as sober lesbians is one way to regain our self-esteem.

Are there amends I still need to make? How can I begin to take responsibility for these actions?

April 4

It is through generating stories of our own crisis and hope and telling them to one another that we light the path. —ROSEMARY RADFORD RUETHER

Twelve-step programs are rooted in the wisdom of Ruether's words. The essence of recovery lies in giving away what we have gained. Unless we are willing to share the experience and hope we have found in recovery, we will lose it.

Sharing our stories, speaking the truth as we have lived it, lights the path both for ourselves and for others. As we share our stories, we grow in self-esteem and confidence. As we share our stories, we come to see the wholeness of our lives. As we share our stories, we discover that we are not alone. And as we share our stories, other lesbians are able to find their path to sobriety through our experiences.

As sober lesbians, we have a responsibility to show the way. Those of us who are already sober must carry the message of hope to our sisters who are still struggling with the burden of their addiction. We are the ones who must tell them that sobriety is worth it. We are the ones who must demonstrate that recovery is possible. We are the ones who must illuminate a path through their denial, allowing them to arrive at their own sense of sanity and hope.

How can I give away the joy that I have found in recovery? With whom do I need to share my story of crisis and hope?

April 5

Truth is the absolute foundation to health. Lies are the absolute foundation to dis-ease.
—THE REV. BRENDA HUNT

Being honest with ourselves is essential to recovery. Being honest with ourselves requires breaking through the denial that characterized our active addictions. This kind of "rigorous honesty," so often discussed in twelve-step programs, challenges us to move beyond easy answers and rationalizations. It calls us to examine ourselves and our relationships, to grapple with our motives, and to clarify our actions.

Dishonesty is dangerous. As Brenda Hunt suggests, when we are dishonest we experience dis-ease, literally a discomfort or an unsettledness within us. When we are dishonest with ourselves, we open our minds to old addictive thinking patterns. When we are dishonest with others, we create barriers that preclude healthy relationships. All of these dynamics lead us back to our active addiction, back to our disease.

The foundation for health was laid when we spoke the truth and acknowledged our addictions. Our ongoing health depends upon continued honesty in recovery.

Are there areas in my life where I feel "diseased"? Have I been fully honest with myself?

April 6

It was as if I had been sleeping all my life until that very instant when I reached out and she met me with her heart.
—CINDY MADRÓN

In a piece entitled "For Maria," Cindy Madrón wonderfully captures the joys of our coming out experiences. I suspect that all of us can vividly recall that moment when we first touched, held, kissed, or made love to another woman.

When lesbians meet each other for the first time, one of the early topics of conversation almost always involves our coming out stories. We delight in sharing them with others, describing the difficulties and complications we put ourselves through and reveling in the joys of finding others like ourselves. We laugh as we share the ways we struggled to ask her out or invite her home, torturing ourselves over whether or not she was attracted to us and wondering who should make the first move.

Sharing our stories builds a bridge to all the other lesbians who have gone before us in this world. Sharing our stories reminds us of the goodness of who we are. Sharing our stories renews our sense of gratitude for all the ways that we have been awakened in our coming out.

Today I will remember and celebrate my first moments of coming out.

April 7

Alcohol doesn't console, it doesn't fill up anyone's psychological gaps, all it replaces is the lack of God.
—MARGUERITE DURAS

In the early stages of our addiction, using substances made us feel better. We knew there was an emptiness inside, and drinking and drugging seemed to fill us. At the very least, we forgot our pain. In recovery we have learned that this belief was an illusion. Drinking and drugging may have helped for the moment, but in the long run we still had to face that haunting emptiness within.

Years ago, Carl Jung wrote to Bill Wilson, the founder of Alcoholics Anonymous, describing alcoholism as a search for God. In doing so, Jung was one of the first to sense that this driving need to fill the emptiness within was really a spiritual quest. This emptiness inside us is about our spiritual need to feel connected.

As sober lesbians, we need to find new ways of responding to our yearnings. We need to find new ways of consoling ourselves and allowing others to console us. We need to find new ways of releasing our spirituality so it can empower and fulfill us.

**Today I will acknowledge the emptiness
I sometimes feel and look for new,
sober ways to fill it.**

April 8

Lately I have let fear lodge in my bones, make a corrosive home for itself inside deep within, out of reach from where I could try and yank it out roots and all.
—MARIA CORA

Fear places a stranglehold on our recovery, choking our spirits and sapping our strength. Sometimes we think ignoring fear will make it go away. We pretend to be unafraid, pushing our feelings aside and acting tough. This approach is rarely successful. When we ignore our fear, it burrows in even deeper, winding its way into the farthest nooks and crevices of our bodies.

Fear has to be recognized and rooted out as it occurs. Naming our fear and sharing it with others robs fear of its power over us. Some fears are stronger than others; they must be rooted out repeatedly. Rooting them out is not easy, but if we ignore them, they will come to rule our lives.

What fears have begun to make a home within me? Can I name them now before they take root and begin to rule my life?

April 9

> There are those who think
> or perhaps don't think
> that children and lesbians
> together can't make a family
> that we create an extension
> of perversion. —PAT PARKER

Our families are as diverse as we are. They come in all shapes and sizes—single lesbian mothers, lesbians without children, lesbian couples who parent together, lesbians who parent with gay men, lesbian grandmothers, lesbians who form extended families with other queer sisters and brothers, biological parents, parents we've adopted as ours—the variations are infinite.

All of our families need validation and affirmation. All of our families deserve to be celebrated. We have faced incredible challenges, and sometimes incredible rejection and disappointment. And yet, we have not given up on the ability to give and get love. In the face of often insurmountable odds, we have created and maintained families for ourselves. We have to exercise the right to define what family is for us. Our families, biological or chosen, are real families.

Today I will celebrate the family I have chosen to be a part of and affirm its basic goodness in my life.

April 10

It's odd that you can get so anesthetized by your own pain or your own problem that you don't quite fully share the hell of someone close to you.
—LADY BIRD JOHNSON

Sometimes we get caught up in our own struggles and fail to notice the pain of those around us. We don't mean to be oblivious to their feelings; we're just preoccupied with our own. We may be so caught up in the difficult day we had at work that we don't notice how bummed out our girlfriend looks. Or we're so focused on the healing work we are doing that we don't listen attentively when our sponsee calls to talk. Or we're so preoccupied with our problems that we forget to show up to meet a friend.

Though we may feel bad when it happens, it is a human experience. It doesn't mean we are a bad person, but it does mean we need to examine what is happening in our recovery. Being so caught up in ourselves that we fail to notice the pain of those we love usually means our focus is out of balance. We need to look for tools to pull us out of ourselves. It might be meetings; it might be disciplining ourselves to spend time with other people; it might be other activities that shift our focus. We do not need to stop working on ourselves, we just need to readjust our perspective.

Am I able to pay attention to the feelings of those I love or is my focus out of balance?

April 11

> I've got the general
> unspecific—no one's
> left me—nothing's
> wrong—Blues.
> —GUDRUN FONFA

This wonderful and humorous poem by Gudrun Fonfa captures the ways we sometimes feel out of sorts for no particular reason. We're not premenstrual, nothing horrible happened at work, we didn't have a fight with our parents or our girlfriend—we're just tired or restless, just generally down in the dumps.

During our addictions, we tried to avoid this feeling. In recovery, we are learning to accept and sit with being out of sorts. We have begun to recognize that feelings aren't facts and feelings don't last forever. Having the blues is not a permament state of being. We are also learning that we do not always need to understand all the ins and outs of why we feel the way we do.

Accepting our feelings, and living lightly with them, makes life easier. I don't have to fight my way through the blues. I can recognize them, rest with the feelings, and maybe even laugh at myself with Fonfa.

Today I am learning to accept and live with my feelings without always needing to understand them.

April 12

> We do all sorts of things for the outside of our bodies, and I'm not gonna say any of that is wrong. But I want to say one thing: we must be concerned about what is on the inside because no matter how well we dress up the outside, it is the inside that needs healing.
> —THE REV. DELORES BERRY

Recovery begins by focusing on the outside: not picking up a drink or a drug, changing addictive behaviors, getting a physical, eating healthy, becoming more responsible. But the real work of recovery is an "inside job." The real work involves changing the attitudes and thought patterns that sustained and enabled our addictions.

It is one thing to stop drinking; it is another to address the anger and resentment that leads us to drink. It is one thing to stop overeating; it is another to address the emptiness that longs to be filled up with food. It is one thing to stop getting high; it is another to address the fear and anxiety that drives our cravings.

Changing the outside is important. We need to feel good about how we look. We need to learn to care for our physical bodies. But the real healing needed to sustain recovery must occur within us.

What areas of my life need healing? How can I recover from the inside out?

April 13

To be a lesbian means to be forever measuring the impact of our truth on other people.
—MARIANA ROMO-CARMONA

We sometimes minimize the continual stress of societal homophobia. If we have not recently encountered violence or overt discrimination, it is easy to play down the more subtle manifestations of oppression and ignore the ways we constantly assess our behavior.

Are we safe hiking this mountain trail? Are we acting too much like dykes in this neighborhood? Will it be okay to have a nice romantic dinner in this restaurant, or will we encounter the subtle stares of homophobia? Are these fears legitimate? Are they real and justified, or do they reflect leftover traces of internalized homophobia?

There are no easy answers. I only know that Mariana is right. We are forever measuring the impact of the truth of our lives. We are forever assessing our safety, forever evaluating the risks and benefits of being "out loud and proud," or even quiet and loving. May the goddess keep us honest and grant us courage in these struggles.

Today I will be gentle with myself, recognizing the ongoing stress of coming out and living honestly in this world.

April 14

A funny thing I've noticed about some of my *amiguitas y amiguitos* who've become half of a pair . . . it's impossible to see them minus their other half.
—GLORIA ANZALDÚA

In a humorous but pointed poem entitled "Old Loyalties," lesbian poet and writer Gloria Anzaldúa discusses a phenomenon in the lesbian community. She describes how entering a new lover relationship often means leaving one's friends behind. We get so busy with new lovers that we no longer have time for old friends. Or, out of fear that our lovers will be jealous, we stop spending time with friends or only see them together with our lover. As Anzaldúa says, we find ourselves caught in a "hierarchy of loyalties," in which our friends usually lose.

There is no easy solution to this dilemma. However, in recovery, we must be as responsible as we can in balancing our relational commitments. Both friends and lovers are important. Being a part of a community and having a sober support network is essential for recovery and for a healthy identity as lesbians.

Have I allowed new relationships to interfere with friendships? Are there ways I can better balance my relationships?

April 15

It is only by living completely in this world that one learns to have faith. —DIETRICH BONHOEFFER

People in the program are always talking about faith. Have faith. Replace fear with faith. Work the third step. Turn it over. Coming to understand what this means for each of us is a long and often painful process.

Before we got sober, the only thing we trusted was our addiction. It made us feel at least a little bit normal. It took the edge off our fears and anxieties. It soothed our insecurities. It quieted our disappointments and losses. It fueled or diminished our anger. This substance that we trusted allowed us to bypass the need for faith, and it did so by taking us out of our feelings and out of this world.

Learning to have faith means we have to become an active participant in our own lives. It means we have to stop running away from our feelings. We have to learn to stand still and deal with whatever is right in front of us, rather than going around it. In program language, learning to have faith is about learning to live in our own skin.

◊

Today I will strive to live in the moment, taking each situation as it occurs.

April 16

I didn't want to be a boy, ever, but I was outraged that his height and intelligence were graces for him and gaucheries for me. —JANE RULE

Most of us understand Jane Rule's outrage. We spent our growing up years caught in the tension between society's rules and expectations and our emerging lesbian identities. Truth of the matter is, some of us did want to be boys. In the process of sorting out our lesbian identities, some of us wondered if we should have been boys or if we really were little boys stuck inside a little girl's body.

As a starting point in this process, we need to hear that these feelings and these struggles are normal and healthy responses to growing up in a homophobic culture. Because of the heterosexism of our society, sorting out gender identity and sexual orientation issues is a major task of our recovery process. Healthy ongoing recovery calls us to grapple with the impact of society's beliefs and rules on our sense of self. We need to understand how growing up lesbian in a straight society affected our sense of ourselves as women and as lesbians. Recovery challenges us to work together to increasingly accept ourselves as the lesbian women that we are.

Today I can be accepting of my struggles to sort out my identity, knowing that I am not alone on this journey.

April 17

If my hands are fully occupied in holding onto something, I can neither give nor receive.
—DOROTHEE SÖLLE

Most of us balk at change. We hang on to old ideas and behaviors, long after they have served out their usefulness. As addicts, we tend to go to great lengths to avoid making changes. One of the truths we learn in recovery is that though it may not be apparent in the moment, letting go and accepting change is the route to receiving something new. When we hang on to the old, we are literally unable to receive anything new.

Willingness to let go is the essence of steps six and seven in twelve-step recovery programs. Are we willing to let go of old beliefs about ourselves in order to find a new sense of self-esteem? Are we willing to let go of old attitudes about others in order to repair and rebuild our relationships? Are we willing to let go of resentment and fear? Are we willing to let go of familiar behaviors that keep us from growing in recovery?

Hanging on keeps us stuck. It keeps us from moving forward and making progress. Learning to let go of old beliefs and behaviors opens us up to the new gifts recovery has to offer us.

What old ideas and actions have I been holding on to simply because they are familiar? How can I begin to let go and open myself to something new?

April 18

When we think of loss we think of the loss, through death, of people we love. But loss is a far more encompassing theme in our life. For we lose not only through death, but also by leaving and being left, by changing and letting go and moving on.

—JUDITH VIORST

Learning to deal with loss, in its broadest meaning, is an important aspect of our recovery. It begins the moment we get sober. Immediately, there is the loss of whatever we used to numb our feelings and cope with life. There are losses of people we used to hang out with, places we used to go, and things we used to do that no longer fit with sobriety.

As lesbians, we experience multiple losses on a daily basis—the loss of societal approval, the loss of family respect and acceptance, the loss of having to hide ourselves and our lovers, the loss of children, the loss of jobs, apartments, promotions.

Each time we experience loss, the current trigger taps into previous losses. It unleashes not only the current feelings, but all of our unresolved feelings from the past as well. As a sober community, we need to find ways to hear and validate one another's sense of loss. We need to create times and places where we can grieve together. We need to acknowledge the pervasive nature of loss, helping one another learn to accept the existence of loss as a part of living.

What losses have I recently experienced? Am I allowing myself to find strength through sharing my pain with others?

April 19

> To pray you open your whole self
> To sky, to earth, to sun, to moon
> To one whole voice that is you.
>
> —JOY HARJO

Joy Harjo's prayer for openness highlights one of the basic tenets of sobriety. Openness is essential to recovery. Being open is what enables us to get sober in the very beginning. Before we became willing to be open, we were hopelessly locked in the prisons of our addiction. Only as we became open were we able to discover the way out.

Continued openness is the key to ongoing growth and change. We need to be open to new understandings about ourselves as lesbians. We need to be open to new beliefs about our strengths and limitations. We need to be open to new ideas about how to be in relationship with friends and lovers.

True openness engages all of our self in the process of change and growth. True openness allows our recovery to permeate every aspect of our being. True openness—to ourselves, to others, and to the world around us—empowers us and makes us whole.

Today I will pray for the openness needed for healthy recovery, recognizing that this is the path to healing and growth.

April 20

We have been thru so much pain that now we have no place to put that pain but to leave it out of our lives.
—NAOMI LITTLEBEAR

"Bottoming out" is a familiar concept to most of us in recovery. We hear others describe the point at which their recovery began as the moment they "hit bottom"—when they became "sick and tired of being sick and tired." In other words, our recovery often begins when we reach a place where we are tired of our addictions, tired of being miserable, tired enough to be willing to give up our addiction to misery, and tired enough to be open to new ideas for a way out.

Recovery, in and of itself, doesn't make all of the pain in our lives go away. Some of us struggle for years after getting sober, with depression, other obsessions, or painful histories of abuse. All of us go through periods of growth, followed by stagnation. All of us have our ups and downs, sometimes mild, sometimes more severe.

Many of us find that there comes a time in our recovery when Naomi Littlebear's words make sense. It is almost like a "bottoming out" on pain. Continuing in our recovery means grappling with how to leave the pain out of our lives. It means we have to let go of old images of ourselves as crazy, messed up victims. We have to be willing now to let go of our addiction to the pain and find new self-identities that go beyond just surviving our past.

◊

Today I will give myself permission to leave the pain out of my life.

April 21

You have to be a little patient if you're an artist, people don't always get you the first time.
—KATE MILLETT

Millett's words are good advice even for those of us who are not artists. We've all had experiences of people who did not, or may still not, appreciate our choices and our lives. Parents who thought it was just a phase. Friends who couldn't believe we broke up with her. Lovers who just didn't get why certain things were important to us.

Often we are tempted to just give in or give up when others fail to understand us. We interpret their lack of knowledge as rejection . . . if they really cared about us, they'd try harder; if they really loved us, they'd "get it."

In reality, it is not easy to truly comprehend another human being. It takes time and consistent effort to learn to listen and discern what someone else values, to clarify how they like to do things, or to come to cherish what they value.

Today I will be patient with those around me, allowing them time to come to know me.

April 22

However confused the scene of our life appears, however torn we may be who now do face that scene, it can be faced, and we can go on to be whole.
—MURIEL RUKEYSER

Weaving together the pieces of our past, sifting through the good and the bad, is one of the challenges of recovery. Many things occurred during our addictions that are confusing to us in recovery. There are events and feelings we would rather not remember. There are people from whom we were alienated or rejected. Sometimes long into recovery we find ourselves still bruised and battered by what transpired earlier. Facing these experiences, and working them through, can be extremely painful.

In the midst of all this, Muriel Rukeyser's words evoke the promise of recovery. It is a promise we need to claim over and over again. The joy of our recovery is that regardless of how broken we feel, we can face our past—the things that we have done and the things that were done to us—and survive. Better than that, we can go on to wholeness. We can do more than just survive our past; we can thrive and grow.

In what ways do I need to face my past and then move on toward wholeness?

April 23

True prayer is not asking God for love; it is learning to love. —MARY BAKER EDDY

Prayer takes many shapes and forms. It is not limited to the obvious practice of talking with God. I have a friend in recovery who says that for her, work is prayer. By this she means that what she does each day and how she does it is a form of communication with her higher power. There are as many different ways of communicating as there are people. We can pray while we are working, playing, making love, sharing a special moment with someone we care about, listening to a friend, or just being quiet by ourselves.

Mary Baker Eddy challenges us to recognize that true communication happens in doing, not in simply talking about something. True communication occurs as we actually learn to love ourselves and others, as opposed to talking about our need to love. True communication with our higher power occurs as we learn to do the work necessary to our own recovery, rather than simply talking about it.

Whatever we need, the real communication occurs as we take the risk to act on our requests. It is not enough to ask for love; we need to learn how to love.

Today I will remember that true prayer or communication with my higher power involves the willingness to act on my requests.

April 24

I didn't steal this. It was "differently-acquired."
—SARA CYTRON

Lesbian comic Sara Cytron humorously highlights how easy it is for us to rationalize our choices and behavior. As addicts, we are experts at rationalizations. For years, we rationalized our actions so that we could maintain our addictions. Over and over again, we found ways to escape taking responsibility: it wasn't our fault; we lost our job because our boss had it in for us; we drank because life was so difficult; if our lover would just get off our back, we wouldn't have to get high so often.

This habit of making excuses for ourselves does not automatically disappear in recovery. Moving beyond rationalization requires honesty with ourselves and others. Am I having trouble at work because my boss is homophobic, or am I contributing to the difficulties in our work relationship? Does my lover have legitimate complaints about my attitudes and behavior? Are my current choices healthy and constructive, or am I rationalizing inappropriate actions in order to get what I want regardless of the consequences?

Today I will be honest with myself. When I am unsure about my motivation, I will seek feedback from those whose judgment I trust.

April 25

Voyager, there are no bridges, one builds them as one walks.
—GLORIA ANZALDÚA

People in twelve-step programs often talk about recovery as a "bridge back to life." Recovery offers us a fresh start. It opens the door to new life. It enables us to begin reconnecting with ourselves and others.

As we continue in our recovery, we increasingly recognize the truth of Anzaldúa's words. This bridge back to life is not handed to us; it does not come ready-made; it cannot be created for us by someone else. This bridge is something we must build.

Each time we take a risk and allow ourselves to be vulnerable with another human being, we are building a bridge back to life. Each time we step out on faith, trusting the resources within us, we are building a bridge back to life. Each time we acknowledge our mistakes and try again, we are building a bridge back to life.

Each action I take today can be a bridge to wholeness and new life.

April 26

What we say and what we do ultimately comes back to us so let us own our responsibility, place it in our hands and carry it with dignity and strength.
—GLORIA ANZALDÚA

During our addiction, we spent a lot of time evading responsibility. We felt overwhelmed and incompetent. We didn't want to show up, act grown-up, or be responsible. It was easier to let somebody else step in and rescue us. We wanted others to take care of things for us.

Being in recovery means beginning to accept responsibility for what we say and do. If we say we will attend a meeting, then we try to show up. If we say we'll finish a task, then we make every effort to get it done. And if it cannot be finished, then we let the appropriate people know this and work with them to strategize options for completing it.

The reward for learning to accept our responsibilities is increased dignity and self-esteem. Each time we show up for a commitment, we gain a sense of self-respect. Each time we complete a project, we gain new self-esteem.

Today I will focus on showing up for myself and owning my responsibilities.

April 27

If you are not afraid of the voices inside you, you will not fear the critics outside you. —NATALIE GOLDBERG

All of us struggle with wanting approval from others. We hand in a paper we have written, and wait anxiously for the instructor's feedback. We submit a proposal for a new program at work, and hang on pins and needles until we hear the boss's reaction. We mail a letter off sharing with someone we love that we are a lesbian, and live in trepidation until we have a response in hand. While we wait, we imagine the worst possible responses.

The truth is, other people can only make us feel inferior or inadequate when we give them this power. Their voices of disapproval and rejection loom large only because they echo the critical voices that live within our own minds. The real critic who has the power to "do us in" lives within us.

Learning to counter, and sometimes live with, the critical side of ourselves is essential to our serenity. If we can make peace with that voice, we will discover we no longer need to live in fear of the voices of others.

Which critical voices still hound me in recovery? How can I begin to make peace with my inner critic?

April 28

Discoveries have reverberations. A new idea about oneself or some aspect of one's relations to others unsettles all one's other ideas . . . No matter how slightly, it shifts one's entire orientation.
—PATRICIA MCLAUGHLIN

Some of us thought that getting sober was just about putting down the drink or the drug. We had no clue about how this simple act would change our lives. Similarly, few of us knew the impact that identifying as a lesbian would come to have in our lives.

Part of why change is so unsettling is that all self-discoveries have an unpredictable impact. When we first begin to acknowledge the revelation, we can rarely predict its full effect. Coming to grips with our self-centeredness, acknowledging our tendency toward perfection, recognizing our incredible survival strength, celebrating our lesbian identity—whatever the discovery, its impact is far-reaching.

Each discovery in sobriety is important. Its value cannot be measured or assessed alongside other discoveries. Each is unique and powerful.

Changes in recovery have a ripple effect; each one touches another, leading me toward healing and growth.

April 29

No partner in a love relationship should feel that she has to give up an essential part of herself to make it viable. —MAY SARTON

Learning how to be ourselves and be with our lovers is something with which we all struggle. The challenges we face in intimate relationships pose a million questions for which there are very few clear or easy answers.

For example, relationships require compromise. There has to be some give-and-take. It can't be all one person's way. How do we decide when to compromise and when compromising might mean giving up something essential of ourselves? Some things may be easier, like where to squeeze the toothpaste or how to put the toilet paper on the roll. But what about tastes in food, or style of dress, or the kinds of friends we enjoy being with, or the way we want to spend our leisure time?

May Sarton's words are not an easy answer, but they do provide a bottom line. If over time, I am losing more and more of me by loving you, then something is out of balance in our love.

Am I paying attention to my needs and likes in my relationships with others? Am I valuing myself as much as I value those I love?

April 30

Those of us who have been forged in the crucibles of difference . . . know that survival is not an academic skill.
—AUDRE LORDE

Growing up lesbian means growing up outside the mainstream, outside of what society defines as normal and acceptable. It means, as Audre Lorde wrote, standing outside "the circle of this society's definition of acceptable women." Those of us who are also Black, Latina, poor, or differently-abled stand even farther outside the mainstream.

Learning how to survive on the margins is not something we were taught in school. We didn't find it in books at the public library. We only sometimes learned it from our families, and even they never taught us much about surviving as lesbians. Survival is something we have learned the hard way—on our own through trial and error.

Our addiction helped us learn to survive. It enabled us to tolerate living on the margins. It helped us push aside the feelings of exclusion, rejection, and abnormality. Whether we used drugs, alcohol, food, or sex, we found it easier to survive.

Today we need to relearn survival, clean and sober. But this time we don't have to do it alone, the hard way. This time we can lean on and learn from one another. Recovery is about surviving together.

How can I reach out today for support from others in recovery?

May 1

> We can make new paths, walk them hand in hand, discover each new road, forge a new world where you can be you and I can be me. —MARIA AMPARO JIMENEZ

We are not confined to the paths that a heterosexist and homophobic society has chosen for us. We are not bound to their expectations for our loves and our lives.

Part of the joy of recovery is being set free from addictive dependence on anything—a substance, a repetitive behavior, our parents, our lovers, or an abusive society. In recovery we no longer need to accept the blatant lies that tell us our love is sinful and perverse. In recovery we no longer need to wait for someone else's blessing before we can stand up for ourselves and take action. In recovery we can take back our power and learn to live our own lives.

The joy of recovery is knowing that we can forge new paths. We are not chained to the old. We can choose new ways of being in this world. And we can do this together, with other lesbians of many colors and many talents. Together, we can forge a new world where there is room enough and love enough for all of us.

Today I will celebrate our abilities to build new paths for ourselves and for our sisters who will follow us.

May 2

Action is the antidote to despair. —JOAN BAEZ

The experience of despair is rooted in feelings of powerlessness and hopelessness. Despair happens when we cannot see a way out. Despair happens when we think our actions are of no consequence, when it seems as if no matter what we do, nothing will change. Despair was something we were all familiar with during our addictions. We drank and drugged and otherwise numbed ourselves because we couldn't imagine another way to survive.

Sometimes despair occurs in recovery. Our lover leaves us and the emptiness is overwhelming; we feel abandoned and isolated, and we can't seem to get beyond our pain. Or we begin dealing with a particular "character defect" and suddenly that's all we can see; change seems impossible; we can't imagine a way out. Or another friend is gay-bashed and we find ourselves wondering what's the point in all this; nothing will ever change.

Taking action is the only route out of despair. Taking action, even the smallest action, marks the beginning of something new. Taking action, and then taking another action, begins to create energy, movement, momentum. Taking action counteracts our sense of powerlessness, in fact, it empowers us. Taking action defies our sense of hopelessness and opens us to new visions for tomorrow.

◇

When I am tempted to despair, I will recall that the way out only becomes evident as I take action.

May 3

I acquired the drinker's face before I drank. Drink only confirmed it. The space for it existed in me.
—MARGUERITE DURAS

When we first get sober, we often identify the onset of our addiction with the moment we picked up drugs and alcohol. As we continue in recovery, our stories tend to change. Many of us come to believe that our addictions began long before we picked up an actual substance. We begin to recognize that we had the attitudes, and even the behaviors, of an addict years before our first drink.

Coming to this awareness is not easy. It means acknowledging that our addiction is deeper than the surface-level behaviors of drinking and drugging. It means grappling with attitudes and behaviors that have become a part of the very fabric of our being. It means confronting the "drinker's face" that tormented us long before we found a way to block it out with chemicals.

Fortunately we do not have to do this alone. There are hundreds of other sober lesbians who have already confronted the pervasive and insidious nature of their disease and have survived. Their sober faces can lead us through the process of healing that addictive space within us.

Today I will reach out and draw upon the wisdom of others as I continue confronting the effects of my addiction.

May 4

The larger question for me is how do we make our relationships safe and nurturing places, where mutual respect marks our beginnings and our endings?
—MONA OIKAWA

In an essay entitled "Safer Sex in Santa Cruz," Mona Oikawa discusses the impact of AIDS and safer sex within the lesbian community. Society has largely ignored our concerns. There has been minimal research regarding our risk of infection. However, we have been complicit in this silence. It has been easier to focus on others and AIDS than to examine our own attitudes, feelings, and sexual behaviors.

As sober lesbians, we must demand research into our concerns. We must initiate conversations within our community about our risk of contracting AIDS. We must begin caring for those among us who are living with AIDS. We must explore new ways to safely and sensually celebrate our sexuality. We cannot afford to remain silent any longer. Breaking the silence marks the beginnings of mutual respect and safety for all of us.

How can I participate more fully in addressing the impact of AIDS in our community?

May 5

I happen to feel that the degree of a person's intelligence is directly reflected by the number of conflicting attitudes she can bring to bear on the same topic.
—LISA ALTHER

No matter how long we have been sober, there will be moments when we feel like using drugs or alcohol. No matter how proud we are of our lesbian identity, there will be times when we wish we could hide. Mixed feelings are a part of being human. Learning to live with this ambivalence, rather than running from it, is essential.

Tolerating ambivalence means we can acknowledge our desire to get high without having to act on it. Tolerating ambivalence means we can recognize our desire to hide our identity without receding completely into the closet. All change involves ambivalence. In recovery we are learning to accept these mixed feelings as a part of being human.

Today I will remember that my ambivalence is a reflection of my humanness.

May 6

Anger stirs and wakes in her; it opens its mouth, and like a hot-mouthed puppy, laps up the dredges of her shame. Anger is better. There is a sense of being in anger. A reality and presence. An awareness of worth.
—TONI MORRISON

One constructive way to utilize our anger is allowing it to transform shame. Shame is a debilitating emotion. When we feel shame, we believe, way down inside, that there is something wrong with us. When we feel shame, we miss the wrong others have done to us; we only see how bad we are. When we feel shame, we are unable to stand up for ourselves or protect ourselves, because we do not believe we deserve protection.

Getting angry can transform that shame. Getting angry means beginning to tell the truth about ourselves and our lives. Getting angry means acknowledging the wrongs that have been done to us. Getting angry means reclaiming the inherent sense of goodness within us.

In contrast to the ways shame paralyzes us, anger is an energizing emotion. Anger motivates us to take action and stand up for our rights. Getting angry can transform our shame about childhood abuse, about being a lesbian in a heterosexist society, or about being an addict. As sober lesbians, we must reclaim anger as a constructive tool for our recovery.

How can I allow my anger to transform the shame I carry?

May 7

Relationships, like houses, can be outgrown or can outgrow the people involved ... We aren't inclined to think of houses left behind as failures ... Most relationships, entered into with good faith and lived with generous responsibility, shouldn't be considered failures if they are not life-long. —JANE RULE

All too often when relationships with lovers and friends end, we tend to see ourselves as failures. We ruminate over what we did wrong or what we could have done differently, berating ourselves for not "getting it right" yet again.

There are all kinds of pressures on lesbian relationships: overt societal discrimination; the absence of affirming rituals like engagement parties, weddings, and anniversary celebrations; family rejection; and insufficient lesbian peer support. Given this, it is amazing any of our relationships survive!

Beyond these factors, there is the more general reality of change. Sometimes we can integrate these changes and maintain our relationship; sometimes we cannot. Sometimes people change and grow in the same direction; sometimes their changes lead them in vastly different directions. Being unable to control these changes does not make us failures.

Are there old relationships that I still perceive as failures? Can I be more gentle with myself by viewing them as a normal part of life's changes and growth?

May 8

Life's challenges are not supposed to paralyze you, they're supposed to help you discover who you are.
—BERNICE JOHNSON REAGON

Some challenges are exciting: a new job, being in love, the possibility of travel, getting to do something you've always dreamed of. Other challenges create mixed emotions: breaking up with a lover and learning how to live alone, giving up an addiction, walking through the grief of losing a close friend to AIDS or cancer.

During my active addiction, almost every challenge, good or bad, seemed overwhelming. I was constantly living "on the edge," just barely getting by, and anything new and different, even if it was good, threatened to upset my extremely fragile equilibrium. Feeling powerless and paralyzed was a way of life.

Recovery from addiction brings the beginnings of sanity. As we discover our ability to maintain sobriety, our image of ourselves begins to shift. Instead of being powerless victims, we find a new source of power and competence. With these changes, we are no longer so easily paralyzed. Challenges become opportunities for growth and self-discovery.

Today I will search out the possibilities for growth and self-discovery in the challenges that face me.

May 9

Adult status is bestowed on those who have a family of their own (read: husband and kids) — all others are eternally children.
—FELICE YESKEL

In describing the journey toward acceptance from her family, Felice Yeskel highlights a phenomenon many of us face. In our society, families grant adult status to children once they marry (heterosexually) and have children of their own. Consequently, as lesbians—whether single or in relationship—we often struggle to establish ourselves as adults in relationship to our families of origin. They may not respect our desire to celebrate holidays at our home with our lovers. They may not view our commitments to friends as seriously as those of our "married" siblings.

If we choose to remain connected to our families, we must be patient with their growth and yet assert our independence. We must recognize the subtle strength of their homophobia without compromising our needs. As we become increasingly confident of our identity as sober, adult lesbians, we must gently, but consistently, insist they treat us in accordance with that identity.

Today I will affirm and respect my identity as a sober, adult lesbian, trusting that as I grow strong in this sense of myself, others will increasingly come to respect my growth.

May 10

The passage is through, not over, not by, not around but through.
—CHERRÍE MORAGA

My first inclination is always to look for the easier, softer way. I suspect that's true for all of us. At first blush, why go through heartache if you can get around it? Why walk through fear if you can jump over it? Why face our difficulties head-on, if we can slyly manage to just slip by them?

Yet so often the way that seems easier and softer at the onset turns out to be more complicated than we thought. Much of the time and energy we invest in figuring out how to go over, by, or around a situation could often be saved if we just jumped into it and waded through to the other side.

Learning this lesson is never easy. Our addictions were about looking for the easy way out of ourselves, our feelings, and our lives. It takes time in recovery to change these behaviors. They won't go away overnight. And they will only go away if we are willing to go through the old patterns on our way to discovering the new.

In what situations am I currently spinning my wheels, trying every solution except walking through the problem?

May 11

Am I like the optimist who, while falling ten stories from a building, says at each story, "I'm all right so far"?
—GRETEL EHRLICH

Learning to ask for help in recovery is a challenge for most of us. We are used to doing things on our own, getting by on our own grit and initiative. Despite the well-intentioned people who tell us it is good for us, we don't like to ask for help. Whether we admit it or not, we tend to think of needing help as a weakness. We think it means there is something wrong with us. And besides, we don't want to "bother" people.

All of this means we are a lot like the optimist in Ehrlich's novel *Heart Mountain*. We cheerfully insist that everything is all right, while we're actually hurtling downward toward self-destruction. At the very least, we tell people, "I'm fine," when the truth is we're hurting.

One reflection of growth in recovery is an increased ability to ask for help when needed. That means we have to begin recognizing when we need help. Then, we have to give ourselves permission to ask. Needing help is about being human. It is not human to insist we are fine when things are going wrong. Being human means acknowledging the truth of our present lives and allowing others to share our pain and our joy.

Have I learned to recognize when I need help? Can I give myself permission to ask for it?

May 12

Everybody must learn this lesson somewhere—that it costs something to be what you are. —SHIRLEY ABBOTT

As lesbians, we know the truth in Shirley Abbott's words. We often know it even before we have experienced it. We know that being who we are can be costly. Long before we first came out to anyone, we intuitively knew the risk involved. Coming out does have its costs. It may mean losing a friend or a family member; it may mean risking our jobs and our children; it may mean having fewer career options, or being denied a promotion.

At the same time, not being what we are has its own costs. Choosing to remain in the closet demands that we constantly monitor what we say and how we say it. Denying our identity robs us of our pride and visibility. Choosing to hide who we are is exhausting; it saps our energies and our creativity.

Either route has its costs. In recovery each of us must weigh the options and make our own choices. Each of us must determine the cost we are willing to pay.

What have my choices been about being who I am? Am I satisfied with the cost?

May 13

The gods bless you. May you sleep then on some tender girl friend's breast.   —SAPPHO

Integrating our sexuality and spirituality is challenging. Who we are and what we believe about our higher power may seem light-years away from what we do in bed with our lovers. Even putting those two concepts in the same sentence may seem strange. Given the society in which we live, it is not surprising that we have so much difficulty imagining our spirituality and sexuality as intertwined.

Yes these words by Sappho, born 612 B.C., offer such an image. Can we envision our sexuality as blessed by the gods? Can we picture the gods blessing us as we snuggle alongside our girlfriend's breast? Can we believe that God truly blesses our relationships? Can we trust that our higher power believes that who we are as lesbians is good? Can we see both our sexuality and our spirituality as a yearning for connection?

How can I begin to experience the wholeness of my sexuality and spirituality?

May 14

We cannot live in the past, nor can we re-create it. Yet as we unravel the past, the future also unfolds before us, as though they are mirrors without which neither can be seen or happen. —JUDY GRAHN

At some point in sobriety, most of us discover a need to go deeper in our recovery work. This next level, often called stage two recovery, generally begins after our second year sober, after we have navigated the basics of getting and living sober.

Stage two recovery involves what lesbian writer Judy Grahn calls "unraveling our past." We begin to delve deeper into our identity, reflecting on how past experiences have shaped us. Those of us who grew up in dysfunctional families often begin to reexamine those experiences. We do this work because we begin to see that some of our unhealthy patterns are not going away simply by staying sober. And we begin to sense that they have some connection to our past.

Surviving stage two recovery is challenging. It means we have to learn to look at the past without living in it. We have to examine our past and yet accept the fact that we cannot re-create it. Difficult as it may be at the time, this work is essential to healthy long term recovery. As Grahn notes, unraveling the past allows the future to unfold before us.

Today I will focus on the importance of unraveling my past so that a healthy, sober future can unfold before me.

May 15

Learning is such a painful business. It requires humility from people at an age where the natural habitat is arrogance.
—MAY SARTON

One definition of humility is "being teachable." To be teachable, we must be open to new information. This means recognizing that we do not have all the facts; we do not know everything. To be teachable, we must be open to one another. We must be willing to listen and learn from the experience of others. To be teachable, we must acknowledge our limitations and allow others to help us with their skills and abilities.

Arrogance is the exact opposite of humility. Arrogance says we already have all the answers; we don't need anyone else's help; we can take care of things just fine. Arrogance aborts the learning process and keeps us ignorant.

We cannot afford this kind of arrogance in recovery. Sobriety is not something we can achieve in isolation. Humility—being teachable—enables us to learn what we need for a healthy recovery.

Am I open and teachable? Am I able to learn from the experience of others?

May 16

The white fathers told us, "I think therefore I am," and the black mothers in each of us—the poets—whisper in our dreams, "I feel therefore I can be free."
—AUDRE LORDE

Learning to trust ourselves and our feelings is essential for our recovery. Homophobic people spend a lot of time and energy telling us how we should think and feel, who we should be, and what is acceptable social behavior. If we are going to break free and take control of our own lives, we must learn to recognize our feelings.

During our addictions, we did whatever we could to numb our feelings. We weren't interested in listening to our feelings; they were too painful. Consequently, it is extremely difficult to trust our feelings in early sobriety; most of the time we can't even recognize them.

It is often several years into recovery before we gain that kind of trust, but we need to begin working on it. Thinking a situation through can be important and helpful, but it is our positive and healthy gut feelings that can motivate us into action. Recognizing and trusting our feelings is scary, but it is the route to freedom in recovery.

Today I will try to acknowledge and affirm my feelings as a way of experiencing the freedom of recovery.

May 17

They ride by our apartment with orgies in their heads, while we cook supper and wash dishes together.
—LOUIE CREW

On a day-to-day basis, there is nothing very radical about our lives. We get up each morning, turn on the coffeepot, fix breakfast, take a shower, feed the cat, pick out something to wear, kiss our lovers and maybe our kids good-bye, and head off to work. During the course of an average day, we run through all the normal feelings everyone encounters: excitement, stress, happiness, disappointment, sadness, hope, and fatigue.

Those who hate us distort our lives. They hear the word "lesbian" and conjure up an image of something other than human, some other kind of being that is consumed by sex, sex, and more sex. Surrounded by these lies, it is all too easy for us to begin to internalize their distorted images of ourselves. Their lies are not the truth. Only we can speak the truth about our lives.

Today I will appreciate the value of my life and refuse to believe those who would distort it.

May 18

We started out being scared of together, but together has chased away all those fears. —HOLLY NEAR

After years of isolation during our addiction, intimacy can be a threatening experience. We are not used to letting others in. We are not used to letting others see the hidden parts of us. Without the shield of drugs or alcohol, we feel exposed and vulnerable. Being together—with lovers, friends, or family—can be terrifying in sobriety.

Holly Near's song "Haven't Grown Tired of Living with You" suggests that if we allow ourselves to slowly experience the reality of being with others, togetherness, in and of itself, can diminish our fears. If we can allow others to be present with us in our joys and our pain, if we can allow others to know our disappointments and share our hopes, over time, those fears will diminish. Rebuilding old relationships and creating new friendships may be scary business, but allowing ourselves to be with others is the key to freedom from our fears of intimacy.

In what ways have I been allowing my fear of intimacy to inhibit my relationships? How can I begin to move beyond these fears?

May 19

Healing depends on listening with the inner ear—stopping the incessant blather, and *listening*. Fear keeps us chattering.
—MARION WOODMAN

Growing up in my family, everyone talked all the time. We talked over one another and around one another. We talked when people were listening and kept right on talking when no one was listening. We talked to cover up our fears. We talked to push aside our anger. We talked to hide behind our words. We talked to step around our pain. We talked till we ran out of breath, and then we paused to talk some more.

Learning to slow down and breathe is important to our healing. Learning to be quiet, to stop the "incessant blather" in our heads, is essential. Our old addictive patterns make us vulnerable to chattering—whether aloud or within us—as a way of sidestepping the things that are really important. This kind of chattering covers up our feelings and keeps us too preoccupied to notice them. In recovery we need to learn to listen carefully. Healing requires our time and our attention. Too much blather can make us crazy.

Today I will remember that my healing depends on my ability to listen to myself and others.

May 20

To assess the damage is a dangerous act. I think of how, even as a feminist lesbian, I have so wanted to ignore my own homophobia, my own hatred of myself for being queer. —CHERRÍE MORAGA

Confronting our own internalized homophobia is a difficult process. Sometimes we would rather just not see the continuing ways that society's heterosexism has permeated our being.

Someone looks at us oddly as we walk down the street with our lover, and we wonder if we look too queer. A coworker makes a comment about the bulldykes in the pride parade, and we secretly wish some of our sisters weren't so obvious. Another friend is diagnosed with AIDS, and a voice we'd rather not acknowledge briefly wonders if this really is a punishment from God.

The homophobia in each of these scenarios is reflected in the ways we blame ourselves for being who we are. None of us are free from the insidious effects of society's heterosexism. Even those of us who have been out for years continue to struggle. Recovering from homophobia necessitates an ongoing assessment of the ways our self-esteem has been, and continues to be, damaged. We must take the blame off ourselves and place it where it truly belongs—on the societal beliefs and structures that perpetuate our oppression as lesbians. Only then can we begin to heal together.

Today I am learning not to blame myself for the continuing effects of society's homophobia.

May 21

In soloing—as in other activities—it is far easier to start something than it is to finish it.
—AMELIA EARHART

For years, I was surrounded by unfinished projects. My life was littered with all kinds of bits and pieces that I had begun but no longer had the motivation to complete. Slowly, in recovery I am learning some lessons that are changing this pattern.

First, I am learning to make my choices more carefully. I no longer take on a hundred projects just because someone else thinks they are a good idea. I am learning to choose the things that I really want to do. Second, I am learning to pace myself, to set small goals that are manageable, to take time out to rest and renew myself. I have learned that jumping into something at a hundred miles an hour almost always leads to burnout. Third, I am learning to live with unfinished projects. Sometimes I still bite off more than I can chew. Sometimes I cannot predict ahead of time just how complicated a project will become. I am learning not to blame myself for this; it is just the way life is sometimes. Starting a task is generally easier than finishing it.

Today I am taking care of myself by learning to balance persistence and acceptance.

May 22

It is this belief in a power larger than myself and other than myself which allows me to venture into the unknown and even the unknowable ...
—MAYA ANGELOU

Finding a working belief in a power greater than ourselves is a difficult task for many of us. Yet this belief is essential in times of crisis and often helpful even in our day-to-day lives. Having a belief in a power greater than ourselves gives us the courage to risk stepping out in faith. Having a power larger than ourselves means that we are not in this all alone. Having a power other than ourselves means that we are not solely responsible for what occurs in our world.

How we define this power is not nearly as important as simply believing in it. What we call it, how it operates, the exact nature of our relationship to it—none of these need precise definitions. We can begin simply by trusting that we are not alone, by trusting that the universe is not dependent upon us. There is something or someone who is larger than we are.

Today I will trust that I am not alone and that there is a power larger than my individual human abilities.

May 23

I am not wrong: Wrong is not my name. My name is my own my own my own. —JUNE JORDAN

When we were children, we had no choice but to let others define our reality. We were powerless, dependent on the adults who surrounded us—dependent on them for love and nurturing, dependent on them for our very physical survival, dependent on their version of the truth. We might have had other ideas, we might have had our own suspicions, but they held the power and the control over our lives and our world. All too often these adults labeled what we did, what we felt, what we said, even who we were, as wrong.

As adults, we no longer need to accept their definitions. In fact, healthy recovery requires that we refuse to allow others to speak and define the world for us. As lesbians in recovery, we have the right to name ourselves, our lovers, and our lives as we see fit. We have a responsibility to speak and accept the truth as we define it. Healthy recovery is about claiming the power we did not have as children and using it responsibly in our growth today.

What truths from the past am I still relying on? What new truths do I need to claim for myself?

May 24

A day spent laughing will bring us closer to God than a day of heavy soul-searching. —TERRY LYNN TAYLOR

When was the last time you really cut loose and laughed? Can you remember moments when you laughed so hard you cried, when you laughed so long you almost couldn't breathe?

Laughter is important in recovery. Laughter frees us; when we are laughing, we tend not to be wrapped up in what someone else thinks about us. Laughter loosens us up; when we're laughing, parts of us can rise to the surface that normally are kept under lock and key. Laughing so hard you cried is not just a metaphor; laughter often does loosen and release our tears. Laughing with other people makes us feel connected. There is something bonding about laughter; that's why public speakers often begin with a joke. Laughing makes us feel good about ourselves. You can't feel miserable and laugh at the same time. After a good, long laugh, our problems generally seem less important and overwhelming.

Today I will look for and welcome the opportunity to laugh, knowing that it will bring me closer to my true self and to God.

May 25

We have come to realize that we are not alone in our struggles nor separate nor autonomous but that we—white black straight queer female male—are connected and interdependent. —GLORIA ANZALDÚA

Isolation was a pervasive and progressive part of our addictions. We spent most of our time feeling like we were all alone, that no one else could understand or share our difficulties. When that old, familiar feeling of isolation starts to creep in, we are in dangerous territory. Feeling isolated sets us up for relapse.

Related to our struggles with isolation are conflicts about independence and dependence. During our addictions, most of us bounced back and forth between the extremes. We were either stubbornly and completely self-sufficient—"I'll take care of it myself, thank you"—or we were irresponsibly and inappropriately dependent on others, expecting them to fix things for us and rescue us from the messes we had created. Rarely could we find a middle ground.

Gloria Anzaldúa's comments, from her introduction to *This Bridge Called My Back*, challenge us to recognize our connection to those around us and work toward healthy interdependence in our relationships with others.

Today I will practice finding balance in my relationships, recognizing my connectedness and striving toward interdependence.

May 26

> We have spent so much time hating ourselves. [It is] time to love ourselves. And that, for all lesbians, as lovers, as comrades, as freedom fighters, is the final resistance.
> —CHERYL CLARKE

Loving ourselves is not only an essential aspect of our recovery process; loving ourselves is the bottom line in our work for liberation. Those who fight against us as lesbians, those who work to malign us and make us invisible, would be all too happy if we continued in our addictive, self-destructive ways. Hating ourselves, and acting that hatred out through self-destructive behavior and relationships, simply plays into the hands of those in society who would just as soon see lesbians disappear off the face of the earth.

The heterosexist world around us wants us to hate ourselves. The homophobic society in which we live wants us to go on destroying ourselves. Choosing to recover is an act of resistance. Choosing to love ourselves is an act of liberation for ourselves and for our community. Our growth and recovery is essential to the liberation of the entire lesbian community.

Today I am beginning to see that loving myself is essential to recovery and liberation.

May 27

Even in knowing a truth communicated to us by others, we must rediscover it within the context of our own experience in order for it to apply to our own survival. —THE REV. SANDRA L. ROBINSON

I had long known the truth of others getting sober, but it was years before I could apply it to my own life. Knowing their truth was not sufficient. I had to discover it for myself before it could become a tool for my survival. Once I had taken it into myself, it was no longer *a* truth, but *my* truth.

Part of our growth in recovery is taking the truths transmitted to us by others and allowing them to empower our own lives. We can know for years the truth of our worth as lesbians, but until we transform it in the context of our own lives, it is useless. Others can repeatedly share with us the truths that have empowered their survival, but until we are willing and able to examine them within our experience, they are meaningless.

Other sober lesbians have a wealth of wisdom and experience to offer us. Our task is to draw upon their resources and reflect on their truths, allowing them to inform and illuminate our own journeys. It is only as we take their truth and experience into our lives that we are empowered for our own survival.

How can I allow the truths of others to empower my own life? In what ways can I transform their truth into the context of my life?

May 28

> Neither passive acceptance nor stoic endurance lead to change. Change occurs when there is action, movement, revolution.
> —BELL HOOKS

Passive acceptance and stoic endurance were tools we used for survival during our addiction. Many of us responded passively to the abuse and oppression experienced during our addictions. We simply lived with whatever happened. Our stoic endurance got us through. When things were bad, we gritted our teeth and stuck it out. Throughout it all, we felt powerless over the events of our lives.

The problem with these coping mechanisms is that they keep us from experiencing change in the present. Growth in recovery, as hooks notes, requires action. When we passively accept our problems, the problems remain. When we simply endure our oppression, the injustice continues.

Real change, whether personal or political, requires action. We must creatively use our power to address the issues of our lives and our community if we want to experience growth.

Have I been passively accepting and enduring my problems? What actions can I take to create the change I desire?

May 29

> Sexual appetite, like all appetites, is not fixed. As our bodies, our needs, and our knowledge grow and change, so do our choices, if not of partners, certainly of practices.
> —JANE RULE

Because we grew up in a sex-negative, sexist, and homophobic culture, developing a positive sense of our sexuality becomes an essential aspect of our recovery journey. As lesbians, most of us grew up believing there was something wrong with our sexual desires and practices. Even if we reject society's prejudices, they can continue to have a subtle impact on our sexual self-esteem.

Like all other aspects of our identity, our sexuality shifts and changes as we develop and mature. What made sense for us in early sobriety may make little sense at all ten years into recovery. What we enjoyed sexually during our addictions may no longer bring fulfillment in recovery.

What is most important is finding the ability to accept and embrace our sexuality with all of its changes and evolutions. Sexuality is not a fixed concept: sexual desire ebbs and flows; choices about sexual practices and partners grow and evolve. As we experience healing and integration in our recovery, our sexuality will continue to change. Our task, as sober lesbians, is to accept and appreciate our growth.

Today I will contribute to my healing in recovery by accepting and embracing my evolving sense of sexuality.

May 30

What keeps this ideal alive as a recurring possibility is the exercise of respect, responsibility, and honesty—commensurate with the nature and depth of the particular relationship.
—JUDITH PLASKOW

Traditional heterosexual values and norms are often of little help in teaching us how to build healthy relationships as sober lesbians. In an essay entitled "Toward a New Theology of Sexuality," Judith Plaskow offers three values that can be helpful: respect, responsibility, and honesty. These three qualities were largely missing from our lives during our addiction. As we recover, we learn to exercise them both toward ourselves and in relationship with others.

Plaskow notes that the way we exercise and experience these qualities varies with the nature of the relationship. In one setting, honesty may mean complete sharing of ourselves; in another, it may simply mean being up-front about our intentions for that interaction. With one person, responsibility may mean lifelong faithfulness; with another, it may simply mean being accountable for the choices we make today.

Learning to exercise these values in our relationships will enhance both our self-esteem and our connectedness to others.

How are these values of honesty, respect, and responsibility reflected in my relationships?

May 31

I have learned to live each day as it comes, and not to borrow trouble by dreading tomorrow. It is the menace of the future that makes cowards of us all.
—DOROTHY DIX

Learning to live each day as it comes is one of the challenges of recovery. Some of us tend to be "fretters." We spend hours worrying about what may or may not happen. We replay imagined situations over and over, trying to prepare ourselves for every possibility. We worry about details that don't even occur to other people. We rarely think positively about the future; our concern is what might go wrong.

This obsessive focus on the future robs us of the present. Sometimes it serves to distract and numb us from our immediate concerns in the same ways substances did during our active addiction. Worrying compulsively about tomorrow can also keep us from taking responsibility for the tasks that are important today. Allowing our imaginations to run wild feeds our fears and immobilizes us.

Learning to let go of our anxieties is part of our overall struggle to learn to live life without relying on addictive substances or patterns. Our obsessions, whether about chemicals or about tomorrow, keep us from changing and growing today.

Today I will strive to let go of my obsessive fears, choosing instead to focus on the present.

June 1

I learned lesbian pride from other lesbians: through reading books like *Rubyfruit Jungle*; on the streets of Berkeley, California; at women's music festivals; and in bed.
— FELICE YESKEL

Very few of us learned lesbian pride when we were younger. It was not something our friends and family taught us while we were growing up. We may have found some during our addictions, but even this was muffled and distorted by the effects of drugs and alcohol. Consequently, an important part of our recovery involves discovering and reclaiming our pride.

Felice Yeskel reminds us that we do not reclaim our pride in a vacuum. We cannot celebrate our lesbian identity in isolation. Lesbian pride is not something we can learn by ourselves; we learn it from, and with, other lesbians.

Community is essential to our recovery as addicts and lesbians. We need to be present with, share with, celebrate and play with other sober lesbians. We need to share in their stories in order to celebrate our own lives. We need the strength of their wisdom in order to develop our own insight and power. We need to learn from their experiences in order to find our own sense of identity and pride.

How can I learn from others today? How can their pride strengthen my own?

June 2

All over the nation our children are watching us to see who we become.   —MELANIE KAYE/KANTROWITZ

Melanie Kaye/Kantrowitz calls us to remember that our children are watching our response to issues of oppression, to see what risks we are willing to take to live more justly with one another. What we say about these issues is not enough; they are watching our lives, waiting to see what we will do.

Who are "our children"? Our children are our biological children, the ones to whom we have given birth. Our children are our adopted children, those for whom we have waited and for whom we have climbed mountains of societal resistance. Our children are our nieces and nephews who visit us and our lovers, clamoring for our attention and affection. Our children are our friends' children, staying with us while their lesbian moms have dinner out alone. Our children are our neighbors' children, dropping by our homes, learning that two women loving each other is family. Our children are the young lesbians just coming out, watching us on the streets, in restaurants, and at the grocery store, trying to decipher what it means to be a dyke. Our children are the young people who see us on talk shows, who see clips of gay pride parades each June, who see lesbian posters on the subway and buses.

These are our children and they are watching us.

Can the children who are watching me see my commitment to recovery? Do they see a sober lesbian working with her community for justice?

June 3

Grief is a circular staircase. —LINDA PASTAN

Grief is an emotion none of us are immune to. Throughout our recovery there will be times when our healing involves working through loss and bereavement. While there are various causes for our loss—violence, addiction, cancer or other illness—the AIDS epidemic has multiplied these losses. Many of us can name dozens, even hundreds, of people we have lost to AIDS.

This kind of multiple loss can be a powerful relapse trigger. Grief, left unattended, festers within us. Pain, left unexpressed, creates depression and despair. Unless we find constructive ways to work through these emotions, we will be at high risk for returning to addictive coping mechanisms.

Grief is not something we can address and be done with. Grief is, as Pastan notes, a "circular staircase." We need other sober people who can share our pain and validate our loss. We need to tell the stories of those we have lost, celebrating our joy and making peace with our pain. Telling these stories, as often as we need to, is the only route to healing.

◊

Today I will try to affirm the importance of acknowledging my grief, recognizing that failing to do so places me at risk for relapse.

June 4

To survive we must begin to know sacredness. The pace which most of us live prevents this. —CHRYSTOS

Chrystos suggests that our survival is intimately connected with our ability to recognize and acknowledge what is sacred. Recognizing the sacred within ourselves requires affirming our inherent worth as lesbians and as women. It requires a willingness to touch those places within us that are most deeply sexual and spiritual. It calls forth the wholeness of our lives.

Recognizing the sacred in one another is about being fully present. It challenges us to set aside our own agendas and listen carefully to one another. It calls us to truly be with one another, sharing both joy and sorrow.

Coming to see the sacred in the world around us means grappling with the ways we are part of creation. It means recognizing life and death, joy and pain, as reflections of the wholeness of life. Recognizing the sacred in ourselves, in others, and in the world connects us to the source of our strength. In this sense, it is our survival.

◊

Today I will pay attention to that which is sacred and whole within myself, in others, and in the world around me.

June 5

It was to her faults that she turned to save herself now. —MADELEINE L'ENGLE

Steps four through seven in twelve-step recovery programs address those personal characteristics that are variously described as defects of character, liabilities, deficits, shortcomings, or weaknesses. In step four, we identify these characteristics. In step five, we share them with God and another human being. Then, in steps six and seven, we begin learning to live with or let go of these unhealthy patterns.

As we remain sober, we often recognize that the very qualities we once thought were negative also have their value. Almost every quality that can be called a "character defect" can sometimes be a strength. Almost every liability is occasionally a great asset. Being stubborn can get us into trouble, but it is also the source of our persistence. Being envious can cause problems in relationships, but it can also motivate us to go out and get the things we want. Being obsessed with details may drive us and others crazy, but it can also mean that we are well prepared for upcoming events.

Learning to reconcile the dual nature of these characteristics is important. Learning to make peace with, and creatively use, our "defects" represents another step toward self-acceptance.

Today I will remember that those characteristics that I tend to view as liabilities can become assets as I learn to use them constructively.

June 6

Life don't clickety-clack down a straight-line track, it come together and it come apart. —FERRON

Things rarely work out exactly the way we plan them. Very little in our lives has followed a "straight"-line track, including our sexuality! There are always twists and turns, curves and bends, detours we didn't plan on, and side trips that can't be avoided.

Time and time again, we map everything out, preparing for any conceivable contingency, only to discover an outcome we couldn't possibly have foreseen. We simply can't account for or control everything. Life just doesn't work that way.

Our inability to accept this truth underlies a big part of our addiction. Substances helped us feel like we were in control. Numbing out made it easier to ignore the ways things were coming apart all around us. And beyond these day-to-day struggles, feeding our addictions helped most of us live with the fact that our sexuality wasn't going along the straight path that everyone around us said it should.

Learning to accept the rhythm of life coming together and coming apart is an essential aspect of our recovery process. Learning to listen to these rhythms, and then "roll with them," enables us to continue moving forward. Learning to accept ourselves and our sexual identities, wherever we are, is essential for healthy recovery.

◇

How can I work with the ups and downs of recovery today instead of fighting against them?

June 7

I think when you pass forty you automatically start thinking about your own mortality ... It's the second half of your life, and you start thinking about what you want to do with it. How you can make it more meaningful.
—JANE FONDA

Most of us struggle with aging. Turning thirty, forty, or fifty years old can be a marker that sparks self-reflection and examination. What have we accomplished thus far? Have we been able to achieve our goals? Are we satisfied with our relationships? Do the things we once valued still have meaning for us?

While these questions are a normal part of human growth and development, they may be more difficult for us as addicts and alcoholics. Our active addiction often consumed the first half of our lives. It may have limited our achievements, caused us to abort relationships, or interfered with career development. We sometimes find ourselves at mid-life feeling as if we wasted our early years in our addictions.

At these times, we need to be careful not to let despair overtake us. While we cannot erase the impact of our addictions, recovery does offer us a second chance. It is not too late to decide how to make our lives more meaningful.

Today I will try to move beyond my regrets, focusing instead on what I want to accomplish with my life.

June 8

Peace and love are always alive in us, but we are not always alive to peace and love. —JULIAN OF NORWICH

This thought from Julian of Norwich, a fourteenth-century mystic, reminds us of the experience of our addiction. Whether or not we recognized it, the ability to experience peace and love was always within us. Our failure to experience these realities was the result of the ways drugs and alcohol deadened our senses.

Much of recovery is about the process of coming back to life, reclaiming our ability to experience our feelings, regaining our capacity for joy and love and peace. As sober lesbians, we have a right to live our lives with serenity. We have a right to find love within ourselves and in those around us. Regaining this right requires the willingness to come alive, to be awakened to the possibilities within us.

No one else can give us peace. No one else can offer us the love we need to nurture and sustain ourselves. We must look within ourselves and find our own source of life. As we work and struggle to live in peace and love with others, we will come to find those qualities within us. As we stay sober, we will discover that we are coming alive to peace and love.

Today I will focus on the ways I am coming alive to life and finding my own peace and love.

June 9

Away, she went away but each place she went pushed her to the other side, al otro lado. —GLORIA ANZALDÚA

These words describe a Latina lesbian's struggle to find an integrated sense of her ethnic and sexual identities. Yet they speak to all of us in our efforts to find a place of belonging. Being pushed aside is a familiar feeling. We experience it all the time from the world around us. You can't be a mother because you are a lesbian. You can't serve in the military and have a lover. You can't be a part of this family if you're going to talk about being queer.

Often we perpetuate this experience among ourselves. You can't be a lesbian because you once slept with men. You can't attend this lesbian gathering because it is not physically accessible. You can't share in this lesbian meeting because we do not have a signer for the hearing-impaired. You can't bring your Latina or Asian self to this queer event. You can't be a real lesbian if you still belong to that crazy church.

Pushed to the other side, left out, constantly searching out a community. As we struggle for our own place of belonging, may we find the courage and the willingness to open up a space where all of us can freely be ourselves.

Today I will look for ways to allow others into my life, rather than pushing them, and thus myself, aside.

June 10

There must be quite a few things a hot bath won't cure, but I don't know many of them. —SYLVIA PLATH

The first time I read this line, I thought to myself, "This must be my lover's guiding principle." And so, after many years, I have learned to look for her in the tub. While a hot bath may not really be the answer to life's complicated problems, there is a certain wisdom in Plath's words.

Many of us have difficulty taking care of ourselves. We know all too well how to care for others, how to listen to them, be present for them, and nurture them. We know how to respond to their needs and encourage their growth. Unfortunately, we often fall short in being able to give ourselves the same kind of attention.

We need to learn how to take time out for ourselves. We need to learn to put our needs first, to listen to our desires, to pay attention to what our soul is longing for. A hot bath may not cure everything, but it will slow us down long enough to begin listening to ourselves.

Today I will focus on taking care of myself and paying attention to my needs.

June 11

When I spoke about having *a* drink, it was a euphemism for having a whole flock of them.
—MARGARET HALSEY

Once we are sober for a while, our denial often returns. We may find ourselves fantasizing about drugs or alcohol, imagining what it would be like to try it one more time. We start to question whether we really were an addict or an alcoholic in the first place. We wonder what the harm would be in having one drink—perhaps a glass of wine over dinner with our lover, or a cold beer after an exhausting game of softball.

Margaret Halsey's comment reminds us that one is never enough. The first was always a prelude to others. Her comment reminds us that no matter how long we have been sober, no matter how much we think we understand the reasons why we drank or drugged, no matter how many personal issues we have worked through—as addicts and alcoholics, we can never have just one drink. One drink or one drug will always lead to the next one and the next one and the one after that. Our fantasies about having one drink are just that—fantasies.

Today I will remember that having one drink or getting high just once is a fantasy that leads me back to my addiction.

June 12

When everyone around you expects you to fail, it seems the easier if more painful thing to do, before too much is invested, before there is too much to lose.
—JANE RULE

Failing at something important to us is a miserable experience. Few of us enjoy the feeling. Yet, as addicts we often have just as much trouble accepting and enjoying our success. We are used to viewing ourselves as failures; seeing ourselves as competent, respected, successful adults is a brand new experience.

When it looks like we might be successful, we are often tempted to sabotage our success. Think about what happens when we meet someone new. We start spending time together; our relationship is going along really well. Then all of a sudden, we get cold feet; it's too good to be true; we're not sure we deserve this; maybe it won't last; maybe we should just get out now while we can, before we love each other too much. The world around us reinforces these fears. Society doesn't expect lesbian relationships to be successful and endure, so why should we? Being afraid of success is a normal part of recovery. But, we don't have to sabotage the good things we accomplish. We can learn to live through our fears.

Are there ways I have been holding back or sabotaging my success? What steps can I take today to begin moving through my fears?

June 13

I have not ceased being fearful, but I have ceased to let fear control me. I have accepted fear as a part of life.
—ERICA JONG

Trying to do away with our fears is a waste of time and energy. Fear is a normal human emotion that is a part of life. Fear comes and goes. No matter how strong and courageous we are, no matter how proud we are about being lesbians, no matter how long we have been sober, we will always experience fear. Recognizing and accepting our fears, instead of fighting against them, can go a long way toward enhancing our serenity.

Our challenge in recovery is not to eliminate our fears but, as Erica Jong points out, to cease to allow fear to control us. Can we acknowledge our fears about being a lesbian mother, without allowing that fear to control our choices? Can we recognize our fears about living with AIDS, without allowing that fear to dominate our relationships? Can we accept our fears about having a Holy Union, without allowing that fear to keep us from celebrating our love? This is the challenge of recovery. Sobriety does not mean we cease being fearful; it simply means we discover the tools necessary to live through and move beyond our fears.

Today I will remember that while fear will always be a part of my life, I no longer need to allow it to control me.

June 14

> **If you fail to imagine your lover,
> you won't recognize her on the street
> when opportunity presents itself
> like a bill in the grass.** —ROBIN BECKER

Lesbian poet Robin Becker humorously reminds us of the importance of imagining the future. She calls us to envision the new things we want in order to be able to recognize them when they occur. She goes on to note, "In order to possess, you must envision."

If we want a lover, we need to begin envisioning ourselves as attractive and lovable. If we want a new job, we must begin imagining ourselves as valuable and worthwhile. If we want to experience sanity and peace, we must begin picturing ourselves free from anxiety. If we want to come out to our families, we must envision ourselves with the confidence and boldness needed for this task.

Being able to imagine the future is one step toward obtaining it. Being able to picture what we want prepares us for taking action. It helps us figure out what steps to take. It enables us to live with, and in, these changes, as they occur.

So start imagining. You wouldn't want to fail to recognize your dream lover when you meet her on the street, would you?

Today I will begin envisioning the things that are important to me in the future.

June 15

You do not notice changes in what is always before you.
—COLETTE

Gradual changes often escape us. We may not notice how our lover's hair is turning gray, or that a lesbian we used to see at meetings hasn't been around for a while, or how much that once-new sofa we like is getting faded and dreary-looking.

We have similar problems seeing our own changes in recovery. We are so close to ourselves and our problems that we have difficulty recognizing changes as they occur. We don't notice the fact that we're not quite as anxious about sharing in meetings as we used to be. We forget how hard it was in early sobriety to get through a dance without drinking. We don't pick up on how easily we handled that last conflict with our girlfriend.

One of the reasons having a sober support network is so important is that other people can often see these changes better than we can. We need other sober lesbians in our lives to help us notice our own growth and development. They can remember how anxious we used to get, how obsessed we used to be with drinking, how difficult it was to survive conflict. And they can point out how different things are today.

Today I will remember that just because I may be the last one to notice my own growth, that doesn't mean I haven't changed.

June 16

I dedicate this work to all women hidden from history whose suffering and triumph have made it possible for me to call my name out loud. —CHERYL CLARKE

Having a sense of herstory is important. It creates a sense of connection with our past, offers role models, provides a context for our present situation, and contributes to a sense of wholeness in our lives.

Much of our herstory, as women and as lesbians, has been hidden. Our stories have been left out of high school history books, skipped over in documentaries, ignored in the official recounting of our culture's growth and development. This is even more true for women of color. As a result, we grew up knowing little of the women who went before us. Their stories were not written down; we can only imagine what they experienced, what was important to them, or how they felt about their lives.

If having a sense of our roots is important to us, we must do the work. We are the ones who must do the research, dig up what has been hidden, and give voice to those who were silenced. Those who have gone before us deserve to be remembered and celebrated. It is, as Cheryl Clarke notes, their suffering and triumph that makes it possible for us to live as proud, visible, and sober lesbians today.

◊

Today I will reflect on the women who went before me—some famous, some unknown to others—recognizing and celebrating the ways they have contributed to my recovery.

June 17

Once we recognize what it is we are feeling, once we recognize we can feel deeply, love deeply, can feel joy, then we will demand that all parts of our lives produce that kind of joy. —AUDRE LORDE

True heartfelt joy is not a feeling we were accustomed to in our addictions. And it may take some of us a long time in recovery to uncover this emotion. Not surprisingly, we may not even recognize it when it first appears.

I can remember the first time it happened sober. I was walking up the street after attending a recovery group, and suddenly I realized that I felt good. This was not a superficial good feeling like the ones I had experienced during my addiction. This was a "way down inside, things are going to be OK, maybe life really isn't so bad" kind of feeling. Sometime later I realized that this was what people meant when they talked about joy.

This initial feeling didn't last forever, but it did have an impact. Once I had experienced this kind of joy, I knew that it existed and that it was accessible to me. From then on, I knew joy was something I could continue to experience, as opposed to something only others could attain.

Today I will allow myself to be open to the joy that recovery offers me.

June 18

God is wherever there is real desire, real longing, for connection . . . God *is* in the connections.
—BEVERLY WILDUNG HARRISON

Our longing for connection, our desire to be in relationship with one another, is part of our spirituality. The isolation and alienation we experienced during our addiction is one manifestation of the spiritual devastation of our disease.

None of us find relationships easy in recovery. We spend our early days feeling incredibly awkward and uncomfortable around people. We have forgotten how to act and interact. We don't know what to say or how to say it. We feel self-conscious and out of place. Sometimes these difficulties plague us well into sobriety.

Our spiritual recovery is dependent on our ability to recognize our need for connectedness with others. Acknowledging our desire and longing for community is a sign that our spirits are waking up, a sign that we are coming back to life. Building community in recovery may not be easy, but it is part of the path toward spiritual growth.

Today I will allow myself to acknowledge my need for community and look for healthy ways to meet that need.

June 19

She had a tremendous impatience with other people's ideas—unless those happened to be exactly like hers.
—GWENDOLYN BROOKS

Most of us find it easy to get along with people who have ideas, beliefs, and preferences similar to ours. These are the people we find it easiest to listen to and learn from. These are the folks we choose to socialize and become friends with. There's nothing wrong with this. It is a normal part of human nature to be attracted to people whose stories and experiences are similar to ours. Twelve-step programs are rooted in this understanding.

However, it is important to learn how to interact with, and appreciate, those who are different from us. While we may be able to choose our friends to fit our beliefs, we are likely to encounter a wide range of varying opinions at work, in community-organizing groups, twelve-step meetings, etc. Learning patience and tolerance for others will make our interactions both more enjoyable and productive. We don't have to agree with everyone else's ideas, but we can learn to listen and try to see things from their perspective.

Today I will practice listening to others with tolerance and compassion.

June 20

The master's tools will never dismantle the master's house. —AUDRE LORDE

In an essay addressing our need to confront racism and other forms of oppression, Audre Lorde makes it clear that we cannot create a new society based on freedom and justice by using oppressive structures and approaches. Dismantling the old requires new tools, new ways of living with ourselves, and new ways of being in relationship with one another.

These truths about society also apply to our recovery. We cannot dismantle our past using the same old skills we learned growing up. Moving beyond our pain and abuse demands new tools, new beliefs, new thinking patterns, and new ways of acting and reacting. Continuing to work out of the old structures and ways of being will only lead to the same old frustrating results.

What old patterns can I dismantle today? Am I still using "the master's tools"? What new tools do I need in recovery?

June 21

> I won't be a heart of destruction
> I won't be a part of the pain, I won't play
> I quit, I won't be the obstruction
> That gets in my way, just gets in my way.
> —FERRON

This song reminds us how we can play into our pain and destruction. The obstacles we encounter in recovery are not only external; some of them are of our own making. Sometimes we become the obstruction that prevents our growth and change.

Self-destructive behaviors keep us locked in a cycle of failure. Negative attitudes and beliefs prevent us from moving forward and accomplishing our goals. Unhealthy relationships hold us back and limit our growth. The refusal to experience joy interferes with serenity and happiness.

Ferron challenges us to let go of these self-destructive patterns. She calls us to join her in refusing to be a part of our pain. She invites us to "get out of our way" and allow the natural healing of recovery to occur.

Today I will try to let go of old self-destructive patterns, allowing myself to experience the joy and growth of recovery.

June 22

I know we can't abolish prejudice through laws, but we can set up guidelines for our actions by legislation.
—BELVA LOCKWOOD

Political action is an important way for many of us to celebrate our identity and reclaim a sense of power and pride. Working together to create societal change enhances our self-esteem and enables us to find a greater sense of purpose and meaning in our lives.

Being effective in our political action requires patience and persistence. There will be moments when things look hopeless, when we wonder if it's "worth it." Even with the passage of civil rights laws, there will still be people who hate and bash lesbians. Effective political action demands the ability to work through these moments of frustration and despair.

It is true that people's attitudes and prejudices aren't necessarily changed through the passage of laws; but legislation regarding acceptable behavior is a beginning. My partner used to say that she didn't care if our teenagers liked doing the dishes; she just wanted the dishes done! In a similar vein, the passage of civil rights legislation may not make everyone like lesbians, but it will go a long way toward demanding that we be treated fairly and with respect.

Today I will remember that working for change can be an important tool for rebuilding self-esteem.

June 23

> I think that for too long [lesbian and gay] people have been told that you have no place with God, that your spirituality doesn't matter. In fact, they've been battered by people using the Bible against them.
> —THE REV. CANDACE SHULTIS

An important part of our recovery includes healing from exposure to negative religious beliefs and attitudes. As lesbians, we have been abused and battered by both the sexism and the heterosexism of religious institutions. We have been excluded and trivialized as women and as lesbians. We have been told that who we are and how we love is sinful. We have been told that God hates our "lifestyle." Even if we vehemently disagree with these beliefs, they affect us. This is true even for those of us who grew up and live our adult lives outside organized religion. Even if our families didn't convey these beliefs, society did.

Healing begins when we speak the truth and acknowledge this abuse. No one has the right to use "God" as a weapon against us. No one has the right to twist and distort our spirituality. No one has the right to batter us with their beliefs and prejudices. Our healing depends on reclaiming the right to define ourselves and our spiritual needs.

How have I been "battered" by homophobic religious beliefs and practices? What steps can I take today to further my healing?

June 24

We are not human beings trying to be spiritual. We are spiritual beings trying to be human.
—JACQUELYN SMALL

Jacquelyn Small offers helpful insight into why we sometimes have difficulty with spirituality. It is because we often have things backward. We think that we have to work at being spiritual, that we have to struggle to understand what this means and then figure out how to make it happen for ourselves. She suggests we begin by acknowledging that we are spiritual beings and then get down to the real challenge: being human.

Recovery is about learning to accept, celebrate, and live within the context of our humanness. As women, we have been socialized to be super-human. As lesbians, we may feel we have to try even harder, to prove that we are real women and real human beings. We often set ourselves up to be and do more than is humanly possible.

Learning to accept and live with our humanness is essential to our serenity. Accepting our humanness is part of accepting ourselves. If we can acknowledge and accept the reality of our humanness, it is possible that our spirituality will fall into place.

Today I will focus on accepting and living my life within the context of my humanness.

June 25

Self-pity in its early stages is as snug as a feather mattress. Only when it hardens does it become uncomfortable.
—MAYA ANGELOU

When things are not going my way, it is easy to fall into self-pity. I begin to think that nobody else has to struggle with this, I am the only one who feels this bad. When I'm feeling miserable, somehow self-pity helps me feel special. If I can't make the uncomfortable feelings go away, I can take comfort in knowing I am unique.

Unfortunately, the long-term cost of this attitude is isolation. If I am unique, no one else can identify with what I am going through. If I am unique, no one else's experience and wisdom can help me. If I am unique, eventually I am alone in my struggles. The ultimate result of self-pity is alienation.

I cannot afford to wallow in self-pity if I want to continue growing in recovery. It may be comfortable for the moment, but eventually it will cut me off from others and strangle my growth and development.

Are there ways in which I am allowing myself to take comfort in self-pity? How can I begin to let go of my "uniqueness" and reach out to others?

June 26

One of the first lessons of power is to be able to walk down the path that is presented to us in our lives.
—LYNN ANDREWS

Can we complete the task that lies in front of us? Can we take the next step? Can we follow through on the things that are most immediate in our lives?

One of the earliest lessons my first sponsor taught me was about showing up. Over and over again, I would find myself completely overwhelmed by the tasks in front of me. Going on a job interview, completing an assignment, or getting through a day at work often seemed impossible. Caught up in my projections of what might happen, I ended up riddled with anxiety, unable to take any actions. My sponsor's advice was always to sort out what small step I could take and then do it.

When we feel powerlessness in the face of the tasks in front of us, we find our power by choosing one task and completing it. If we can just show up for ourselves and take the first step, the rest of the path often takes care of itself. Taking any action breaks the cycle of immobility and creates power that we can draw upon to keep ourselves moving forward.

Today I am learning to draw upon my own power by showing up for myself and doing the next thing that needs to be done.

June 27

> **Sister, I am calling you**
> **from distant lands, I am calling you**
> **sending you strength**
> **for your survival.**
>
> —VICTORIA LENA MANYARROWS

We find our strength in many ways. During our addictions, it often came in the form of drugs, alcohol, another substance, or dependence on people. It was a false strength, a strength that held us up and held us together, for the moment. In recovery we are finding new ways to call upon the strength within ourselves and in others.

A friend of mine says that her mental health is dependent upon a certain quota per year of large lesbian events, that several times a year she needs to be in the middle of hundreds of dykes. Surrounded by others like her, she finds strength. She draws upon their energy, is mobilized by their creativity, finds hope in their survival. She finds fresh courage and pride in this experience of being "in the majority." We find our strength in many ways.

In recovery we learn to draw upon our own inner resources. We learn to lean upon others without draining them. We learn to give of ourselves without giving ourselves away.

Today I will allow myself to draw upon the strength of my sisters and share my resources with them.

June 28

Stonewall is not just about yesterday; for us it must also be about tomorrow. —VIRGINIA APUZZO

On the anniversary of the riots at the Stonewall bar in New York City, we need to remember those who stood up to the police and fought for our right to be who we are today. We need to recall the courage of butches and femmes, bull dykes and fairies, drag kings and drag queens. We need to honor the lesbians, gay men, bisexual and transgendered persons who were not afraid to say to the world, "I am who I am; I will love whom I choose; you can no longer define or silence me."

We also need to take from our remembering those things that enlighten and empower us for the future. We need to recall with honesty who was present at the Stonewall riots and continue our fight for the rights of all people to live and love as they choose, especially those on the margins of society. We need to learn from their courage and speak out in the present when injustice manifests itself.

Our recovery is rooted in the past, but it must lead us through the present and into our future.

Today I will look for the opportunity to honor the efforts of all who work for liberation and justice.

June 29

> Coming out has to be better for the soul than passing through life in various shades of invisibility. It can be uncomfortable and even frightening at times. But not to do so leaves us disconnected. —RACHEL WAHBA

Living in "various shades of invisibility" as a lesbian parallels what we experienced during our addiction. As our substance use progressed, we became increasingly out of touch with our true selves. We became more and more alienated from those around us. What we valued, what our hopes and dreams were, who we really were, gradually became invisible. Getting sober marked our coming out of that fog. Sobriety meant becoming visible, to ourselves and one another, once again.

Having to hide in recovery is dangerous. It takes us back to the sense of alienation we experienced during our addiction. Once we are sober, having to act invisible feels out of sync with our new values of honesty and integrity. Having to hide our lesbian identity in recovery leaves us feeling disconnected from ourselves and others. While coming out is not always easy, moving in that direction is the route toward wholeness and integration.

Are there places where I feel invisible? What steps can I take to experience a greater sense of integration and wholeness?

June 30

> The awakening of consciousness is not unlike the crossing of a frontier—one step and you are in another country.
> —ADRIENNE RICH

At the time, it may not have seemed so clear-cut, but in retrospect, we can see that our choice to recover was an awakening of consciousness. One day we were buried in denial and insanity, alone, isolated, and hopeless. The next day marked a new beginning, filled with the possibilities of acceptance, soundness of mind, belonging, and hope. Recovery opened the door to a whole new world.

Staying in recovery brings a continuing series of these experiences. One day we are locked in our resentments, unable to experience the freedom of acceptance; the next day we begin to let go and move forward with our lives. One day we are paralyzed by our fears, unable to reach out or risk; the next day we begin to take action, trusting ourselves and those around us. One day we are overwhelmed with grief, unable to accept our losses; the next day we begin to find a sense of peace even in the midst of our pain.

When we are in the midst of our struggles, it doesn't always seem so easy. We don't always realize that we have stepped over the border into another country. Our awakenings are not always apparent as they occur.

I will acknowledge the possibility that today may mark a new beginning in my journey toward healing.

July 1

I still miss those I loved who are no longer with me but I find I am grateful for having loved them. The gratitude has finally conquered the loss.
—RITA MAE BROWN

I keep a picture on my desk of a colleague who died of AIDS. Initially, I placed it there because I missed him, and having his photograph at hand somehow made me feel closer to him. As time went by, I had several opportunities to do some closure about his death. I thought about putting his picture away, but never got around to it. Recently I realized that while I placed it there out of loss, I keep it now for gratitude—gratitude for the opportunity of loving him and for the lessons I learned through my relationship with him.

Moving beyond our losses and allowing them to be transformed into gratitude is not easy. It takes time and patience. The process cannot be rushed. Often there is work we need to do—closure that needs to occur, healing of the painful parts of our relationship, reconciliation of the "good and bad" qualities of the one we loved, and movement toward integrating the truths we learned about ourselves. This work can be painful, but in the end, having our loved ones near us out of gratitude will heal our sense of loss.

What steps can I take to transform my losses into gratitude? What healing work do I need to do?

July 2

We discovered that peace at any price is no peace at all.
–ÉVE CURIE

Many of us were raised to be nice girls, pressured to "not make waves," to keep the peace, to be silent rather than risk creating conflict. We were taught that peace is the absence of conflict, that peace means everyone agrees, or at least pretends to agree. We learned that keeping the peace was more important than our own individual needs, and certainly more important than resolving diverse needs and choices.

In recovery we are learning that peace rooted in denial is not true peace. Peace that demands our silence and invisibility is not true peace. This kind of false peace is an illusion. In recovery we are learning to speak out and speak up, to speak our minds, to speak the truth, to make our choices known, even at the risk of not being "nice." In recovery we are learning that we do not need to settle for the illusion of peace. We are learning that people will not die from conflict. We are learning that disagreement can be healthy and is often necessary if we are ever going to arrive at true consensus.

Today I am learning to recognize the difference between the illusion of peace and the true resolution of differences.

July 3

It is the creative potential itself in human beings that is the image of God. —MARY DALY

Mary Daly provides important clues in our search for a new and healthy spirituality. Discovering the image of divinity within us challenges us to accept and celebrate ourselves for who we are. If God is within us, then our lives and our very selves are inherently worthy, good, and valuable. Recognizing our creative potential as a reflection of the divine enables us to celebrate our ability to change and grow.

Our creative potential gives us the ability to transform even the most painful and oppressive of situations into resilience and strength. We have survived, sometimes against incredible odds. And we have not only survived, we have emerged with pride and beauty and courage.

Our creative potential gives us the ability to transform words like "dyke" and "queer" into words that no longer diminish and demean us, but instead celebrate and affirm our identity. Our creative potential moves us beyond the slavery of our addictions into the freedom of our recovery.

Today I will celebrate my survival and growth as a reflection of that which is good and divine within me.

July 4

I want to know why people are threatened by us. We represent no danger, no harm. We represent gifts and resources for the whole nation. The nation is depriving itself of its treasures by rejecting gay and lesbian people.
—THE REV. LARRY UHRIG

Do we truly believe that we represent "gifts and resources" for the whole nation? Are we sober enough to recognize our unique strengths and abilities? Can we celebrate our survival and lesbian ways of loving as gifts to be shared?

In their homophobia, other people are often threatened by us. Myths and stereotypes tell them that we will steal their wives, molest their children, pervert their religions, and generally undo the values upon which society rests. Viewed through this lens, we represent extreme danger. Yet, in accepting these lies, people deprive themselves of our skills and abilities; they deprive themselves of the gift of our friendship; they deprive themselves of the wisdom and strength gained in our struggle for survival; they deprive themselves of our creativity by forcing us to waste our energies hiding our lives; and they deprive society of the fullness of our presence.

Even if others continue to hold on to their fears, we can recognize our gifts and abilities. We can reclaim our ways of loving as good. We can celebrate one another's presence in this society.

Today I will celebrate the unique gifts and resources I have to offer the world as a sober lesbian.

July 5

Mama exhorted her children at every opportunity to "jump at de sun." We might not land on the sun, but at least we would get off the ground.

—ZORA NEALE HURSTON

This line from Hurston's novel *Dust Tracks on a Road* reminds us of our need for balance. If we want to grow and change, we need to set goals. We need to challenge ourselves to do better this time than we did the last time. In Hurston's words, we need to "jump at the sun."

However, this desire to excel must be balanced with the recognition that we may not accomplish everything we planned. We may not achieve all our goals. The challenge in recovery is to keep on jumping at the sun, while at the same time being willing to accept just getting off the ground.

Our goal may be creating a greater consciousness about addiction in our community; can we be happy today with scheduling one sober lesbian dance? Our goal may be changing the sodomy laws in our state; can we be happy today with meeting with one senator? Our goal may be building new friendships; can we be happy today with extending ourselves to one new lesbian at a twelve-step meeting?

Today I will set goals for myself, remembering that each achievement is one step closer to their reality than yesterday.

July 6

Nora robbed herself for everyone; incapable of giving herself warning, she was continually turning about to find herself diminished.
—DJUNA BARNES

As women, we have been socialized to be like Nora, a character in Djuna Barnes's novel *Nightwood*. We have been trained to give ourselves away for others. We have been brought up with the belief that caring for others is more important than taking care of ourselves. This heterosexual socialization affects us, even as lesbians.

Getting sober is the first step in breaking these patterns. Getting sober is about taking care of ourselves. However, getting sober is only the first step. This tendency to give ourselves away for others is a pattern that we must confront repeatedly.

In recovery we are learning that most of the time others are quite capable of taking care of themselves. And even if they are not, it is not necessarily our job to do this for them. In recovery we are learning that it is perfectly acceptable, and often necessary, to put our needs first. In recovery we are learning that robbing ourselves for everyone else ensures that eventually no one gets anything. Giving ourselves away for others does nothing to empower them and only serves to diminish us.

◇

Have I been giving myself away trying to take care of others? How can I begin to replenish my own resources?

July 7

There's a glorious, ecstatic feeling in being seen, in being out there, especially after so many years of hiding. This is me, come and take it. —SARA CYTRON

One of the first times I came out to someone was during a game of Scrabble. She was a straight coworker on whom I had an intense crush. We had begun to get to know each other fairly well, and yet there was a huge secret inside me. I was terrified that if she knew who I really was, she would no longer want to be my friend. We went back and forth, with me saying there was something I wanted to tell her, and she encouraging me to go ahead and say it. After what seemed like an eternity, I spelled out the word "lesbian" on the game board and the secret was out. What an incredible release!

Coming out can be a freeing experience. Take a few minutes to reflect on the time when you barely had a sense of who you were, when you knew you were somehow different but didn't yet have a name for it. Can you recall your feelings the first time you recognized yourself as a lesbian? Can you remember those early experiences of sharing your secret with others? Despite the ways in which these early glimpses of ourselves were often fraught with fear and anxiety, they eventually became our liberation.

Today I am grateful for the freedom I have found in coming out, in giving myself permission to be who I am.

July 8

As we do at such times, I turned on my automatic pilot and went through the motions of normalcy on the outside, so that I could concentrate all my powers on surviving the near-mortal wound inside.

—SONIA JOHNSON

Being able to switch into "automatic pilot" mode is a skill many of us learned as children. It served us well then, and played a major role in our survival during our addictions. It enabled us to "keep on keeping on," even when it seemed as if we were coming apart.

Sometimes it still serves us well. If our lover threatens to break up with us over the phone at work, we may need to switch into automatic pilot to get through the rest of the day. If our best friend is dying of breast cancer, we may need to occasionally use our automatic pilot switch in order to keep moving through the pain.

This coping mechanism becomes a problem when we cease to have a choice about when we want to use it. When our automatic pilot switch gets stuck, we are in trouble. If all we do is shut off our feelings to push our way through life, we run the risk of losing touch with both our feelings and our very selves. Eventually this can lead us back to our addiction. Being able to go on automatic pilot can be helpful now and then, but it is not a permanent solution.

Do I have a choice about when and where I want to make use of my ability to shut down my feelings? Do I need to look for other coping mechanisms?

July 9

Faith is not *being sure*. It is *not being sure*, but betting with your last cent. —MARY JEAN IRION

Too often when we hear people in recovery talk about having faith, we have the mistaken notion this means being one hundred percent sure of things. We think faith means never having doubts, never having questions, and never wondering if things will work out all right. We think having faith means never worrying about whether our lover will leave us. We think it means being perfectly sure that our children will love us even after we come out to them. We think it means not having any doubts about handling a new position at work.

In reality, faith is about *not being sure* and taking the actions anyway. Faith means trusting our commitment to our lover, even if we do have a few worries now and then. Faith means taking the risk of coming out to our kids despite our fears. Faith means showing up for the first day in our new job, in spite of our anxieties. If we could be completely sure, there would be no need for faith. Real faith is about knowing we can never be one hundred percent sure of anything, but being willing to take the risk anyway.

Today I will remember that having faith is not about being sure; it is about being willing to trust despite my uncertainty.

July 10

I was ashamed to admit the extent of our violence.
—KATE HURLEY

In an essay on violence in lesbian relationships, Kate Hurley describes how shame prevents us from acknowledging our pain. It is not easy to talk about the existence of battering and abuse within the lesbian community. We would rather believe that women can't hurt one another like this. We don't want to face the violence within us.

We need to confront this denial so that our relationships can become safe for all of us. Those of us who have been, or are, in abusive relationships need to be able to speak the truth about our lives. We need to feel safe to reach out and ask for help. We need to be able to trust that the community will believe us.

Recovering from violence, like all recovery, begins with letting go of our denial and shame. Healing continues as we find others who can share our stories, listen to our pain, and support us in our changes. All of us are at risk for violence. All of us must be part of the healing process.

◊

Today I will remember that denial only perpetuates abuse, shame, and isolation. Speaking the truth is the first step toward healing.

July 11

A friend can tell you things you don't want to tell yourself. —FRANCES WARD WELLER

Building a sober lesbian support network is essential to our recovery. Staying sober by ourselves doesn't work very well. In order to truly establish a sober lesbian identity, we need the support of others who share our experiences.

This need for a sober support network continues throughout our sobriety. We need others who understand the challenges of recovery. One reason this is so important is reflected in Frances Weller's comment. Other lesbians who know us, who have watched our growth and healing, can often see things about us that we would just as soon ignore. They can often identify our rationalizations long before we notice them. They can often point out the dangers of choices we are about to make. They can often recognize old, unhealthy behavior patterns as they begin to occur.

Even when we do not want to listen, we need their feedback. We need the insight and wisdom they have to offer us. Getting sober required letting others in and allowing them to point the way. Continuing to grow in recovery demands no less.

Am I listening to the sober wisdom of my lesbian sisters? Am I willing to receive their feedback in my ongoing recovery?

July 12

Read the Book, Go to Meetings, Sleep in the Nude.
—ANNE S.

Shortly before I reached one year sober, my sponsor handed me a button with the above sentiment and, with a twinkle in her eye, told me that this was her "serious sponsorly advice" on how to get through the crazies of my first anniversary.

I've kept that button as a reminder of how important it is for us to maintain a sense of humor in our recovery. Getting sober is hard work. Maintaining an active program of recovery requires constant and consistent effort. Our disease is always out there waiting for us to ease up, to get complacent.

At the same time, those of us who struggle with addictions have a tendency to take ourselves and our circumstances too seriously. We find it difficult, if not impossible, to "lighten up." Using was often the only way we could ease up on ourselves or take a break from the struggles of our day-to-day lives.

Discovering the lighter side of life is absolutely essential. Learning how to balance hard work with hard play is an ongoing part of our recovery process. Yes, we need to read the Big Book, work the steps, and go to meetings. But we also need to learn to take it easy, read a fun book, go to the movies, walk in the park, or maybe even just do nothing for an afternoon. Healthy, long-term recovery requires a sense of balance.

Today I will practice finding balance by taking time out for myself.

July 13

I'm not afraid of storms, for I'm learning how to sail my ship.　　　—LOUISA MAY ALCOTT

Early in recovery, everything seems overwhelming. Each task must be faced without our old coping mechanisms, each new situation confronted without the buffer of our addiction.

Gradually we begin to build a sober frame of reference. We begin to realize that we actually are weathering the storms and surviving the crises, sometimes in spite of ourselves. These experiences of survival can help us develop a sense of trust in ourselves. Getting through a challenging task without relying on our old addictive behaviors is empowering.

During our addictions, many of us failed to grasp the fact that learning is a process. Whether the outcome is success or failure, each time we navigate a new situation, we are learning. We need to trust this process and allow it to nurture our trust in ourselves. In recovery, we are discovering we can survive whatever comes our way.

◊

Today I will be grateful for the sober frame of reference I have begun to develop in recovery.

July 14

Sharing is sometimes more demanding than giving.
—MARY CATHERINE BATESON

Recently I heard a woman speak about her experience of making amends in recovery. She explained that for her, amends had been about accepting shared responsibility for what had occurred, as opposed to her addictive pattern of assuming all responsibility and blame for the mistakes. In recovery she was learning that relationships are a two-way street. We each play a part in what transpires, be it good or bad.

Mary Catherine Bateson is right. Sharing—our resources, our experience, our power to act responsibly—is sometimes more difficult. It is often easier to give people what we think they need, rather than help them become clear about their own needs. It is often easier to tell them what we believe they should do, rather than work with them to sort out their own choices. It is often easier to accept all the blame for what has gone awry, rather than work through our shared abilities and responsibilities.

In recovery I am learning to share my experience, strength, and hope with others, rather than simply giving myself away.

July 15

For months, for years, each of us had felt her own yes growing in her. —ADRIENNE RICH

Aside from the occasional "good time," our addictions were characterized by misery and isolation. Our attempts to get out of ourselves and our feelings were desperate. We hated the actions that our need for drugs and other substances forced us to take. As we continued to abuse ourselves, we became more and more isolated from others.

Yet, even in the worst moments of our addiction, something was driving us closer to recovery; something was driving us closer to the possibilities of healing. Almost in spite of ourselves, and often without our knowledge, we were moving toward recovery.

In recovery we are learning to recognize this spirit within us. It is the spirit which says, "Yes" to self-acceptance and sanity, "Yes" to honesty and integrity, "Yes" to community and healthy relationships, and "Yes" to integration and wholeness.

How can I nurture the spirit within me that moves toward self-acceptance and healing?

July 16

Nature has created us with the capacity to know God, to experience God. —ALICE WALKER

God seems very evident as I sit here amid the beauty of rural New Hampshire, with its lakes and mountains. It is easy to recognize my limitations as a human being, easy to feel a sense of connection to the world, easy to acknowledge the presence of a larger force at work in the universe.

However, much of the time this certainty and sense of connection is difficult. We grew up with many beliefs about the nature of God, some of them nurturing and comforting, others rejecting and punishing. At best, these ideas were often contradictory.

In recovery we need to be open to new ways of thinking about God, what this God wants for us, and how this God is at work in our lives. God can be the wisdom of sober friends, the collective energies of lesbian community, the force that keeps the universe running, the spirit within us that makes us laugh, our commitment to recovery, or anything else that brings us a sense of spiritual connection to our world. Connectedness is what God is all about.

In recovery I am opening myself to new ways of imagining the divine.

July 17

The moment you judge, you stop loving and you separate yourself from God. —ANONYMOUS

Judging others creates a barrier between ourselves and others. It makes us separate from others by saying we are right and they are wrong. They are different. They are not like us. While we may not always agree with other people, when we place a judgment upon them, we are setting them apart from us.

These judgments create a spiritual and emotional barrier. What we often do not realize at the time is that these human separations always create a wall between ourselves and the divine. In judging others, we diminish our own self-worth. In judging others, we place ourselves at risk of being judged. In judging others, we separate ourselves from the spark of the divine that is within all of us.

Recovery demands a sense of spiritual and emotional connection. We cannot afford to risk creating any more walls within ourselves than the ones that already exist.

Today when I feel tempted to judge another, I will remember that doing so separates me from my higher power.

July 18

> Build for yourself a strong-box,
> Fashion each part with care;
> When it's strong as your hand can make it,
> Put all your troubles there.
> —BERTHA ADAMS BACKUS

One tool for gaining serenity in recovery is learning to let go of things and set them aside. We don't need to be constantly working on, or worrying about, something. Even if something major is going on in our life, it is okay to take a break from it once in a while. Some people use "worry jars," or "worry dolls," or imagine placing their thoughts and feelings in a box and putting them up on a shelf out of reach.

It is important to work on our issues. We do need to plan ahead and be prepared for things. But we do not need to work, or worry, or even feel, all the time. In fact, we are likely to go crazy if we try. One key to serenity is learning to take a break. After all, we can always take our worries down off the shelf when we're ready to go at them again.

Are there thoughts or feelings from which I could use a break today? How can I give myself permission to take time off?

July 19

An error means a child needs help, not a reprimand or ridicule for doing something wrong.
—MARVA COLLINS

Too many of us were reprimanded and ridiculed as children. When we made mistakes or failed to accomplish our goals, the adults in our lives criticized and belittled us. These experiences continue to affect us as adults. Because of these experiences, we have difficulty identifying our need for help in recovery; we do not believe we deserve assistance; we are afraid to reach out and ask for help.

We need to take Marva Collins's observation to heart. When children make mistakes, they deserve compassionate help from the adults in their lives. This is no less true for us today. When we make a mistake in recovery, we deserve understanding and support. We deserve direction and advice from other sober lesbians. We deserve help and assistance with our difficulties, not reprimands or rejection.

I need to move beyond childhood experiences of ridicule or reprimand, and allow myself to receive the help I need and deserve in recovery.

July 20

Underground issues from one relationship or context invariably fuel our fires in another. —HARRIET LERNER

This comment from Harriet Lerner's book *The Dance of Anger* highlights one of the difficulties we encounter as we seek to build healthy relationships in recovery. It might be easier if we could create ourselves anew each time we entered a relationship. As it is, we bring ourselves and all of our past experiences with us.

As lesbians, this means we bring all our experiences of homophobia—both external and internalized. It means we bring all the tools, healthy and unhealthy, that we have utilized for survival in an oppressive society. It means we bring all the lessons we learned about being open versus being closeted, as well as about "acceptable" versus "unacceptable" ways of expressing our sexuality.

Learning to build healthy relationships in recovery means confronting the old messages we received about who we are and how we are supposed to be in this world. Learning to build healthy relationships means we need to talk with one another about the effects of our oppression. Confronting these issues and doing this work is the only way we can keep from carrying baggage from one relationship into another.

◊

What underground issues are affecting my present relationships? How can I begin to address them constructively?

July 21

After many years of struggling to be someone else's image of who I am supposed to be, I am coming to accept myself as I am. And I am the better for it.
—JUANITA RAMOS

Self-acceptance is the key to serenity. Learning to accept ourselves as we are, not as someone else wants us to be, is essential to our recovery.

Many people gave us messages about what they wished us to be. They made their expectations clear in both overt and subtle ways. They made their approval and love contingent on our fulfilling their expectations. They chose to see us as they thought we were, regardless of what we said or did to the contrary.

Learning to recognize their demands is the first step in our recovery. This is followed by learning to identify our real wants and needs, even in the face of someone else's demands. Accepting ourselves, as we are, is the only path to growth. And it is the only way we can come to truly accept others.

Recovery opens the door to self-acceptance, enabling me to let go of other people's beliefs about who I should be.

July 22

> I cried as loud as I could and cried as much as I wanted to . . . Then, after I cried it out, this pain in my heart, I felt better. —MOUNTAIN WOLF WOMAN

Pain that we avoid tends to go underground. Buried within us, it transforms itself, often into anger, resentment, or bitterness. We may convince ourselves that we have moved beyond it, but if we have suppressed the emotion, it will reappear at a later point. Avoiding pain only prolongs its impact.

In recovery it helps to deal with our emotions as they emerge. There is nothing wrong with tears. They can be cleansing and healing. When we experience great pain or profound grief, tears are a natural human response. Forcing them aside is what we did during our addictions. It represents a pattern that needs altering if we want a healthy recovery.

When we experience pain, we need to give ourselves the time and space to deal with our feelings. We need to give ourselves permission to cry when we need or want to cry.

Am I able to give myself permission to cry when necessary? What steps can I take to deal more effectively with painful feelings?

July 23

Part of having a strong sense of self is to be accountable for one's actions. No matter how much we explore motives or lack of motives, we are what we do.
—JANET GERINGER WOTITZ

During our addictions, we gave away our ability to freely choose our actions. Much of what we said and did was driven by our obsessions. This repeated process of giving away our ability to choose and act freely diminished our sense of self. Over time, this inability to be accountable for our actions led to an increasing loss of ourselves.

Rebuilding a sense of our self in recovery occurs as we discover the ability to choose and act rightly in relationship to ourselves and others. Each time we identify our needs and communicate them directly to those around us, we are rebuilding our sense of self. Each time we affirm the goodness of ourselves as lesbians and act honestly on this awareness, we are rebuilding our sense of self. Each time we choose to do the thing that is healthy despite our impulse toward self-destruction, we are rebuilding a sense of self.

Sobriety enables us to be accountable for our actions. The ability to make choices and take actions, coupled with the increasing awareness of ourselves as the initiators, empowers us and rebuilds our self-esteem.

Today I will be grateful for my increasing ability to be accountable for my actions in recovery.

July 24

One never notices what has been done; one can only see what remains to be done. —MARIE CURIE

Many of us are plagued by the phenomenon expressed by Marie Curie. We can only see the things we have not achieved and are unable to appreciate what we have accomplished. When we review our "To Do" list at the end of each day, our focus is on the items without any marks; we hardly notice the items we have crossed off our list.

This kind of skewed vision means we are constantly harping on ourselves, pushing ourselves to go further and do more, yet never allowing ourselves the replenishing that comes with our accomplishments. No matter how much progress we make, it is never enough. We are never quite satisfied.

Increasing our serenity in recovery requires changing this pattern. Perhaps instead of only using a "To Do" list, we could take a few minutes at the end of each day and write an accomplishment list, identifying all the positive actions we were able to take that day. This could be the beginning of learning to focus on the things we have accomplished, allowing ourselves to take satisfaction in these achievements.

Today I will practice the ability to notice the things I have accomplished, rather than focusing on the things that are undone.

July 25

Never doubt that a small group of thoughtful, committed citizens can change the world. Indeed, it is the only thing that ever has.   —MARGARET MEAD

Sometimes social problems seem insurmountable: the devastating effects of poverty, the pervasive dynamics of racism and other oppressions, the ongoing battles for our basic civil rights. When we are in the midst of these struggles, it is easy to become overwhelmed. Margaret Mead's words challenge us to remain faithful to our vision for change. She calls us to keep working for justice and reminds us that all change occurs slowly, one step at a time.

Creating social change requires three things: a vision of something different, a small group of people committed to making that change a reality, and lots of persistent action. Twelve-step recovery wisdom urges us, "Don't give up before the miracle happens!" Do we want the legal right to "marry" our lovers? Do we want the right to maintain our jobs without the threat of discrimination based on our sexual orientation? Do we want lesbians to have the right to serve in the military if they choose, regardless of our own personal preferences? These "miracles" will only occur if we are willing to keep taking action together to make them happen.

What changes would I like to see happen? Are there steps I can take today to move toward the reality of my visions?

July 26

Goddess grant me the serenity to accept the lovers I cannot change, courage to change the ones I can, and wisdom to know the difference. —KAREN E. DAVIS

Too often we get caught up in trying to make the women in our life act the way we want them to act. We spend our mental and emotional energy trying to make them think the way we think or strategizing how to get them to do what we want them to do.

This tongue-in-cheek comment by Karen Davis in an essay on lesbian humor reminds us not to take ourselves and our relationships too seriously. It reminds us that we have little control over what our friends and lovers think, feel, or do. Our lives are our own, and their lives belong to them. In a playful way, Davis challenges us to keep the focus on ourselves and our recovery.

In reality, we will probably always want to change the one we love. That tendency is not likely to go away completely. But we can learn to recognize and resist it, for our sanity and the health of those we love.

Am I trying to change my friends and lovers to meet my needs? Am I asking them to give up their real selves in order to be with me?

July 27

If we live in that condition of alienation, we will love or desire or pursue obsessively anything which gives us a feeling of connection to ourselves, to one another, to our environment. —JUDITH MCDANIEL

Disconnectedness from ourselves and others was both the driving force behind, and the cumulative effect of, our addiction. In the beginning, drugs and alcohol eased our alienation, enabling us to feel a sense of belonging and connection with our world. But as we continued to abuse substances, we found ourselves farther and farther away from our world and ourselves. As lesbians, this sense of alienation was exacerbated by the heterosexist systems and structures that oppress us and separate us from one another.

These feelings do not automatically disappear when we get sober. We must learn how to break through our isolation and establish healthy relationships. If we do not find this healing, we will continue to obsessively pursue anything and anyone that makes us feel connected. In other words, in the absence of chemicals, we will continue our addictive patterns in our relationships with others. Becoming a part of a sober lesbian community, and allowing that community to nurture and empower us, is essential. Only in community can we begin to heal the devastating effects of isolation and alienation.

How does my sense of alienation continue to motivate my actions in relationships? What steps can I take to further my own healing?

July 28

There ain't no answer. There ain't going to be any answer. There never has been an answer. That's the answer.
—GERTRUDE STEIN

I sometimes have a tendency to spend a lot of time figuring out why things happen the way they do. Why this? Why now? Why here? Why me? Slowly, I am learning that some questions just do not have answers, at least not easy or certain ones.

Accepting the present reality of a situation is the first step toward changing it. Then, if we still want to ask questions, the more useful question may be "How?" How can I get through this situation? How do I want to deal with this turn of events? How important is this to me? How can I make a difference?

We cannot control all the things that happen in our lives. What we do have control over is our response. How I am going to deal with a person or situation is the one question to which I can find an answer.

Today I will try to let go of needing to know why and focus instead on how I want to act or respond to events.

July 29

I can't afford to be afraid of you, nor you of me. If it takes head-on collisions, let's do it: this polite timidity is killing us.
—CHERRÍE MORAGA

Sometimes we are simply too polite. We dance around the truth, so worried about what everyone else might think that we never manage to say what we believe. We make excuses for people. We get inside their heads and try to figure out what they need from us instead of asking them. We spend our energies trying to protect others from the truths they need, and probably can stand, to hear.

My mother always told me, "If you don't have something nice to say, don't say anything." Well, she may have had a point, but the wisdom does not apply to all situations. Sometimes the truth is not nice. And sometimes the truth needs to be spoken.

In recovery we need to learn how and when to speak the truth. We need to learn to speak up and stand up for ourselves and one another. And we need to learn to tackle things directly when that is what the situation calls for. Despite our fears, neither we, nor those close to us, are likely to die from the truth.

Where have I been unnecessarily protecting others, withholding or reframing the truth, in an effort to be nice?

July 30

Why the fuck should you and I feel shame over a situation where we were totally powerless?
—LANUOLA ASIASIGA

These words are written in response to the overwhelming effects of child abuse in the lives of women. Many of us know these feelings. Many of us carry the shame of incidents and situations over which we had no power, both as children and later in life.

Those of us who struggle with substance addictions often have a similar shame. We mistakenly think that we were responsible for becoming addicts, that we made this happen, that we could have prevented ourselves from developing this disease.

Some of us still carry this kind of shame about our identity as lesbians. We may act proud, but somewhere deep inside we are still not sure that it is truly OK to be who we are.

This kind of shame is useless and debilitating. It paralyzes us. It isolates us from other people. We need to allow our collective anger to make us outraged enough to give up this shame.

In recovery I am learning to let go of the shame imposed on me by others.

July 31

When we were children, we used to think that when we were grown-up we would no longer be vulnerable. But to grow up is to accept vulnerability . . . To be alive is to be vulnerable. —MADELEINE L'ENGLE

As an adolescent, I often acted fearless: walking across gas pipes suspended twenty feet in the air, playing chicken on the nearby railroad tracks, lighting up a joint before the principal was even out of sight, placing myself in remote and desolate places where almost anything could happen. I thought I had achieved my childhood dream; I believed I was invulnerable.

My addictions helped me carry this illusion of invulnerability into adulthood. They made me feel safe, powerful, untouchable. Nothing and nobody could hurt me. I thought being vulnerable was the equivalent of being powerless, being a victim. My addictions shielded me, or so I believed at the time, from these feelings.

Much of my recovery has been about growing up and accepting the realities that are part of being human. Vulnerability is one of those realities.

Today I am beginning to recognize and accept my vulnerability. I am learning to be open to life.

August 1

I don't know what I am; no one's ever told me that I'm different and yet I know that I'm different.
—RADCLYFFE HALL

Long before we had words to describe ourselves, most of us sensed we were different. Years before we heard the labels "lesbian," "dyke," or "queer," we knew we didn't quite fit in. For some of us, it was knowing we would never marry; for others it was a sense that we would not have children; for others it was realizing we didn't seem to feel the same way about boys as other girls our age did.

Addiction and experiences of abuse add to these feelings. In fact, being different often functioned as part of our denial before we got sober. Being different meant our problems and our addiction were not as bad as the person next to us (or were worse); being different meant nobody else would understand; being different kept us from reaching out for help.

This sense of being different often follows us years into recovery or coming out. Because we, as lesbians, are different, and because as addicts we have specialized in being different, this sense of not belonging has gotten into our souls. In other words, we have internalized this myth. In recovery we cannot always trust our own perceptions about belonging. We may need a reality check from those close to us.

Today I will pay attention to my perceptions about not fitting in and check them out with those I trust.

August 2

There's something contagious about demanding freedom.
—ROBIN MORGAN

Today I want others to see the recovery I am experiencing. I want others to look at my choices and see the release and freedom I have been granted. I want them to look at my life and see a glimpse of the sanity and serenity that is possible in recovery. I want them to know that there is more to life than being a victim. I want them to know that survival is possible and healing can happen. I want them to see that we don't have to do it all alone, that letting others in doesn't have to mean pain and disappointment.

Sharing our recovery, giving out of our strength and growth, is how we continue to move forward in our journeys. Hoarding the gifts we have gained locks us up within ourselves and blocks our growth. When I was in my addiction, I didn't want anyone to know anything about me. I just wanted to be left alone. Today I am eager to be with others and to share what I have received through recovery. I want the freedom I have worked so hard for to be contagious.

Today I will look for an opportunity to share with someone else who is still struggling for her freedom.

August 3

> The chains are here
> no metal—no clang
> chains of ignorance and fear
> chains here—causing pain
> how do i break these chains —PAT PARKER

Pat Parker's poem entitled "Questions" describes the many ways people are oppressed—as women, people of color, lesbians and gay men. Over and over again, she asks the question "How do I break these chains?" These chains are not made of metal. They are the oppressive societal structures and systems, the prejudices and stereotypes, the ignorance and fear, that we encounter in our day-to-day lives.

How do we break these chains? How do we move beyond the fears that keep us trapped in our own self-consciousness and isolation? How do we get free of the chains of self-hatred and distrust? How do we break the chains of drug and alcohol abuse that threaten to kill so many in our community?

One thing is certain. We cannot do it alone. We cannot break these chains by ourselves. We need one another. We need the strength and wisdom of sober lesbians. We need the experience of others who are committed to their own growth and to the healing of the whole lesbian community.

In what ways am I still enchained by fear and ignorance? How can I seek the support of others to break these chains?

August 4

You cannot make yourself feel something you do not feel, but you can make yourself do right in spite of your feelings.
—PEARL BUCK

Feelings, in and of themselves, are not right or wrong. There is nothing inherently good or bad in feeling angry, sad, happy, or scared. It just happens to be the way we feel at the moment. It is also true that our emotions are something over which we have very little control. When we are afraid, we feel afraid. When we are sad, we feel sad. There's generally not a whole lot we can do to change our feelings.

However, we do have control over the choices we make. We may not be able to change feeling angry with our lover, but we can choose how to express our anger. We may not be able to make our loneliness go away, but we can choose to go out and be with friends rather than isolate. We may have little control over feeling afraid, but we do have choices about how we respond to our fears.

Learning to make healthy choices in spite of how we feel in the moment is essential in recovery. Acknowledging our feelings is important, but we do not need to let them control all of our choices and actions.

Today I will remember that while I cannot always change my feelings, I do have the power to act in spite of them.

August 5

> The battle is to hold to the vision I know I must express, but the confidence to do it, where does that come from?
> —HONOR MOORE

All of us have visions, images of the future, hopes and dreams that offer something different from our present reality. Maybe it is a vision of ourselves strong and sober. Or a vision of relationships that are healthy, loving, and empowering. Or a vision of lesbian community celebrating both our differences and our commonalities. These visions are important to our survival. We need to hold on to them regardless of the challenges we encounter.

Finding the confidence to express and work toward these visions occurs in community. As we speak our visions aloud, sharing them with one another, they move one step closer to becoming a reality. As we listen to one another's visions, our own become clearer. As others acknowledge our visions, we find the energy and the commitment to work together to make them happen. We cannot hold on to our visions in isolation.

What are my visions of the future? How can I share them with others?

August 6

> Could be the famine, could be the feast,
> could be the pusher, could be the priest,
> Always ourselves we love the least,
> That's the burden of the angel/beast.
> —BRUCE COCKBURN

I was an incredibly self-conscious adolescent, especially about my body. I hated my emerging breasts, the sudden hairiness of my legs, my short fingers, my incredibly pale white skin, my long and awkward body. I wore long-sleeved shirts and long pants all the time, no matter how hot and muggy the weather. I would do almost anything to avoid suiting up for our high school swimming class.

At the time I didn't have a clue that most of my classmates felt similarly. I did not understand that self-esteem is a struggle common to all humanity. Somehow I believed that I was the only one so afflicted.

My perceptions of myself are light-years away from what they once were. They are still not always accurate, but I have a clearer understanding of the roots of my self-consciousness and a greater awareness of the commonness of my struggle for self-acceptance.

In recovery I am learning that I am not alone in my journey toward acceptance and self-love.

August 7

There is no one who will feed the yearning. Face it. You will have to do, do it yourself. —GLORIA ANZALDÚA

During our addictions, we craved many things. It may have been drugs, alcohol, sex, food, or other substances. It may have been involvement with or dependence on other people. No matter how much we had, we wanted more, in a desperate effort to fill up the emptiness we felt inside of us. Despite our frantic efforts, it was never enough.

Sometimes we carry this into recovery and continue trying to get other people to "fix" us. If we can gain their approval, we will feel better about ourselves. If they care for us, we will feel valued and worthwhile. If we can get them to love us enough, we will come to love ourselves.

Slowly we are learning that this emptiness inside us is a spiritual and emotional yearning that cannot be filled by other people and substances. We are the only ones who can fill this yearning. We will have to do.

Today I am taking responsibility for the emptiness inside me, learning to nurture and care for myself.

August 8

Fear is not a good teacher. The lessons of fear are quickly forgotten. —MARY CATHERINE BATESON

Fear ruled our lives during our addictions, but it did very little to get us sober. We may have been terrified of what would happen if we got drunk again, but that didn't stop us from drinking. Once the fear wore off, we went back to doing what we had been doing. Our fears about the physical, mental, emotional, and spiritual consequences of our addictions rarely contributed to our ability to get sober.

Fear is not a good teacher. In fact, we learn best in the absence of fear. Fear immobilizes us and makes it impossible for us to learn. Fear ties up our mental and emotional energies, leaving us too exhausted to absorb new information. Fear isolates us, cutting us off from the wisdom and experience of others.

Children learn best in a nurturing and supportive environment. They learn most quickly when surrounded by people who believe in them and in their abilities. Sober adult lesbians are no different. Like children, we learn best when we are surrounded by others in recovery who believe in us and are able to bring out the best in us. Patience and love are always better teachers than fear.

Today I will try to let go of my fears and instead surround myself with others who can nurture and support my learning in recovery.

August 9

Those who do not know how to weep with their whole heart don't know how to laugh either. —GOLDA MEIR

During our addictions, we rarely understood the ways our feelings are interconnected. We thought we could turn off our pain and still feel our joy. We thought we could bury our anger and still experience our strength. We thought we could ignore our losses and still celebrate our loves.

In recovery we are discovering that feelings are connected; they spring from the same source. Consequently, we cannot turn off one feeling without shutting them all down. We cannot brush aside the feelings we find uncomfortable or painful without losing some depth in those we consider enjoyable.

Learning to weep with our whole heart sets us free to laugh from the depths of our souls. Learning to grieve and mourn our losses moves us toward acceptance and healing. Learning to rage at injustice empowers us to act fully toward right relationship.

Today I will be grateful for my tears, recognizing them as part of my path to laughter and healing.

August 10

The game was just to find something about everything to be glad about—no matter what 'twas . . . You see, when you're hunting for the glad things, you sort of forget the other kind. —ELEANOR H. PORTER

Regardless of how simplistic we may think Eleanor Porter's story of Pollyanna is, it does teach us something about the development and practice of gratitude. Gratitude rarely comes naturally. It is too easy to focus on the negative things about our lives, only noticing the things we wish were different. It takes practice, and lots of it, to begin noticing all the little things we like about ourselves and our sober lives.

Practicing an attitude of gratitude is important to our happiness in recovery. One way to begin is to start each day with a conscious appreciation for being sober. Continuing in an attitude of gratitude means learning to notice the positive changes we have made in recovery, rather than dwelling on the issues with which we continue to struggle. It means learning to recognize the positive qualities of others, instead of focusing on the negative.

Practicing an attitude of gratitude is not easy, but the rewards are tremendous. Over the long haul, we will discover a greater capacity for appreciation and joy in our lives.

How can I begin practicing an attitude of gratitude in my recovery?

August 11

I'm giving the gifts back, one by one. I'm tearing the pages of my past. I'm turning my back. I'm turning them down.
—JOAN LARKIN

Letting go of the past is a task all of us face in recovery. It may be the pain and rejection we experienced in our families of origin. It may be the exclusion we felt with so-called friends or coworkers. It may be the disappointments of jobs lost, lovers who left us, plans that just never worked out.

Whatever the particular wreckage of our past may be, we don't need to continue carrying it around in recovery. We can choose to let it go, leave it behind us, and begin to move forward into a clean and sober future. Continuing to carry it around with us only weighs us down. Today is a new day. Today, in recovery, we have choices. We can choose which pieces of our past we wish to keep and which pieces are better left behind. We can give back the gifts no longer needed, the lessons learned that are now unhealthy, and move forward to create a new tomorrow.

Today I will pray for the wisdom and ability to let go of those pieces of my past that weigh me down in recovery.

August 12

Many of us know former drunks who have given up alcohol and changed nothing else in their lives, who have been unable to alter the patterns of insanity that compulsive drinking induces. —JUDITH MCDANIEL

In her book *Metamorphosis*, Judith McDaniel discusses our need to both stop drinking and drugging and be restored to sanity. Once we are in recovery, most of us recognize that it is not enough to simply stop using chemicals. If we truly want a healthy recovery, we must embark on a journey of change. We must begin addressing what McDaniel calls the "patterns of insanity" that were woven into our lives during our active addiction.

Being restored to sanity requires, first of all, that we choose sanity, that we see sanity as something to be desired. Choosing sanity is about our willingness to change. As sober lesbians, this means facing the thoughts and beliefs that perpetuated our addiction, as well as the self-destructive attitudes and behaviors that persist after we have stopped ingesting chemicals.

If our sobriety is only about staying away from drugs and alcohol, we will shortchange ourselves. The full joys and blessings of recovery come as we are willing to change, moving closer and closer to the sanity that restores us to ourselves and our world.

How am I being restored to sanity? What steps am I taking to create the necessary changes in my life?

August 13

We need to demystify the forces that have told us what we should be before we can value what we are.
—GLORIA STEINEM

Living up to the expectations of other people is exhausting. Many of us spent years trying to fulfill them or fighting against them: being the good little girls society wanted us to be, taking care of others and putting their needs first, trying to be normal—in other words, looking and acting straight.

Attempting to live out someone else's expectations of us wears us down. It robs our energy. It strips our creativity. It takes away our power and our ability to be responsible in our own lives.

Recovery is about taking back that power and responsibility. Recovery is about deciding who we are and faithfully living out that identity. Recovery is about being honest with ourselves and others, even if it means we disappoint their expectations. Recovery is about accepting the fact that our expectations of ourselves are the ones that count the most.

Today I will accept myself for who I am and live by my own expectations of myself.

August 14

The word religion means to bind together, and the bonds of religious faith, for those who take them seriously, are as intimate as family ties.
—BARBARA ZANOTTI

Those of us who grew up in families with intense religious commitments know the truth of Zanotti's observation. She goes on to note that given the intimacy of these connections, a betrayal of trust by the religious community or its leaders can be as shattering as betrayal by one's family. Healing from these kinds of experiences can be slow and painful.

Often it seems easier to deny our past connection rather than do the hard work that real healing demands. When we come out as lesbians, it may seem easier to walk away from religion. It may seem less painful to seal over the past, to act tough and say it doesn't matter anymore; we're done with it.

The truth is, closing off the past rarely engenders healing. True recovery requires acknowledging and resolving our pain. We need time and space to grieve our losses. We need others who understand the betrayal we felt and share our journey toward wholeness.

Are there losses from my past that I have sealed over? How can I open myself to further healing?

August 15

She suddenly felt quite safe. It was a very strange feeling, and she found it indescribably nice. What was there to worry over? The disaster had come at last.
—TOVE JANSSON

Many of us spend our lives waiting for the other shoe to drop. No matter how good things are in the present, we "know" it won't last. Sooner or later, something bad is bound to happen. Maybe coming out to our father went better than we expected, but we "know" it can't be this good. Maybe the things we said to our lover seemed all right yesterday, but we "know" they will eventually backfire on us. It's almost as if we are waiting for the disaster to happen.

Much of this is because disasters are familiar to us. We spent years during our addiction getting ourselves out of one scrape after another. Those of us who grew up in dysfunctional families were conditioned to expect the worst from an early age, and the worst generally happened. Anticipating the negative feels safe and comfortable.

The problem with this old coping mechanism is that it robs us of the joys of the moment. We can never be happy with the present. We are always looking ahead, waiting for the next problem to occur, anticipating the negative, unable to appreciate the positive. Learning to live in the moment requires risk and trust.

Today I will try to stay in the present, enjoying each moment as it comes, without waiting for the other shoe to drop.

August 16

All of us would do well to stop fighting each other for space at the bottom, because there ain't no more room.
—CHERYL CLARKE

Sometimes in the effort to grapple with the realities of our oppression, we get caught in a "victim mentality." The first step in healing always involves speaking the truth about what has occurred. Absorbing the full impact of oppression means coming to terms with the many ways we have been victimized.

Sometimes we become unable, or unwilling, to see ourselves as anything other than victims. We compete with others, arguing about who has experienced the greater oppression. We attempt to achieve identity and self-worth through our battle scars.

Lesbian writer Cheryl Clarke challenges us to move beyond identifying ourselves as victims. She challenges us to stop comparing oppressions, to stop fighting about whose life experiences have been the most devastating.

Healing means we need to be honest about the ways we have been victimized. But recovery requires seeing ourselves as more than victims. It demands the ability to see ourselves as survivors who can thrive despite the painful experiences of our past.

Are there ways in which being "the victim" makes me feel more important and valuable? How can I begin to find a more positive and fulfilling identity?

August 17

Sometimes it happens before you even know it. You find yourself passing through life quietly, politely not "flaunting" those differences about yourself that the other person may not easily understand, integrate, or like.
—RACHEL WAHBA

In an essay entitled "Hiding Is Unhealthy for the Soul," Rachel Wahba describes the ways we sometimes find ourselves "passing" without having made a conscious or deliberate decision to be closeted. We leave our lover out of a conversation about our recent vacation. We forget to include a piece of information that might disclose our lesbian identity. We fail to insist that others celebrate the anniversary of our relationship. We realize after the fact that we somehow did not wear our "wedding ring" to that important business event.

Societal pressure to be straight is so strong that in the moment, we sometimes do not realize we are "passing." The expectation of heterosexism is so pervasive that we sometimes do not recognize the ways we are "being polite," in an effort to fit in. No matter how long we have been out as lesbians, no matter how proud we are of our identity, the heterosexism and homophobia of the society around us is constantly at work to silence us.

◊

Recognizing the powerful impact of society's heterosexism and homophobia, today I will look for ways to celebrate and affirm my identity as a lesbian.

August 18

Power can be taken, but not given. The process of the taking is empowerment in itself. —GLORIA STEINEM

No matter how much we might have liked it, no one was able to give us the power we needed to get sober. We were the only ones who could eventually take that power and use it for our own recovery. No one else can give us the power to feel proud of ourselves as sober lesbians. They may nurture us along the way, but ultimately we are the ones who must take back the power to be proud of ourselves.

Taking back our power is what recovery is all about. During our addictions, we were continually giving our power away—to drugs and alcohol, to our families, to friends and lovers. Getting sober was the first step in reclaiming our power. It was the first step toward taking back the power needed to nurture and care for ourselves.

When we feel powerless, we need to step back and examine what is going on. Are we expecting others to give us a sense of power? Are we feeling powerless because we have given away our power? If so, then the only solution is to once again take back the power that is rightfully ours. If we wait for others to hand it to us, we will never be empowered.

Am I learning to appropriately use the power I have regained in recovery?

August 19

Generally by the time you are Real, most of your hair has been loved off, and your eyes drop out, and you get loose in the joints and very shabby. But these things don't matter at all, because once you are Real, you can't be ugly, except to people who don't understand.
—MARGERY WILLIAMS

In this quote from Margery Williams's children's story *The Velveteen Rabbit*, the skin horse describes the process of becoming real to the velveteen rabbit. Becoming real is a lot like getting sober. In fact, recovering from our addiction is about becoming real.

Recovery is about moving from a false understanding of ourselves to an honest and realistic sense of who we are. Recovery is about letting go of our need for pretensions and being willing to be who we are. Recovery is about allowing others to get close to us and come to know and love us. Recovery is about being willing to change and grow, even if that means having our rough spots rubbed off or becoming loose in the joints.

When we first get sober, most of us are terrified about what will happen to us. We cannot imagine life without chemicals. We worry that being sober means our life is over, that other people won't like us anymore. We are terrified that we won't be the same once we're sober. In truth, we are not the same; we are becoming real.

Today I will remember that recovery is a process of becoming real; it may not always be comfortable, but the end results are worth it.

August 20

There is no way to take the danger out of human relationships.
—BARBARA G. HARRISON

Part of the isolation during our addiction resulted from our fears of risk-taking in relationships. If we were drunk or high, we could generally navigate the risks required for socializing and building friendships. However, as our disease progressed, so too did our disease with others.

Barbara Harrison is right: all relationships require risk-taking. If we want to know whether that cute dyke over there likes us, we will have to take some risks. If we want to know what our lover's commitment to this relationship is, we will have to take some risks. If we want to know whether our friends or family will still accept us once they know we are lesbians, we will have to take some risks.

Living sober, in and of itself, is a risk. There are no guarantees in recovery. Being connected to one another will always require risks. If we can survive sobriety, maybe we can survive risking ourselves with one another.

Are there relationships where I have been allowing my fears to control me? What risks do I want to begin taking instead?

August 21

In order to feel fully safe, I need to feel known.
—EVELYN TORTON BECK

When we are holding on to secrets, it is difficult to feel safe. There is always the danger that the truth will be discovered. As lesbians, we tend to feel safer with others like us, or at least with those who know and accept our lesbian selves. It is difficult to feel truly safe when we are in a situation where we have to constantly hide our sexual identity.

As addicts in recovery, we learn the importance of self-disclosure in the fifth step. Having completed an inventory of ourselves, in the fifth step we are encouraged to share our assessment with our higher power and with another human being. This means revealing things about ourselves that we kept hidden during our addictions.

The importance of the fifth step is that it enables us to become more fully known by someone else, and thus we find a greater sense of safety in recovery. Sharing ourselves with someone else diminishes the isolation created during our addictions. In the process of becoming safe, we are empowered to continue building sober relationships.

What actions do I need to take to allow trusted others to more fully know me?

August 22

The surprise and delight of making love to her that night still fills me. What was supposed to be queer, perverted and debased was, I found, lovely, sacred and healing.
—THE REV. NANCY L. WILSON

Nancy Wilson's description of her first experience of making love with another woman reminds us that old beliefs and ideas are often wrong. Many of us were taught that our feelings for other women were wrong. We believed acting on these feelings was perverted. And yet, many of us also shared Nancy Wilson's discovery the first time we made love to a woman. Much to our surprise, what we had been taught was perverted and debased turned out to be healing, sacred, and liberating.

The willingness to let go of old ideas and beliefs remains an important aspect of our recovery. The messages we received about our lesbianism are not the only ones that are inaccurate. Many of us continue to believe that we are somehow less than others, that our feelings are a sign of weakness, that coming out will destroy our families, or that we don't really deserve to be successful. Recovery challenges us to disprove these ideas and beliefs and to be surprised by new truths. In these surprises, we will find our healing and our growth.

What old ideas and beliefs have I been hanging on to? How can I begin to disprove them, allowing myself to be surprised by the healing power of new truths?

August 23

> I know in the end it will be better than it was an' cannot berate myself cause of limited survival mechanisms; I am gettin' up and gettin' on, Comin' home! and don't want no static bout where I been.
> —SAPPHIRE

Learning to forgive ourselves is an important lesson in recovery. We cannot go back and rewrite the past. We cannot change the ways we interacted with others during our addiction. While we need to take responsibility for our actions, living in those failures serves no purpose. Living in the past only immobilizes us in the present. As Sapphire says, we have to be about "gettin' up and gettin' on."

Recognizing the limited nature of our past survival mechanisms is a useful tool for learning to forgive ourselves. Most of the time, we did the best we could with what we had. If we weren't always loving in our past relationships, it was probably due in part to the ways we had not been loved and nurtured. If we didn't always act honestly and responsibly with others, it was probably due in part to how little we understood about being honest and responsible. We do not need to berate ourselves for the past. It is more helpful to concentrate on learning new survival mechanisms in the present.

Are there things for which I still have difficulty forgiving myself? Can I recognize my limited survival mechanisms in these situations?

August 24

> I realized finally that if I couldn't relate to religious rituals, prayer groups, or feminist liturgies, it wasn't because there was something wrong with me . . . It was—and is—because my spiritual experiences and needs are different.
> —MARY MENDOLA

Finding a healthy sense of spirituality that works for us as sober lesbians is a challenging task. Sometimes in the process of sorting out our needs, we compare ourselves to those around us. Sometimes we think what works for them ought to work for us. When this fails, we wonder what is wrong with us . . . Why can't I relate to a Mother God image? Why can't I make my peace and stay in the church? Why can't I feel comfortable in the gay and lesbian synagogue? Why can't I find fulfillment in women's rituals?

The answer may be that our spiritual needs are not like everyone else's; they are uniquely ours. Each of us needs to explore the varieties of spiritual experiences available to lesbians in order to discover what is most helpful for us. We also need to remember that our spiritual desires and needs change over time. What was helpful in early sobriety may not be so fulfilling later on in our recovery. We must accept and embrace our unique sense of spirituality, in order to discover the best route to our spiritual fulfillment.

◇

Have I been trying to express my spirituality through other women's ways? What new experiences might be better suited to me?

August 25

Indifference is the invincible giant of the world.
—OUIDA

Recently I was driving down a country road where I encountered a series of signs alerting me to bridge construction ahead. They began with a sign stating that it was two miles ahead, then one mile, then a half mile, then a quarter mile. Additional notices appeared along the way informing me that there was only one lane open on this bridge, warning me to prepare to stop. Clearly the folks of this small town did not want anyone to come upon this bridge unprepared.

Maintaining our recovery demands that we learn to recognize the "warning signs" in our own lives. We have to learn to see our own trouble spots, the attitudes and behaviors that warn us of a possible relapse ahead.

Indifference is perhaps one of the most glaring warning signs. When I don't care anymore—about myself, my work, my family, my friends—my recovery is jeopardized and I am in trouble. Failing to pay attention to this warning sign can destroy all that I have achieved in recovery.

Today I will focus on maintaining my recovery by paying attention to the warning signs within and around me.

August 26

It is a hard quest worth making to find a comrade through whose presence one becomes steadily the person one desires to be. —ANNA LOUISE STRONG

Building healthy relationships is a critical component of our ongoing recovery. Many of us enter recovery with little idea of what constitutes a healthy relationship, let alone how to go about establishing and maintaining one. Anna Strong offers one piece of advice that we can use in reflecting on our current relationships, as well as in thinking about those we would like to develop.

In a healthy relationship we are able to be ourselves. We can make choices freely, unafraid of rejection or punishment. We can express our likes and dislikes. We don't feel like we have to give up some piece of ourselves in order to gain the other person's approval or respect.

In a healthy relationship, there is also room for us to grow; change is recognized as normal. This means that the other person wants what is best for us, wants us to become our very best self, and will work to help us achieve that, even if it means changes in the nature of the relationship.

Am I able to be myself in my relationships? Are there people in my life who enable me to be the sober and growing lesbian I want to be?

August 27

Folks bring their pain, their insecurities, and their crazies with them wherever they go—to work, to church, to meetings, to relationships. How we treat one another reflects how we feel about ourselves.
—SUSAN TAYLOR

Sometimes we are critical and judgmental toward others. We don't want to deal with the chairperson who seems to have "issues" with control. We get tired of listening to people whose lives are constantly in crisis. We feel impatient with the sponsee who keeps relapsing. We get irritated with what we perceive to be our lover's refusal to change.

These patterns and behaviors, on the part of ourselves and others, reflect the ways we struggle with old issues and insecurities. We carry past feelings and experiences into the present, allowing these dynamics to affect our current relationships and commitments.

Susan Taylor reminds us that our level of compassion for others is a reflection of our compassion toward ourselves. Developing tolerance and compassion for others is a sign of growth in recovery. It is a sign that we are becoming more accepting and compassionate of ourselves.

Today I will remember that compassion for others begins with compassion for myself.

August 28

To cope with hurt and control my fears, I grew a thick skin. Oh, the many names of power—pride, arrogance, control.
—GLORIA ANZALDÚA

Some of us know the pain and terror of an abusive childhood. Many of us have struggled with the difficulties of growing up in an environment that failed to nurture our self-esteem and autonomy. All of us as lesbians know the fears of coming out and the pain of being different.

As our addictions took control of our lives, these dynamics were exacerbated. Disappointment, fear, anxiety, and depression became a way of life. Surviving all of this required a thick skin. We learned how to protect ourselves from rejection by others, disillusionment with ourselves, and seeming abandonment by any kind of God. We assumed a kind of pretend power—acting tough, looking like we had it all together, putting others down—in an increasingly desperate effort to fend off painful feelings within us.

In recovery we are challenged to give up this illusion of power, to set aside the unhealthy pride that keeps us from asking for help, the desire for power over others, the obsession to be on top of everything. Recovery challenges us to put down these old ways of coping with fear and pain that keep others at a distance.

Today I will look within myself for power and allow myself to be empowered through relationships with others.

August 29

There were no role models for female singer-songwriters when I began in the early sixties and fewer for young lesbians.
—JANIS IAN

Janis Ian's observation applies to all of us. As young lesbians, we had few role models. Until very recently, there were no visible, positive images of lesbians in the larger society. Few of us knew such women in our families and neighborhoods. Few of us had sober, positive, older lesbians who could mentor and teach us how to survive and thrive as young lesbians. We had to figure it out for ourselves, often through a very painful process of trial and error.

Today things have begun to change. As more and more women come out, younger lesbians are beginning to have role models—lesbians they can look at and say, "I want to be like her when I grow up."

As lesbians in recovery, we have the opportunity to become role models for others. We have the opportunity to give others some of what we missed. We can share the wisdom and knowledge gained through our life experiences and through our recovery. Our willingness to be visible can assure that younger lesbians will not feel invisible.

Am I willing to allow my recovery to be an example for younger lesbians? How can I share my experience and wisdom with others?

August 30

Spiritual empowerment is evidenced in our lives by our willingness to tell ourselves the truth, to listen to the truth when it's told to us, and to dispense truth as lovingly as possible, when we feel compelled to talk from the heart. —CHRISTINA BALDWIN

During our addictions, the truth was something we wanted as little to do with as possible. Facing the truth of our lives, as it was unfolding, was painful. We did not want to see the ways we were becoming powerless. We did not want to hear the truth of how we were destroying those we loved. We suppressed as much as possible the truth we needed to speak to others, and when it reached a boiling point, we often exploded in anger.

One way to recognize our growth in recovery is how we respond to the truth. Are we increasingly able to tell ourselves the truth? Are we able to face and confront the realities of our lives? Can we listen to the truth more easily when others speak? Are we able to hear from others how our behavior affects them? When we need to speak the truth to someone else, can we do it honestly and compassionately? Can we speak the truth simply for what it is, without using the truth as a weapon?

◊

Today I will focus on my ability to speak and listen to the truth, within myself and in my relationships with others.

August 31

A glimpse of two women in love is a gratuitous gift from God, a miracle of courage, daring and integrity.
—LORNA HOCHSTEIN

It is amazing any of us form intimate relationships with other women. We are frequently forced to find one another and begin our relationships in secret. Our commitments are often made in the face of family opposition, or at the very least, silence and subtle disapproval. We are excluded from the rituals that affirm and celebrate heterosexual unions. We receive virtually none of the legal benefits available to straight married couples. In light of this, our survival is a miracle.

Our continued survival and health demands that we find ways to recognize and affirm our relationships. We must celebrate one another's courage and daring. We must honor one another's integrity. We must bless one another's love and nurture one another's ongoing commitments.

Our relationships cannot survive in a vacuum. Amid the overt homophobia and the permeating heterosexism of our society, we need to know that the lesbian community values and respects our integrity. In the absence of societal support and validation, we need to know that the lesbian community celebrates our courage, daring, and integrity.

Today I will celebrate the miracles of courage, daring, and integrity reflected in my relationships.

September 1

By the time I understood that I was queer, that habit of hiding was deeply set in me, so deeply that it was not a choice but an instinct. —DOROTHY ALLISON

Long before we have the vocabulary to name ourselves, we intuit the need to hide for survival. Without being told, we sense that who we are is unacceptable, even dangerous. Before anyone says out loud that being a lesbian is wrong, sinful, dirty, or perverted, we intuit these beliefs and "know" they apply to us. And so we hide ourselves.

Coming out of hiding in recovery can be scary and painful. Even those of us who were out as lesbians during our addiction discover that there is yet more coming out in recovery. Coming out means confronting our instinct to hide. Coming out means challenging our fears and breaking old habits. Coming out and being visible means learning new tools for survival.

How did I learn to hide myself growing up? What new survival tools have I gained in recovery?

September 2

What is destructive is impatience, haste, expecting too much too fast.
—MAY SARTON

Often we hear old-timers in twelve-step meetings wish newcomers a "long and slow" recovery. Though this sounds odd initially, the longer we are in recovery, the more we understand the old-timer's intent.

As addicts, we have a tendency to want the world and want it right now. We sometimes think that since we've gotten sober, the rest should be easy. We begin to get a glimpse of the promises of recovery, and we want to experience them as quickly as possible. We want immediate serenity. We expect relationships with lovers and family to be rebuilt in a day. We're ready to let go of our "character defects" and don't understand why they haven't already disappeared.

Sometimes we need to be reminded that it took years for us to become an addict and it will take time for us to experience the fullness of recovery. We need others with long-term sobriety to give us permission to slow down, to not be so hard on ourselves, and to ease up on our expectations of the healing process. Being impatient with ourselves will only make the journey difficult.

Today I will remember that healing takes time; I cannot expect myself to recover overnight.

September 3

Early sobriety is tough stuff—being bombarded by the memories that denial so conveniently repressed, struggling to deal with dozens of new situations sober. The point is be gentle—this is going to be hard, so try to take it easy.
—SUSAN D. YARBER

These words, written from one sober lesbian to another, remind us of the importance of learning to be gentle with ourselves in recovery. Learning to live sober, learning to live honestly with ourselves and others, learning to take responsibility for our needs and our actions, is no easy task. Recovery is hard work, perhaps the hardest work we have ever done. Sobriety, whether early or later, can be "tough stuff." Being hard on ourselves only makes the journey more difficult.

Being gentle with ourselves and learning to "take it easy" is essential to our serenity. We have all the time in the world for recovery. We have the rest of our lives for sobriety. We do not need to learn or accomplish everything today. Pacing ourselves, taking things one step at a time, learning to balance hard work with time out for play, is an important part of the journey.

Recognizing that recovery is hard work, today I will practice being gentle with myself.

September 4

Surely the earth can be saved by all the people who insist on love.
—ALICE WALKER

Insisting on love means learning to care for, value, and respect ourselves as sober lesbians. Insisting on love means giving others the respect and honesty they deserve. Insisting on love means celebrating our diversity as well as affirming our commonalties. Insisting on love means bringing forth the very best from one another and ourselves. Insisting on love involves recognizing the interconnectedness of love and justice.

Insisting on this kind of love may not change the world overnight, but it will begin to build communities of accountability and respect. Insisting on this kind of love will create relationships where we have the freedom to be ourselves and yet be connected to others. Insisting on this kind of love will move us out of ourselves and into communities where we are able to find ourselves in one another. This kind of love is what getting sober is all about.

How can I insist on love as I move through the events and interactions of this day?

September 5

I can see that there are many problems that lesbians face that physicians have yet to address. We have to train our nation's physicians to ask the right questions and to offer lesbians advice that is appropriate to them. —FORMER U.S. SURGEON GENERAL JOCELYN ELDERS

With a considerable amount of fear and trepidation as a young lesbian, I arrived for my first appointment with a gynecologist. "Are you on the pill?" he asked. "No," I answered. "So, what kind of birth control are you using?" "None," I replied. I was completely unprepared for the ridiculing tone of his next query: "What's wrong with you? Don't you ever have sex?"

I have since learned that my experience was a common one. The medical profession is often uneducated about the needs of lesbians. Little research has been done on our health-care issues. We are often rendered invisible by the profession's heterosexist assumptions.

Taking care of our physical selves is important. If we are going to receive the medical care we need and deserve, we must educate ourselves. We need to work as a community to raise the issues that are important to us as lesbians. We must come out and demand that the medical profession recognize us.

Today I will not allow someone else's heterosexism and ignorance to intimidate me or rob me of the information and treatment I need to remain healthy in recovery.

September 6

I made a decision—or the decision shining in the soft, brutal darkness took hold of me—to live.
—JOAN LARKIN

In a poem entitled "Clifton," these words poignantly describe the moment when a young woman moved from the depths of alcoholism into the beginnings of recovery. For all of us, the decision to recover is a decision to live. Sometimes we know we have made that decision, and other times it is as if the decision were made for us. In either case, recovery is about choosing life, choosing life instead of the never-ending cycle of addiction, despair, and death.

It is important to keep this moment fresh in our heart and mind. We need to remember what it was like during our addiction in order to be thankful for what we have gained in recovery. We need to maintain a constant sense of gratitude for that moment in time when we said, "This is enough. I have had enough. I am ready to look for a way out of this despair."

Today I will be grateful for that first moment when I began to choose to live.

September 7

My makeup wasn't smeared, I wasn't disheveled, I behaved politely, and I never finished off a bottle, so how could I be alcoholic? —BETTY FORD

Betty Ford's openness about her journey contributed much toward breaking down the myths and stereotypes surrounding addiction. Many of us faced similar struggles with our own denial: I didn't drink in the morning; I only used on weekends; I didn't use needles; I never touched hard liquor, I never got nasty when I used—how could I be an addict or an alcoholic?

Today we understand that it is not how much or how often we used drugs or alcohol, but what happened when we drank or drugged—what the consequences were and at what point we became powerless to stop using.

Despite our awakening, there is still tremendous denial within the lesbian community about the nature and extent of addiction. Most research indicates that drug and alcohol use is two-to-three times higher in our community than in the larger society. Those of us who are already sober need to carry the message of recovery to the still sick and suffering. Sharing our experience, strength, and hope, when appropriate, can help others break through their denial.

As an expression of my gratitude for recovery, I will look for an opportunity to share the message of hope with someone else today.

September 8

The price of peace is to abandon fear and replace it with faith.
—PEACE PILGRIM

Fear was a familiar feeling in our addictions, and most of us struggle with it long into recovery. We are afraid we won't get the job, afraid our lover will fall in love with someone new, afraid our sister won't talk to us after we tell her we're a lesbian, afraid we'll lose our kids if our ex-husband finds out we're a dyke or afraid our kids will hate us if they find out, afraid people will look at us funny if we don't drink at the party tonight.

Replacing fear with faith requires developing a sense of trust in ourselves. Trusting ourselves is about relying on our own inner resources. It means trusting that we will be able to stay sober and get through each situation as it occurs. This kind of self-trust is extremely difficult in early recovery. Developing a sense of trust for others in our sober support system can be a helpful first step. If we cannot trust ourselves, maybe we can begin to trust the wisdom and experience of other lesbians who have stayed sober longer than we have. As we gain trust in our friends and ourselves, it will become easier to replace fear with faith.

Today I will remember that replacing fear with faith requires trusting myself and those who are close to me.

September 9

Family life! The United Nations is child's play compared to the tugs and splits and need to understand and forgive in any family. —MAY SARTON

Television families gave too many of us the wrong ideas about what it means to be family. We've had too many storybook images and not enough truth about how complex real family life actually is. And besides all the missing routine heterosexual complexities, no one ever came out on "the Brady Bunch," Donna Reed never had a lesbian lover, and even on "Roseanne," Darlene didn't grow up to be a dyke.

All families have conflicts and struggles. Relationships between parents and children, between siblings, between other relatives and multiple generations are never smooth and easy. If we want to remain connected to our families, we need to acknowledge that it will not be perfect. Even if our mother likes our new girlfriend, she still may expect us to spend the holidays at home. Even if our sister still talks to us after we come out to her, that may not change the fact that she thinks we're too lenient with our kids.

Dismantling the myths we grew up with and recognizing the truth about families won't necessarily fix things, but it may help us be more patient with ourselves and our loved ones.

Today I will try to remember that my struggles with family are common ones; they are part of being human.

September 10

If you haven't forgiven yourself something, how can you forgive others? —DELORES HUERTA

Learning to forgive ourselves is an important aspect of our recovery. During our addictions, and even afterward, all of us said and did things we later regretted. All of us have things in our past we wish had been different. Carrying these into the present and continuing to berate ourselves only weighs us down.

Many of us carry guilt and shame about things for which we were not even responsible. As children, we perceive everything as our fault. People dying, parents divorcing, abuses done to us—whatever the problem, children feel responsible. Some of us continue to carry that responsibility into adulthood. We need to learn to forgive ourselves, to let ourselves off the hook. Some of us even need to forgive ourselves for being lesbians, despite the fact that we "know" there is nothing wrong with who we are.

Guilt and shame are useless burdens. They prevent us from loving ourselves and others. Forgiving ourselves frees us for moving on in recovery.

Are there things from my past that I continue to feel guilty about? How can I begin to free myself through forgiveness?

September 11

Suddenly, I was happy to be free of the responsibility to be dully the same as anyone. I felt a deeper responsibility to grow, and most importantly, to live.
—THE REV. SANDRA L. ROBINSON

The freedom to be ourselves is one of the joys of coming out. When we finally recognize ourselves as lesbians and allow ourselves to begin living out that reality, we discover a freedom that we never knew existed. Discovering who we are sets us free from being "dully the same" anymore.

We have similar experiences in recovery. In fact, it is in recovery that the joys of coming out to ourselves and others can most fully be realized. The entire process of recovery is about rediscovering our true selves—finding out who we are, what we like, how we feel, what we value and treasure. It is about rediscovering our emotions and being restored to sanity. In recovery we are challenged to be ourselves, and only ourselves.

Sobriety sets us free to take responsibility for ourselves, for living out our true identity as we understand it. With that freedom comes a deeper responsibility—that of growth and change, all in an effort to live fully as the proud sober lesbians we were created to be.

Today I will celebrate the joys of being set free to be myself, appreciating how I no longer need to be "dully the same" as anyone else.

September 12

To the degree that I have put together the various parts of my being—Puerto Rican, Woman, Black, Poor, Lesbian, Christian, etc.—the clearer my vision of God has become. —ALTAGRACIA PÉREZ MACEIRA

Our understanding of God is related to our self-esteem. If we are critical of ourselves, our image of God will likely be judgmental. If we have difficulty loving ourselves, we will rarely view God as a loving being. If our understanding of ourselves is fragmented, we will tend to see God as one who might love some parts of us and reject others.

By contrast, as we come to value our strengths and limitations, we will find it easier to view God as a loving and accepting force in our lives. As we are able to accept and integrate the varying aspects of our identity, we will come to experience God as a healing and nurturing presence. Learning to value and cherish the wholeness of our identity, rather than cutting off parts of ourselves in order to "be acceptable," is essential to our spiritual growth. Finding new and healthier visions of God requires continued integration of our self-identity.

How do my images of the divine reflect my own struggles for self-esteem? What steps can I take toward healthier views of myself and God?

September 13

Sometimes, it's like a hair across your cheek. You can't see it, you can't find it with your fingers, but you keep brushing at it because the feel of it is irritating.
—MARIAN ANDERSON

Overt homophobia is easy to recognize: being discharged from the military, having your parents disown you, losing out on a promotion at work, being denied a family membership at the gym.

Sometimes this obvious discrimination blinds us to the more subtle effects of society's heterosexism and homophobia: feeling uncomfortable holding our lover's hand on the street, wondering if someone is staring at us because we look like dykes, being silent when our family ignores our lover.

Marian Anderson's words remind us that the subtle manifestations of oppression can be equally irritating and destructive. While they may not be as easily identified, their presence is a constant source of tension and stress. Acknowledging these "hairs across our cheek" is crucial to our sanity. Ignoring them can make us think we are crazy, that there's something wrong with us, that we're just making a big deal out of nothing. As lesbians in recovery, we need to recognize and respond to both overt and subtle homophobia.

Are there ways in which I have been brushing off the more subtle experiences of homophobia, telling myself "it's not a big deal"?

September 14

The important point is that where feeling is evaded, where anger is hidden or goes unattended, masking itself, there the power of love, the power to act, to deepen relation, atrophies and dies.
—BEVERLY WILDUNG HARRISON

During our addictions, we spent much time and energy ignoring, hiding, and evading our feelings. We used chemicals and other substances or behaviors to mask our real feelings. At the time, we rarely realized the extent to which burying and avoiding our feelings was affecting us.

As Beverly Harrison points out, our feelings are the source of our connectedness to those around us. When we avoid our feelings, we are unable to be fully present in our lives. When we hide our true feelings, we are forced into superficial relationships with others. When we disregard our feelings, we are unable to make honest choices about what we value and how we wish to live and be in this world. Avoiding our feelings cuts us off from the source of our power and growth.

What feelings have I been avoiding lately? Are my relationships with others stagnant because I am hiding from or masking my true feelings? What feelings do I need to acknowledge and accept in order to deepen my connectedness with those I love?

My feelings are the source of my life and power. Today I will allow them to deepen my relationships with others.

September 15

It is imperative that a woman keep her sense of humor intact and at the ready ... Women should be tough, tender, laugh as much as possible, and live long lives.
—MAYA ANGELOU

We need a sense of humor in our lives. Humor helps us maintain a sense of perspective about ourselves. It keeps us from taking ourselves and our plans and schemes too seriously. Being able to laugh at ourselves helps us learn to be patient with ourselves; it takes the edge off our inherent self-criticism.

Humor brings a sense of balance to our relationship with the world. It cuts through all the craziness around us and keeps us from getting lost in the pain and injustice that is part of this world.

Humor reminds us not to "sweat the small stuff." It helps us keep the important things in focus and allows us to let go of the details that don't really matter in the long run.

Humor keeps our passion for one another alive. Sharing a good joke or a funny story creates a bond between us. It brings us together and helps us find our common humanity.

Today I will nurture my recovery by valuing and exercising my sense of humor.

September 16

Insanity is doing the same thing over and over again, but expecting different results. —RITA MAE BROWN

Having heard this saying repeatedly in recovery, I was delighted when I discovered it originated with a lesbian! I was also struck, once again, by the many ways we are invisible to the world around us. While hundreds of people in twelve-step rooms know this quote, few recognize that it originated in our community.

Sometimes invisibility is forced upon us. Most of us are not obviously lesbian. We don't wear "flashing lavender signs." This means we can pass if we choose. Sometimes we are made invisible when others ignore our lesbianism or fail to acknowledge the contributions of identified lesbians. A friend told me he studied Adrienne Rich's poetry in college, but no one mentioned the fact that she was a lesbian.

We may not be able to be out all the time. But choosing to remain invisible while expecting straight people to recognize and respect us reflects the insanity Rita Mae Brown describes. Choosing not to come out, over and over again, while at the same time expecting society to change, is insanity. If we want to be treated differently, if we want different results for our lives, then we, as sober lesbians, need to make different choices.

Today I will remember that doing the same thing over and over generally yields the same results.

September 17

In our addictive state, we forget that the poet, the lover, the healer, the Wise One is within us.
                                                    —CHARLOTTE DAVIS KASL

Regardless of what our addiction was or how our addictive behaviors continue to manifest themselves, at root these patterns are about using something or someone outside of us to try and fill up the emptiness we feel inside.

During our addictions, we were constantly searching outside ourselves for something that would make us feel less lonely, less anxious about being good enough, less dependent on others' approval, and more confident about our abilities. Our addictions often helped us forget how hard it felt to be a lesbian. We believed that if we could just find a new job, the perfect lover, the right apartment, everything would be OK.

In recovery we learn that there are no magical solutions, and that the "answers" are not outside us. In recovery we learn to recognize the resources within us. We discover that only by accepting ourselves can we begin to feel at peace with our lives.

Today I will recognize and honor the poet, lover, healer, and Wise One within me.

September 18

The easiest kind of relationship for me is with ten thousand people. The hardest is with one. —JOAN BAEZ

Creating intimacy is a challenge for all of us in recovery, regardless of what form our addiction took. Many of us learned very little about healthy intimacy growing up. What we saw around us often represented the extremes: distance and neglect, or enmeshment and codependency.

As our addictions progressed, we became less and less capable of true intimacy with others. Some of us became so isolated that there were very few people, if any, left in our lives by the time we hit bottom. Others of us had people in our lives, but we became more and more emotionally isolated; we may have interacted, but we never really let anyone know who we were.

Taking risks, sharing ourselves, and opening our lives to others is a part of our recovery journeys. Learning how to be honest with ourselves and others, learning how to be close to you and not lose me are major recovery tasks. For many of us, this process of creating healthy intimacy is one of the hardest lessons to learn.

Today in recovery I am learning how to build healthy relationships with those around me.

September 19

I've got to relearn what I was supposed to have learned. —SYLVIA ASHTON-WARNER

Life is full of moments when we end up needing to relearn what we were "supposed" to have learned a long time ago. In seventh grade, I had at least five different math teachers. Years later I had to relearn the skills I was supposed to have figured out in junior high.

Being a lesbian means we didn't get the same opportunities to practice social skills as heterosexual adolescents do. As addicts, we were often too busy being drunk or high to learn how to interact with people. Consequently, as adults, we find ourselves relearning how to build healthy relationships.

We need to be careful not to berate ourselves for these struggles. Relearning is a normal part of recovery. In reality, it is part of being human.

Today I will try to be accepting of my need to learn new truths and skills in recovery.

September 20

I have a right to my anger, and I don't want anybody telling me I shouldn't be, that it's not nice to be, and that something's wrong with me because I get angry.
—MAXINE WATERS

Many of us were taught that nice girls don't get angry. We were told to act polite and only say nice things about others. We were often taught to forgive others and not be angry with them, as if anger and forgiveness were mutually exclusive. Consequently, as adults we tend to deny or bypass our anger. We would rather pretend it does not exist, than face it, deal with it, or God forbid, express it.

In recovery we are learning that anger is a normal, healthy human emotion. We are learning that we have a right to our anger. We are learning, as lesbians, that there are a lot of things about which we have every right to be angry. And we are learning that if we deny that anger, it will not go away. It will return to haunt us and our mental health. Our emotional well-being in recovery depends upon our ability to acknowledge our anger and find constructive ways to express it and utilize it in our lives and work.

Today I recognize my right to be angry, refusing to allow others to force me into denial of my feelings.

September 21

Parents can only give good advice or put them on the right path, but the final forming of a person's character lies in their own hands. —ANNE FRANK

Some of us had parents who gave good advice and put us on the right path. Some of us did not. Either way, as sober lesbians, we need to grapple with Anne Frank's reflection that regardless of what we learned or did not learn as children, we are now the ones who are responsible for our lives. This does not mean that we were not affected, sometimes drastically, by the events of our childhood. But it does mean that, regardless of the experiences we encountered growing up, ultimately we must take responsibility for who we are and for the choices we make.

Coming to this awareness is often difficult. It may seem easier to blame someone else, rather than to assume full responsibility for our lives. Sometimes we shift the blame—from parents to ex-lovers to lovers, and back to our parents again—in an effort to put off dealing with ourselves.

When we entered recovery, we took responsibility for our addiction and for beginning to change our lives. Now we need to continue the process, reflecting on who we are and how we live our lives, and taking responsibility for making the changes necessary to our own growth in recovery.

In what ways have I been reluctant to assume responsibility for my own life? How can I begin to do this more effectively?

September 22

You have to accept whatever comes and the only important thing is that you meet it with the best you have to give.
—ELEANOR ROOSEVELT

Learning to "accept whatever comes" is an essential lesson of recovery. Acceptance means we stop turning ourselves inside out trying to control everything in our lives. Acceptance means letting go of those around us and allowing them to live their own lives. Acceptance means giving up our frantic efforts to project the future and learning to deal with things when they occur.

However, acceptance is not about being a doormat. It is not the same as giving in or giving up. Acceptance doesn't mean we become "good little girls," or passive, disempowered lesbians who take anything the straight world might dish out.

Genuine acceptance is about facing what is real, in our lives and in our world. It is about seeing the truth of our lives. It is only as we face, see, and accept what is real that we can begin to choose how to act with courage.

◊

Today I am learning to see the truth of my life, confronting and accepting the reality that surrounds me.

September 23

The great thing and the hard thing is to stick to things when you have outlived the first interest, and not yet got the second which comes with a sort of mastery.
—JANET ERSKINE STUART

Some of the most awkward moments in recovery occur during those periods when we have given up an old behavior, but have not yet gained or gotten comfortable with the new. It may be that we are letting go of a self-image marked by internalized homophobia, but have not quite discovered how to celebrate our lesbian identity. It may be that we have begun to reach out and connect with the sober lesbian community, but still feel awkward interacting with other women. It may be that we have chosen to stop acting out our anger in self-destructive ways, but haven't quite figured out how to express it constructively.

The awkwardness we experience at these times is a normal part of change. Feeling lost or out of place makes sense when we are giving up an old behavior and struggling to replace it with something new. As uncomfortable as we may feel in these moments, we can move on to experience serenity and growth.

Today I will remind myself that all changes take time. Giving up old behaviors and finding new ones requires patience and persistence.

September 24

I am the welder. I am taking the power into my own hands.
—CHERRÍE MORAGA

When we were still using drugs and alcohol, we were powerless over much of what happened in our lives. We moved through each day, dealing (or not dealing) with whatever came along. We may have had lots of dreams, but the ability to realize them eluded us.

We were powerless because we had turned our power, our will, our very selves over to our addiction. It ruled our lives. It decided what we could and could not accomplish. It determined whether we could show up and follow through, or whether we'd miss out once again.

Recognizing our powerlessness over our addictions is the first step in taking back our power. Recognizing our inability to control our use of drugs, alcohol, money, or our interactions with other people enables us to begin making choices about the things we can control. Recognizing our powerlessness empowers us to take responsibility for ourselves and our lives.

Recovery means accepting the things we cannot control and learning to take back the power for the things we can control. As sober lesbians, we may not be able to change the whole world today, but we can become the welders of our own lives.

Which situations are beyond my control today? What things are appropriately within my control?

September 25

In the unraveling, the threads become more apparent, each one with its distinct color and texture. And as I unravel, I also weave. I am the storyteller and the story.
— BETH BRANT

Recovery has moments when we feel like we are unraveling, times when it seems as if the events of our lives, and our very selves, are coming apart at the seams. Finding ourselves unraveling is an unsettling feeling, full of fear and uncertainty.

This unraveling is part of the path toward growth. Sometimes things have to come apart before they can be put together in new and healthy ways. Sometimes we need to unravel our stories in order to understand their significance. Sometimes we need to pull apart the events of our lives before we can weave a new tapestry.

As sober lesbians, we are both the story and the storyteller. Recovery offers us a new beginning. Recovery gives us the power to re-create our lives, to weave a new cloth, to create a new ending.

Though the unraveling may feel unsettling, it is an opportunity to see more clearly and choose new ways to weave the pieces of my life together.

September 26

The bitterest tears shed over graves are for words left unsaid and deeds left undone.
—HARRIET BEECHER STOWE

We all have unfinished business in our lives: people who moved on without an opportunity to say good-bye, relationships that ended without resolution, life situations that changed before we had a chance to finish all we had hoped or planned for them. In some of these situations, we might have made different choices if we could have predicted the impending change or ending. In some, we were given no opportunity for resolution.

Living with regret is a part of our recovery. Some endings can be re-created. In some situations we can go back and repair the damage of the past. In others, all we can do is draw from our experiences and move forward. The lessons of the past can empower us to make new choices in the present. We can resolve to say and do those things that are important to us. We can resolve to act as if change might be just around the corner, instead of leaving things until tomorrow.

Are there people in my life with whom I have not yet said the things I need to say? Are there things I might wish I had done if these relationships were to end abruptly?

September 27

I am the dialogue between my Self and *el espíritu del mundo*. I change myself, I change the world.
—GLORIA ANZALDÚA

So often we spend enormous amounts of energy changing other people, convincing them to do things our way, trying, in essence, to make them like us. We rarely get exactly what we want, and for all our efforts, we end up frustrated and dissatisfied.

Family therapists who work from a systems perspective suggest that when just one person is changed, others will change in response to the new dynamics. That doesn't necessarily mean the changes will be exactly what we want, but there will be change.

When faced with behavior by others that upsets us, we must remember two things. First, the only person we have any control over is ourselves. Second, if we change our reactions and behavior, this is likely to provoke some change in others.

Today I will focus on changing my behavior rather than on expending energy trying to make others change.

September 28

The only merciful thing about drug abuse is the speed with which it devastates you. Alcoholics can take decades to destroy themselves and everyone they touch. The drug addict can accomplish this in a year or two. Of course, suicide is even more efficient.

—RITA MAE BROWN

Though we did not recognize it at the time, our alcoholism and drug addiction were killing us. We may not have been consciously suicidal, but in recovery we have come to see that our addiction was a slow, drawn-out death wish. Day by day, with each drink or drug, we were killing ourselves—physically, emotionally, and spiritually. Our self-hatred was propelling us toward self-destruction.

Once in recovery, we are confronted with our self-hatred and its self-destructive drive. We are forced to grapple with the way we view ourselves and how we feel about who we are. We are compelled to examine our internalized homophobia, racism, sexism, and whatever else has contributed to our negative image of ourselves. We are challenged to learn how to live, instead of waiting for, and enabling, our death.

As sober lesbians, we are compelled to find a way to live. Survival, through sobriety, replaces our slow suicidal fantasies.

Today I will be grateful for the ways sobriety has given me back my life.

September 29

To say something nice about themselves, this is the hardest thing in the world for people to do. They'd rather take their clothes off.   —NANCY FRIDAY

When is the last time you were able to receive a compliment by saying, "thank you," without having to discredit or minimize what the person said? How easy is it for you to fill out the section about your strengths on an application? Can you quickly identify ten positive qualities about yourself that you appreciate and enjoy?

Most of us find it easier to focus on what we perceive to be our weaknesses rather than to focus on our strengths. Even if we can identify positive qualities about ourselves, we may struggle with the idea of speaking these out loud to another human being. Some of this is based in old and inaccurate ideas about humility. Most of it is rooted in our lack of self-esteem.

Learning to appreciate ourselves as sober, competent, worthwhile lesbians is essential to our recovery. Being able to say something nice about ourselves is a sign that our self-esteem is growing. Being able to simply receive a compliment tells us that our view of ourselves is changing. Learning to like ourselves is one of the joys of recovery.

Today I will try to identify five qualities about myself that I appreciate and share one with a friend.

September 30

Sexuality is a sacrament. —STARHAWK

In religious language, a sacrament is an outward and visible sign of an inward and spiritual reality. It is a visual, and often tactile, reminder of those truths that we might easily forget. A sacrament serves both to remind us of these realities, as well as to make them real for us in the moment; it is a way of experiencing the divine in all of us.

Being open to the recognition of our sexuality as sacrament, especially as lesbians, can be a freeing and healing experience. Sexuality as sacrament reminds us of our humanness. Sexuality as sacrament brings us back to the inherent goodness of our physical bodies. Sexuality as sacrament empowers us to recognize our desire as right and holy. Sexuality as sacrament visually and tactilely reminds us of our need and longing for connection—to ourselves, to others, and to the spirit.

Regardless of our personal religious beliefs, we can come to see our sexuality as an outward and visible reminder of the goodness and wholeness of our lives. When we do this, our sexuality can become a channel for continued healing in recovery.

How can I more fully experience my sexuality as a source of healing?

October 1

For a long time, I just didn't know who I was, where I belonged, what people I belonged to. —JULIA PÉREZ

Developing a sense of identity and belonging are core issues for all addicts. Given the homophobic society in which we live, they are even more critical for us as lesbians. Acknowledging factors of race, ethnic background, class, religion, differing abilities, and others, can make the process of finding a sober identity and a sense of belonging even more challenging. It is especially difficult when it seems that various aspects of our identity are in conflict, such as how to be an Asian lesbian, or a Baptist lesbian, or a Black Latina lesbian. This sense of needing to trade off or give up parts of our identities in order to fit in makes the process of self-esteem and self-acceptance extremely difficult.

Recovery offers us a starting point, a place to begin our search for ourselves and our communities. Recovery provides a new identity and offers a community where we can find acceptance and support. As we stay sober and continue accepting our lesbian identity, we are empowered to seek out and integrate other aspects of ourselves. For all of us, this is an ongoing life process.

What steps can I take to find support for my journey toward acceptance and belonging?

October 2

Cleaving is an activity which should be left to snails for cleaning ponds and aquariums. —JANE RULE

In a continuation of our addictive patterns, we often latch on to someone or something to make us feel complete. We jump from one lover to another to avoid our loneliness. We hang in with a job that makes us crazy because it also makes us feel worthwhile. We hang on to lovers long after they have left us because the drama distracts us from ourselves. We go from one project to the next in a desperate effort to fill up the emptiness inside us.

Clinging to others in an effort to make ourselves fulfilled never works. Using people or projects to avoid ourselves hinders our recovery. Hanging on, when we really need to let go, keeps us from finding the freedom and serenity that recovery offers.

As difficult as it may be, the real work of recovery occurs as we let go of our distractions and begin to face ourselves. Letting go of our obsessive need for other people and projects sets us free to find our true, sober selves.

In what ways have I been hanging on to other people and things in an effort to fill up my emptiness? How can I begin to let go?

October 3

If we want there to be a place for older lesbians, now is the time to prepare the way for that change.
—MATILE POOR

Regardless of how old any of us are today, the reality is that we are aging, and at some point all of us will be older lesbians. In our process of taking responsibility for ourselves, Matile Poor encourages us to think about what it is we might want as older lesbians and begin working toward that reality today.

How will we wish to be viewed by the younger lesbian community? How will we want to be treated? What might our needs be as we age? In what ways might our values and goals change? How can we ensure that we will be taken care of and treated with dignity and respect?

Beginning to reflect on these questions is the first step toward a community that is better prepared to care for and enjoy its older lesbian members. Given the homophobia of the society in which we live, no one else is likely to do this work for us. Taking the time to begin this process is something we owe ourselves and all of our community.

How can I begin to make a place within my life for the older lesbians I know, recognizing that in doing so, I will also be making a space for myself?

October 4

It is hard to fight an enemy who has outposts in your head.
—SALLY KEMPTON

One of the reasons recovery is so difficult for us to grasp initially lies in the way it is both an external and an internal process. If recovery were only about fighting off external things like alcohol, drugs, food, sex, or overdependence on others, the journey would be a lot easier. If it were just about choosing not to drink or overeat, we might have gotten sober a lot sooner.

The real difficulty lies in the fact that addiction is not just about external behaviors. It is also about our internal thought processes. The ways we think about ourselves, the inner critic inside our head, the mistaken perceptions we have about the world around us, the lies we were taught about our relationships—all these conspire to lead us to the external behaviors of our addiction.

Getting sober requires not only changing our behaviors. It also demands that we tackle "the enemy" with outposts in our own head. We have to change our thoughts and beliefs about ourselves, our relationships, and our world.

Today I am learning to recognize and refute the inner critic who sabotages my growth and wholeness.

October 5

Challenges make you discover things about yourself that you never really knew. They're what make the instrument stretch—what make you go beyond the norm.
—CICELY TYSON

Trying new things is part of how we grow and develop. When we start out, we are often unsure of our ability to complete a task. But as we move through it, we learn and grow. We may have to gain new knowledge and information. We may need new skills. We may discover abilities within ourselves that we never knew existed before. Trying something new is almost always anxiety-provoking, but it is the only way to keep changing and growing.

Getting sober seemed impossible in the beginning. We were sure we wouldn't be able to maintain our recovery for the long haul. Yet, in the course of our recovery, we have learned that we can be competent, responsible adults. We have learned our beliefs and experience can be helpful to others. We are learning to live with our feelings and to celebrate our identity as lesbians. We are learning how to reach out and ask for help when needed.

All of these new things are occurring because we were willing to take on the challenge of sobriety and allow ourselves to be stretched by the continuing process of recovery.

What new challenges am I currently facing? Can I allow excitement to replace fear as I imagine the new skills these challenges may bring?

October 6

> I say to gays and lesbians all over the world, don't let people define who you are . . . Don't cease being spiritual people just because somebody else is trying to define you. Don't give permission to someone else to define your spirituality. —THE REV. TROY PERRY

On this date in 1968, eight months before the Stonewall Riots in New York City, the Rev. Troy Perry founded the Universal Fellowship of Metropolitan Community Churches as a spiritual home for the lesbian and gay community. The impetus for beginning what was ridiculed as a "queer church" emerged out of Perry's refusal to allow others to define his own, or anyone else's, spirituality. This message remains an important one for us today.

Too many of us believed that coming out meant we had to cease being spiritual. We thought celebrating our lesbian identities meant we had to give up our connectedness to God. Because of societal homophobia, we thought loving another woman precluded our ability to experience the divine. None of this is true.

As sober lesbians, we have the right to define our own spirituality. Our healing in recovery rests on our connectedness to others, to the world around us, and to what we experience as the divine. Defining our spirituality is our right and our responsibility.

Have I allowed others to define my spirituality? How can I take back my rights and responsibilities in recovery?

October 7

Parents learn a lot from their children about coping with life.
—MURIEL SPARK

Whether or not we happen to literally be lesbian mothers, there is a lot we can learn from children about coping with life. Parenting—whether they are our children or the children of family and friends—can be a tremendous force for healing in our own lives. Nurturing children and participating in raising healthy children can go a long ways toward learning to nurture and re-parent ourselves.

Watching young children interact and play often helps us recognize how adorable and vulnerable we were as children. Watching them may slowly help us let ourselves off the hook; recognizing their innocence may help us stop blaming ourselves. Showering them with unconditional love and affection often has a rebound effect: we discover that our own "little kid" is being nurtured. Taking care of them teaches us how to care for ourselves.

Our society has often kept children from us, denying us the right to parent. Some of us have internalized homophobic myths and keep ourselves away from children. In reality, being with children can be healthy for our lives and theirs.

Have I affirmed my right to be with children if I choose? What lessons can I learn from the children in my life?

October 8

Being a lesbian is by definition an act of treason against our cultural values. —JUANITA RAMOS

Our culture values conformity. It values women who define themselves by their relationships with men. It values women who are quiet, submissive, passive. It values people who do not challenge the status quo. It values people who fit the dominant white male heterosexual world. Consequently, our very existence as lesbians is, as Juanita Ramos states, an "act of treason."

Surviving as lesbians creates two challenges. First, we must establish our own values. We must name what is important to us, what we will value, and what goals we will strive for. The values of a society that rejects us simply will not work any longer. Second, being forced to live outside society's blessing requires living without the approval of others. We must learn to value our own approval of ourselves and discover ways, as a community, to bless one another's loves and lives.

Today I will take action in keeping with my values without worrying about having someone else's approval.

October 9

We've all known each other so long there's not even anyone to flirt with. —ELEANOR PERRY

Whether we live in rural, suburban, or large urban areas, most of us have at some point encountered the "smallness" of the lesbian community. The recovering lesbian community can be even smaller. We can't go to lesbian dances without seeing ex-lovers. We can't go to twelve-step meetings without running into our lover's ex-lover. We can't attend the local women's conference without encountering our therapist. Wherever we go, we are bound to run into someone we know!

The joys of being connected to one another can sometimes be challenging. As sober lesbians, we need a sense of community. We need to feel connected to one another. We need each other's support and affirmation. We need to know that there are others who share our experiences and struggles.

At the same time, we need to respect each other's need to be separate and autonomous. We need to acknowledge and appreciate each other's differences. And, especially in light of how small our community can feel sometimes, we need to work at creating enough room for everyone—the women we want to run into and those we'd rather not see today.

Today I will be grateful for the sense of community I have found in recovery and look for ways to make it big enough for everyone.

October 10

When we begin to take our failures non-seriously, it means we are ceasing to be afraid of them. It is of immense importance to learn to laugh at ourselves.
—KATHERINE MANSFIELD

Learning to live with failure is an essential life skill. Yet many of us grew up in environments where failure was not tolerated. Someone made us feel stupid when we failed or accused us of not trying hard enough. Experiencing failure as adults can also leave us fearful of trying new things.

However, failure is a normal part of learning. Few skills can be acquired without the risk, and generally the reality, of at least a few failures along the way. Taking these failures too seriously leaves us fearful of further trial and error and short-circuits the learning process. If we are afraid of failure, we will never try to accomplish something new, we will never venture out into the unknown, and we will never know what might have been accomplished. Willingness to grow requires an openness to failure.

Today I will accept my failures as a normal part of the human learning process.

October 11

No matter how far in or out of the closet you are—you have a next step.
—AD SLOGAN, NATIONAL MARCH ON WASHINGTON, 1987

We have lived in denial too long, as addicts and as lesbians. Most of us discover in recovery that coming out is healthy for us. Since one of the most basic tenets of recovery is honesty, we often find that hiding ourselves and our loves no longer works as well once we begin to recover from our addictions.

Some of us have been out as lesbians for a long time and then get into recovery. Others of us start the coming out process after recovering from our addictions. Either way, coming out is a never-ending process. The slogan is right—there is always a next step. It may be our parents, our relatives, our coworkers, our friends, our neighbors, or our plumber, dentist, or grocer.

Speaking the truth about ourselves challenges the bits and pieces of society's homophobia that we have internalized. Speaking the truth frees us from other people's expectations and their attempts to silence us. Speaking the truth moves us closer to integration and wholeness.

What next step can I take? How can I continue to challenge my denial and fear of who I am?

October 12

The one important thing I have learned over the years is the difference between taking one's work seriously and taking one's self seriously. The first is imperative and the second is disastrous. —MARGOT FONTEYN

Most of us have problems differentiating between taking our work seriously and taking ourselves seriously. As addicts, we are women of extremes. Generally we swing from taking nothing seriously to viewing everything—work, play, sobriety, ourselves—with far more seriousness than the situation demands.

Taking our work seriously means we attempt to do our best. It means that in our relationships, our recovery, or on our jobs, we take responsibility for our thoughts and actions. It means remembering that we, not others, are responsible for our feelings and reactions.

Not taking ourselves too seriously means that in all of the above situations, we recognize our humanness. We are not perfect; no one is. Even when we have done our best, things sometimes go awry. Not taking ourselves too seriously means remembering that we can only take responsibility for our actions; we cannot control the outcome.

Today I will strive to maintain a balance between doing my best and not taking myself too seriously.

October 13

The demand for equal rights in every vocation of life is just and fair, but, after all, the most vital right is the right to love and be loved. —EMMA GOLDMAN

We deserve basic civil rights. We deserve the right to serve in the military if we choose. We deserve the right to employment without fear of discrimination. We deserve the right to legally marry our partners if we choose to do so. We deserve the right to hold our lover's hand without the threat of violence. In recovery, we have the opportunity to work toward and achieve these rights.

Emma Goldman suggests that while these basic civil rights are essential, the most vital right is our right to love and be loved. In the midst of our political work for justice, in the midst of our fight to attain civil rights, we must remember that we are the only ones who can ensure our right to love and be loved. We must believe that we deserve the right to be loved. We must believe that we deserve the right to love whom we choose. No one else can give us this right. It is ours only as we believe we deserve it.

Do I truly believe I deserve the right to love and be loved?

October 14

What difference do it make if the thing you scared of is real or not?
—TONI MORRISON

Sometimes we are afraid of things that have a genuine basis in reality. The first time we go to a social event where alcohol is present, it makes sense to be afraid we might drink. If we have never driven a car before, it makes sense to feel anxious the first time we get behind the wheel. The first time we have sex sober, it's logical to feel scared and uncomfortable.

On other occasions we are afraid and there doesn't appear to be a logical reason for our fears. We've done a particular task a hundred times, and this time we're anxious but can't figure out why. We've taken our lover home to visit our parents repeatedly, but tonight we're worried without any particular reason to feel this way.

Funny thing is, it doesn't seem to matter whether we can find a "rational" reason for our fears. Fear is an emotion that is not necessarily rooted in reality. Our fears are not always rational; sometimes they just are. And figuring out their reasons doesn't necessarily help us deal with them. The best we can sometimes do is acknowledge them and figure out how to move through them.

Recognizing that my fears may or may not be rooted in reality, today I will focus on getting through them rather than on figuring them out.

October 15

Realizing I was a lesbian made me feel as if I was throwing a huge wrench into the parental plan. I thought about killing myself every day. How could I destroy my parent's happiness? —FELICE YESKEL

Other people often have expectations about us. Sometimes they are clearly spoken aloud; other times they are more subtly communicated, or go unspoken until we have disappointed them. Either way, we often discover that coming to be ourselves, and coming out, does not fit with what others have expected of us.

Realizing that we have disappointed those we love is painful. We may feel as if we let them down or betrayed them. They may lead us to believe that we have destroyed their happiness.

In recovery we are learning that we are responsible for our own happiness. We are responsible for our own expectations. We need to learn to live with expectations that go unfulfilled. No one's happiness is dependent on our ability to fulfill their expectations. They are responsible for their own serenity.

Today I will remember that despite what others say, I am only responsible for my recovery, growth, and happiness.

October 16

I'd rather have roses on my table than diamonds on my neck.
—EMMA GOLDMAN

It is easy to get caught up in what we want, what we do not have, what we think we need in order to survive, or what others have that we haven't yet obtained. Sometimes we get so wrapped up in all of this that we forget what is really important. Sometimes we forget how little we had in our addictions and how much we have gained in recovery.

Experiencing joy in recovery is dependent upon maintaining a sense of balance. If we are focused on what is missing in our lives, we are unable to appreciate what we have. If we are focused on getting more and more out of life, we are unable to value the things we have already obtained. If material things begin to overtake our life, we lose sight of the emotional and spiritual values that lead to joy and fulfillment. If we can begin each day with an appreciation of what we have, we will be able to celebrate whatever accomplishments come our way.

Today I will be grateful for the real joys that I am able to experience in recovery.

October 17

The growth of understanding follows an ascending spiral rather than a straight line.   —JOANNA FIELD

One of the most frustrating experiences in recovery is thinking that we have "worked through" an issue, only to have it resurface at a later time. We think we've resolved our issues of childhood abuse, finished grieving for a lover who's left us, or let go of our unrealistic expectations for love and approval. And then, often when we're least expecting it, the feelings and conflicts surface again. When this happens, we are tempted to despair—haven't we made any progress at all?

In reality, we probably have made progress. The problem is that healing and growth in recovery is more like a spiral than a straight line. When we move in a spiral, we circle around and around, revisiting issues and challenges each time we pass that point on the staircase. Our view of these dynamics may seem the same, but things are different—this time we are one step above the place where we stood last time around. Learning to accept this process can bring us closer to serenity in recovery.

Today I will try to remember that all change occurs in a spiral fashion. I may need to revisit my emotions and behaviors many times as I wind my way toward healing.

October 18

> **Nobody, but nobody
> Can make it out here alone.**
> —MAYA ANGELOU

Trying to make it on our own generally gets us into trouble. Many of us tried for years to get sober by ourselves; we thought we could handle our drinking and drugging just fine; we didn't need anybody's help. Realizing that we could not get sober by ourselves was one of the first steps in our recovery.

This need for interdependence on others continues into the present. Even in sobriety, we can't make it by ourselves. Trying to celebrate our lesbian identity without knowing any other lesbians doesn't work very well. Trying to function effectively as a lesbian mother without the support of others who are facing similar situations isn't easy. Learning how to reach out and ask for help from other sober women doesn't happen very easily unless we have some role models. We need the support and encouragement, the wisdom and experience, of others in recovery.

Today I will remember that I was not created to "make it on my own"; we all need support from others in recovery.

October 19

The real lesson is how to see and act clearly. To learn from the past so that we do not repeat it, without getting stuck in the past so that we do not repeat it.
—BERNICE MENNIS

Recently I was part of a conversation in which people were debating the merits of being able to go back in time. If they had the opportunity, would they want to be fifteen, eighteen, twenty-five, or thirty years old all over again? The consensus was that they would do it only if they could go back with the benefit of what they had learned in recovery since that time.

Our past is filled with a wide range of experiences—some that we might want to repeat and others that we would never care to relive. Being able to learn from our past, without getting stuck in the past, is one of the challenges of recovery.

Reflecting on our past experiences—with ourselves, in relationships, within our community—is important. We need to learn to identify what we did well and where we need new skills. We need to celebrate our past accomplishments and move forward toward new goals and ideas. As sober lesbians, we can learn from our past without living in the past.

What lessons can I learn from past experiences? How can they help me in my present recovery?

October 20

I'm nobody! Who are you? Are you nobody too?
—EMILY DICKINSON

Twelve-step recovery programs stress the importance of humility. Yet too often these words from Emily Dickinson describe our definition and understanding of the word "humility." We think that being humble means we have to grovel. We think becoming humble is achieved through a series of humiliating experiences. We think being humble precludes having a sense of pride or confidence. No wonder so many of us rebel against this aspect of twelve-step programs!

True humility is not about obliterating our sense of self. It is not about acting as if we are "nobodys" and deserving of nothing. It is not about viewing ourselves as less than the rest of the world.

Real humility means developing an accurate sense of ourselves. It is rooted in an honest inventory of our strengths and limitations. It requires an accurate assessment of our progress and identification of the areas in which we need continued healing and growth. Real humility is about knowing who we are. Only by starting with who we presently are can we hope to become all we wish to be.

Have I equated humility with poor self-esteem? How can I begin to change my understanding of this concept?

October 21

I was told that if you liked doing something, it wasn't worth pursuing.
—AMY TAN

Many of us grew up with and adopted this philosophy. We learned along the way that if we really wanted something, we didn't deserve to have it. We came to believe that having dreams and wanting more was wrong. We internalized the idea that enjoying life is wrong, that real life is always hard work, and if we are not struggling, we must be doing something wrong.

Learning to find satisfaction in recovery demands that we give up these old ideas and reject them as untrue. Lesbian author Rita Mae Brown offers an alternative in her comment "I finally figured out the only reason to be alive is to enjoy it." Living is about more than simply surviving. There is nothing inherently wrong with liking our work and, even, liking ourselves. There is nothing inherently wrong about pursuing those things that bring us joy. In fact, doing so is what sustains us in the struggle.

Am I still hanging on to old ideas that prevent me from experiencing joy and celebration in my life?

October 22

If we do not stop killing the other in ourselves, the self we hate in others, soon we shall all lie in the same direction. —AUDRE LORDE

When we feel judgmental toward others, it can be a sign that they remind us of ourselves or reflect a quality we have difficulty accepting in ourselves. We are most impatient with those things we cannot tolerate in ourselves. It is easier to get angry at someone else's mistakes than to be accepting of our own errors. It is easier to be judgmental of another's need for approval than to face and accept our own needs.

Learning patience and tolerance for others is part of learning love and acceptance for ourselves. Showing compassion toward others enables us to be more compassionate with ourselves. Accepting the weaknesses of those around us goes a long way toward our being able to accept our own limitations.

Today I will remember that showing acceptance and tolerance toward others can help me learn to love myself.

October 23

I keep saying to myself, what's wrong with choosing lesbianism. Maybe some of us were born that way and maybe some of us chose it. I keep trying to figure out what's wrong with choosing it. I think it's a fabulous choice. What a great idea! —JOANN LOULAN

It is not clear how we arrive at an understanding of our sexual orientation. Some women seem to have been born lesbians. Others piece together their identity as children or adolescents. Still others are straight-identified for years before coming to an awareness of their lesbianism.

Rather than getting caught up in confusion, or being thrown off guard by the questions of others, we need to celebrate the fact that we have made it. Despite society's homophobia, we have found our identity.

Our fears of acknowledging the choices implicit in some of our stories are rooted in lingering shreds of internalized homophobia. If we truly believe that who we are as lesbians is good and right, then what could possibly be wrong with choosing it?

Today I will strive to accept and celebrate my lesbian identity, including the uniqueness of all of our stories.

October 24

Some couples go over their budgets very carefully every month, others just go over them. –SALLY POPLIN

The next time we find ourselves arguing with family, friends, or lovers about money, we can remember that dealing with financial matters is a difficult aspect of everyone's recovery. Money is a loaded issue. During our active addictions, we often ignored financial matters. Once in recovery, we worry about having enough money. We struggle with whether we deserve what we have or can afford what we want. Making choices about how to handle our finances is an ongoing process.

Negotiating these choices with another person is a separate challenge. We can begin by recognizing that we probably grew up with different beliefs about and experiences with money. These continue to influence us as adults. Our present sense of self-esteem and competence also plays a major role in our ability to handle financial issues constructively. We need to clarify our values about money and how we want to handle it. We cannot effectively negotiate with someone else until we are clear about what is important to ourselves.

◇

What are my beliefs and values about money? How do these affect my ability to negotiate effectively with others?

October 25

I've come to realize my greatest task is to unlock the prison doors which are of my own making.
—ALETICIA TIJERINA

As lesbians, we are intimately acquainted with the oppression of a heterosexist and homophobic society. We know what it is like to grow up within the prison of isolation and despair. We are well versed in the intricacies of living in fear and silence, hiding our loves and lovers. However, in recovery we are discovering that not all of the oppression we experience comes from the outside world.

What doors within my heart and mind have I kept shut off from new ideas and new growth? What walls have I constructed to keep myself in and others out? What are the many passages and labyrinths I have designed to keep my isolation intact, barring others from entrance to my soul? How does denial keep me running in circles, repeating the same old patterns one more time? Where are the hidden chambers of old horrors into which even I am ashamed to venture?

Today I will begin to unlock the doors, opening myself up to true freedom and serenity.

October 26

Where so many hours have been spent in convincing myself that I am right, is there not some reason to fear I may be wrong?
—JANE AUSTEN

Our tendency to rationalize our way into unhealthy behaviors does not go away simply because we are in recovery. Old patterns die hard. Continuing growth in sobriety demands that we learn to recognize our rationalizations when they occur. Jane Austen's question offers us a clue to this process.

When we spend days convincing ourselves that this relationship is all right, it might be that we are making an unhealthy situation seem less dangerous than it is. If we find ourselves arguing and arguing with our sponsor about a recent decision, it might be that we are rationalizing our way out of doing what is healthy for our recovery.

Anytime we have a long list of justifications, it is a signal to take a second look at our choices. Anytime we feel the need to rationalize our behaviors, it is a clue that something is amiss. Learning to recognize this pattern is essential to healthy growth and recovery.

Today I will pay attention to my actions, looking especially for times when I feel the need to justify my choices.

October 27

Sure, you create your joy, but you have to overcome a lot of pain to get there. Many people just can't. There's nothing sadder than an old alcoholic dyke unless it's an old alcoholic queen. —RITA MAE BROWN

Years of using substances creates a demand for instant gratification, for getting what we want without having to work for it. Consequently, as addicts we tend to want a lot of things, but we don't like having to put in the work it takes to obtain them.

We want sobriety, but we don't want to face life without something to fall back on. We want to feel better about ourselves as lesbians, but we don't want to deal with our internalized homophobia. We want our families' acceptance, but we don't want to struggle through the process of coming out to them and helping them deal with their homophobia. We want the passage of civil rights laws, but we don't want to do the painstaking political work it takes to achieve them.

Assuming responsibility for ourselves means learning to do the work necessary for achieving our goals. Rita Mae Brown is right: we can create our own joy, but it takes work. It doesn't happen magically. And sometimes the process includes working out old pain and loss before we can relax and enjoy our healing and growth.

Today I will remember that change is a process. Getting what I want in recovery, though ultimately worthwhile, will take work.

October 28

My mother's definition of spiritual was to care for and act on behalf of life, to keep people alive. Religion, she said, is not sacred; people and life are sacred.
—MARTA BENAVIDES

Our spiritual awakening in recovery emerges from our increasing ability to care for and act on behalf of life. Getting sober is our first act on behalf of life. Staying sober reflects our desire to care for and nurture our own lives. Accepting our sexual orientation is another act of caring for ourselves. Letting go of societal lies about ourselves challenges and empowers our lives.

Sharing our experience and hope with others nurtures our own spiritual growth. As we care for their recovery, we grow by acting on behalf of life. Sharing our coming out stories, speaking with another struggling addict, volunteering within the lesbian community, working for justice and liberation—all of these are ways to act on behalf of life, ways of keeping people alive.

Remembering that people and life are sacred, I will look for ways to act on behalf of my life and the lives of those around me.

October 29

Turning it over, takes so much practice, but it's making me sane. So I'm turning it over and over and over again and again. —MEG CHRISTIAN

Learning to "turn it over" is a key principle of twelve-step programs. In reflecting on her own recovery, lesbian singer and songwriter Meg Christian shares about the challenges of applying and living out this principle. Defining this concept is not easy. What does it mean to turn something over? Can turning it over be a way to avoid taking responsibility for our lives? If we turn something over, does that mean we no longer need to struggle with and work through the feelings generated by that situation?

There are no easy answers to our questions. However, there are some clues in our shared stories of recovery. Turning it over means letting go of our need to be in control of every possibility. It means we stop manipulating others and events in order to make things turn out the way we want. It means taking responsibility for our part and no more. Having done our best, we no longer need to hang on to our fears and anxieties about the outcome.

Learning to let go of our desire for the illusion of control, while simultaneously assuming responsibility for our part, takes practice. Ultimately, it is the only route back to sanity.

As I move through today, I will try to focus on being responsible for my part and then let go of my desire to control the outcome.

October 30

You mustn't force sex to do the work of love or love to do the work of sex. —MARY McCARTHY

As women and as lesbians, we received mixed messages about sexuality from our families and society. Some of the relationship problems we encountered during our addictions, or even in recovery, are the result of confusing the concepts of sex, sensuality, and intimacy.

For example, sometimes we go looking for sex when what we really need and want is intimacy. Other times we jump into a relationship that goes on for years and gives us all kinds of intimacy when what we really wanted was a good night's sex. Or we think that sex has to follow sensuality; we don't understand that it is okay to be sensuous for the joy of it, without adding sex to the picture.

Learning to sort out these differences is essential to our sexual recovery and to our ability to get what we want and need in relationships. We need to find places where we can feel free, as lesbians, to talk about our struggles with these issues. We need to clarify our own definitions. We need to sort out what is important to us and what we want in our relationships. Asking sex alone to do the full work of intimacy rarely works.

In what ways do I need clarity about my definitions of sex, sensuality, and intimacy?

October 31

It has come, the time and I—WOMAN STRENGTH-ENED reclaiming what is mine; redeeming PRIDE on my terms.
          —MICHELE CHAI

Michele Chai writes of a young lesbian whose sexual innocence was stolen from her by the men in her life. She describes the ways this violation filled her with shame and left her isolated and afraid. These experiences of violence and exploitation are familiar ones. There are ways in which we all have felt this shame and alienation, whether it be from specific experiences of actual abuse, or from the more subtle ways our culture violates our being by refusing to acknowledge the existence and the goodness of our identity as lesbians.

Recovery enables us to begin moving beyond these experiences. Recovery opens the door to healing and new ways of living our lives. Recovery allows us to step out of our roles as victims and reclaim the power that is within us. Those who once victimized us no longer define our reality. Indeed, the time has come. The time has come for each of us, strengthened by our varying life experiences, to reclaim what was stolen and take back our lesbian pride on our own terms.

Today I am living my own life, reclaiming my identity and pride on my terms.

November 1

Believing is seeing. —THE REV. PAT BUMGARDNER

In a recent sermon on faith, my pastor suggested that the old adage "seeing is believing" was backward. She said that faith was best described by flipping the adage around.

Most of us cling to the expression "I'll believe it when I see it!" After all, it is easier to believe something that we can actually see, hear, touch, or feel. It is a whole lot easier to believe my boss's promise of a raise once I have the paycheck in hand. It is a lot easier to believe that my relationship with my lover will survive once the argument is over.

Real faith works differently. First, real faith demands that we believe in order to see. Real faith requires me to trust in the enduring power of the love my partner and I share; otherwise I won't even risk entering into the argument. Second, real faith suggests that as we choose to believe, we will become able to see more clearly. When I entered recovery, I chose to believe that sobriety was possible. I chose to believe that there was a way out of my insanity, even though this was incomprehensible to me at the time. As I trusted the wisdom and experience of those around me, I came to see that they were right. I was becoming sane and sober.

Today I choose to believe my way into new faith and new ways of experiencing the world.

November 2

It was a gradual process that took several months. But I can remember writing in my journal: I'm a lesbian and I can no longer deny it. —TORIE OSBORN

Torie Osborn reminds us that coming to know and accept ourselves as lesbians is a process. It doesn't happen overnight. It takes some of us years of exploration and discovery. In a similar manner, coming to understand our addiction was a process. It was years before we could easily say to ourselves, "I am an addict."

Self-discovery always takes time. It doesn't matter whether the discovery is our addiction, our lesbian identity, our career choices, what we want in relationships, or how we want to interact with family. All of these discoveries occur over time. We cannot rush the process. There are actions we can take to explore our choices or try out different options, but we cannot force the moment of decision. It occurs on its own time frame. It occurs as we have examined, reflected upon, and internalized all that is necessary to attaining clarity about ourselves.

Today I will remember to be patient with myself, allowing myself time to clarify my choices and self-discoveries.

November 3

The hardest thing we are asked to do in this world is to remain aware of suffering, suffering about which we can do nothing.   —MAY SARTON

During our addictions, we had a buffer between ourselves and the pain around us. It kept us from getting too close to others and the struggles they were experiencing.

In recovery that buffer is gone. Today we have to confront the friend who is drinking herself into oblivion because she can't cope with being queer, the sister lying in the hospital suffering with cancer or AIDS, the lover who keeps sabotaging her growth and progress because she can't believe that she is worth something better, the friend who lives her life in isolation, fearing relationships because a long time ago someone violated and abused her trust.

Staying aware of their suffering is one of the hardest tasks we face in recovery, largely because it means confronting our own powerlessness. In recovery I have to accept that I cannot make someone else get sober; I cannot cure someone else's illness; I cannot convince someone else of their worth; and I cannot make someone else feel safe and loved.

Today I will accept my powerlessness to change the lives of others, recognizing that what I can do is to be present with them in their struggles.

November 4

A life of reaction is a life of slavery, intellectually and spiritually. One must fight for a life of action, not reaction.
— RITA MAE BROWN

Before we began this journey of recovery, we were prisoners of circumstance. We felt, and often were, powerless over the events of our lives. Someone criticized us, and we retaliated with rage. We were abused, and we reacted with humiliation. Situations didn't turn out the way we planned, and we became depressed. People let us down, and we withdrew into isolation. They told us being lesbian was wrong, and we believed them, hiding ourselves and our relationships.

In our recovery, we begin to see that there is a difference between reacting to what happens around us and choosing to act. We learn to step back, evaluate the experiences of our lives, and then choose how we wish to respond. We discover the freedom of being proactive in our own lives, as opposed to the powerlessness of simply reacting. As sober lesbians, we begin to celebrate this freedom, choosing to fight for our right to be who we are in this world, regardless of the beliefs and actions of others.

Today I will pray for the ability to pause before I react, so that I can experience the freedom of choosing my actions.

November 5

> If I had to name one quality as the genius of patriarchy, it would be compartmentalization, the capacity for institutionalizing disconnection. Intellect severed from emotion. Thought separated from action . . .
> —ROBIN MORGAN

Growing up lesbian in a heterosexist society teaches us to split off parts of ourselves, to build separate compartments for our sexual thoughts, attractions, and feelings. Experiences of addiction and abuse further hone these skills. We learn to hide our addictions. We split off experiences that are too painful to remember. Over time, our thoughts and feelings become so compartmentalized that we aren't even sure what we think or feel anymore.

These skills that were once so essential to our survival become problematic in recovery. Being sober is about being present for our lives, and it is hard to be truly present when everything inside is disconnected. It is difficult to be truly present when our immediate reaction to any uncomfortable feeling is to dissociate. Bridging this gap begins when we reclaim our sexual selves and refuse to allow others to compartmentalize our lives.

Today I am recognizing that old skills no longer work. In recovery I need to try new ideas and choices if I want to continue changing and growing.

November 6

The human soul has need of security and also of risk.
—SIMONE WEIL

Steady and consistent growth requires finding a balance between security and risk. If we don't have some sense of security, we cannot find the courage to risk. However, if we settle for security alone, we will never grow and change in recovery.

Coming out offers a useful analogy. In order to risk coming out to others—family, friends, coworkers—we generally need to feel some sense of security in our own identity. We need to be sure of who we are as lesbians, and it helps to have reached a point in our identity where we feel good about who we are. The higher the risk, the more security we need.

In recovery we are constantly challenged to let go of old patterns and risk trying something new. If we reach a place where we are resisting the risks, it may be useful to take stock of how secure we feel. Maybe the reason we are reluctant to risk is that old insecurities need attention. Learning to find a balance between risk and security is the key to continued growth in recovery.

Am I taking the risks necessary to growth? Am I paying attention to my sense of security so that I can take these risks?

November 7

Love doesn't just sit there, like a stone; it has to be made, like bread; re-made all the time, made new.
—URSULA K. LEGUIN

One of the reasons being in, and staying in, relationship with one another is so challenging is that relationships are not static. We cannot build a friendship one day and expect that it will continue forever. People are constantly changing and evolving. Our interests and abilities shift and change. Our levels of commitment to one another and to our common goals ebb and flow.

Maintaining a relationship requires constant attention and effort. If we want to continue our friendship, then we must be responsible for sharing our stories and keeping one another updated on the changes in our lives. Continuing a friendship means maintaining and nurturing our sense of commitment to one another.

As sober lesbians, our love for one another—whether as friends, lovers, or sisters in recovery—has to be made and re-made all the time.

What actions can I take today to nurture my commitment to those I love and care about?

November 8

Because of my lack of awareness about what the range of symptoms of alcoholism are/can be, I had never grasped that depression as such is a physical/spiritual expression of the disease. —BEVERLY W. HARRISON

Many of us struggle with symptoms of depression at some point in our recovery. They may occur during early recovery when we are still physically and emotionally detoxing from chemicals. They may affect us as we get into the real work of recovery and begin examining who we are and how we have lived our lives. Sometimes issues of loss and grief overwhelm us and we find ourselves dealing with depression.

We need to recognize that we are not alone in our struggles. Neither are we to blame. Recent research increasingly documents a correlation between addiction and depression. In the same way that we were not to blame for being an addict, it is not our fault that we are depressed.

When we experience depression, we need to find healthy ways to care for ourselves: reaching out to others with similar experiences, finding lesbian-positive medical professionals who are knowledgeable about addiction and depression, or working with an experienced lesbian therapist. Just as we are recovering from our addictions, we can recover from depression.

When I find myself dealing with depression in recovery, I will remember that I am not alone; there are others who can help me through my struggles.

November 9

The lesbian part of my childhood was like a silent movie. There were clues, and pictures, but no words were spoken.
—THE REV. NANCY L. WILSON

Few of us had words for our lesbian selves during childhood. We may have sensed that we were different, we may have had some early inkling of our attractions to other women, but rarely did we have the vocabulary needed to make sense of our intuitions. Our early lesbian selves were shrouded in silence.

Part of the healing work in recovery involves sifting through our childhood memories and making sense of what we intuited back then. It means taking the vocabulary we now have and reinterpreting the truths we knew as children. Using Nancy Wilson's analogy, it means writing the missing dialogue for the once-silent movie of our early lesbian identity.

This process of giving voice to our early memories is critical. While we cannot re-create the past, going back and giving voice to it enables healing. Breaking the silences of our past empowers us for the present. Piecing together the clues and the images of our early intuitions creates a sense of wholeness in our lives. It weaves the past and the present into one seamless fabric, empowering us to more fully be ourselves today.

Are there ways I can empower myself by giving voice to the early, silent images of my lesbian self?

November 10

There are only two or three human stories, and they go on repeating themselves as fiercely as if they had never happened before. —WILLA CATHER

Those of us who are addicts tend to suffer from what is sometimes called "terminal uniqueness." Despite evidence to the contrary, we tend to think that what we have gone through, or are currently going through, is different from everyone else's experience. This is a good example of addictive thinking.

In reality, there are very few new human experiences. Regardless of our particular life struggles or challenges, someone else has experienced similar ones before us. Regardless of the paths that life has laid before us, someone else has forged the way. In reality, we are not unique.

As difficult as it sometimes is in recovery to acknowledge this truth, there is a freedom in acceptance. If we are not unique, then we are not alone. If we are not unique, then there are others who can share our pain and nurture our journey. Uniqueness keeps us isolated. Recognizing our common bonds and experiences allows us to rejoin the human race.

In recovery I am learning to place my story in the context of the stories of those around me.

November 11

It's easier to act your way into new ways of feeling than to feel yourself into new ways of acting.
—SUSAN GLASER

During my addiction, I was plagued with the pattern of waiting for the "right time," waiting for myself to feel less depressed, waiting for things to "go right," waiting for that elusive feeling of competence and self-esteem.

I put off phone calls I felt anxious about, waiting for that magical moment when I would no longer feel anxious. I put off necessary conversations and confrontations with others, waiting for the moment when I would feel strong enough to begin them. I put off jobs that felt overwhelming, until I felt a little more confident and capable. I thought that I had to feel my way into action.

Today I know that I won't always feel capable and competent. Sometimes feeling anxious and overwhelmed is just the way it is for now. In recovery I have learned that feelings aren't facts. I can choose to act capable even when I don't feel that way. I've learned to show up for myself and my life despite my fears and insecurities. If I wait for the "right feelings," I may never take any actions.

What actions am I putting off? How can I begin to act my way into new feelings?

November 12

The worst walls are never the ones you find in your way. The worst walls are the ones you put there—you build your-self. Those are the high ones, the thick ones, the ones with no doors in. —URSULA K. LE GUIN

We encounter many obstacles in recovery. Some are placed there by the racist, sexist, and homophobic society in which we live. Some are put there by people who know us, perhaps to sabotage our growth or keep us from changing more quickly than they can tolerate. LeGuin suggests that the most troublesome obstacles are the ones we have built. Scaling these walls can be incredibly difficult.

They may be walls built during our addiction, walls that kept others out, enabling us to maintain our addictions. They may be walls built to protect ourselves, to block out the anguish of not knowing who we were, or separate us from our feelings of loss and grief. They may be walls of resentment, piled high with anger and pain. They may be walls of neglect, of abusing ourselves and those we love.

Whatever the nature and size of these walls, their continued presence blocks our way. We cannot travel forward toward healing and recovery without tearing down these walls. Whatever it takes, they must be torn down.

Are there walls I have built, even to protect myself, that now must be torn down in order to go forward?

November 13

I must take the responsibility of standing up for my rights and those of other oppressed people as well. I can only take this responsibility when I have come to terms with my past. —JUANITA RAMOS

Learning to stand up for ourselves is not an easy task. As women, most of us were socialized to let others take power, define our reality, and name our truths. In recovery we are learning that if we do not stand up for ourselves, no one else will. We are the ones who must define ourselves, claim our rights, and create a space for those who follow. We are also learning that claiming our right to be must go hand in hand with claiming the rights of all others who are oppressed.

Being able to stand up for ourselves and others requires an honest, sober understanding of our lives. I cannot stand up for you if I am still in denial about my racism. You cannot stand with me if you are still blaming yourself for the abuse you have experienced. We cannot stand up for anyone if we continue to see ourselves as victims. Coming to terms with our past is the only way we will be effective in our work toward liberation for ourselves and others.

Today I will strive to see the ways my past has limited my view of myself and others and begin to own my current responsibilities.

November 14

Ah, the relationships we get into just to get out of the ones we are not brave enough to say are over.
—JULIA PHILLIPS

Rarely have we had the opportunity to learn the skills necessary for navigating friendships and relationships with lovers. It would be nice if it was as easy as signing up for a course in "Lesbian Relationships 101," but most of the time we have to pick it up as we go along. Those of us who are in recovery have an even tougher time—we have to get sober, figure out what we want, what we are feeling, and how to communicate this—all at the same time, and generally while we are in the midst of the relationships!

Given this, it is not surprising that some relationships come to an end. Sometimes we have outgrown them, and sometimes we simply do not have the skills needed to rebuild and go forward. Ending a relationship does not mean that we are failures. It simply means we need to move on.

Getting out of a relationship rarely feels good or comfortable for anyone. As sober lesbians, we need to try and do this in the most compassionate and honest way possible. Being brave enough to move on, when a relationship has truly ended, may be the best solution for everyone.

Am I willing to be as compassionate and honest as possible when my relationships need to change or come to an end?

November 15

All dope can do is kill you the long hard way. And it can kill the people you love right along with you.
—BILLIE HOLIDAY

No matter how long we have been sober, we are not immune from thoughts about drinking or drugging. Addiction is a disease of denial, and that denial can return at any point in our recovery. We are especially susceptible to it during times of stress. The addict in us may suggest that using will make it better, that having just one won't hurt, that we have been sober long enough to handle it now.

Billie Holiday forcefully reminds us that there is nothing to be gained from returning to our addictive patterns. Returning to substance use will not "fix" anything. In fact, it will sabotage what we have gained in recovery. It will wipe out the progress we have made. It will damage our relationships with others. And eventually it will kill us. Her reminder is a valuable tool for responding to our denial.

No matter how long I have been in recovery, I need to remain alert to the ways denial may return to tempt me.

November 16

Sometimes a person has to go back, really back — to have a sense, an understanding of all that's gone to make them — before they can go forward.
— PAULE MARSHALL

Most of us enter sobriety feeling beaten up and torn apart, amazed at our very survival. Our lives tend to be confused and broken during early recovery, littered with what twelve-step programs call the "wreckage of our past."

Making amends demands all the faith and courage we have. Left to our own devices, our thoughts and fears will easily overwhelm us: I'm not strong enough; what if they don't listen to me; I can't bear to go back there and face them; what I did was too shameful to acknowledge to anyone. If we get stuck in these reactions and emotions, we will never be able to do the work required of making amends.

Faced with the wreckage of our past, whether accumulated in our addictions or in sobriety, we need a message of hope. We need to be reminded that the purpose of "going back" is to move forward freely, unencumbered by past behaviors. We need the assurance of other sober lesbians that we can go back to make amends, and then move on to wholeness.

Am I maintaining a balance of addressing my past so I can make amends, yet not getting stuck in the past?

November 17

Nobody sees a flower really; it is so small. We haven't time, and to see takes time—like to have a friend takes time.
—GEORGIA O'KEEFFE

During our addiction, we paid little attention to the world around us. We rarely noticed the brilliance of sunsets, the glistening light of rainbows, or the intricate colors of flowers and trees. We were caught up in surviving from one moment to the next. We were so busy numbing ourselves and blocking out the horrors of our lives, that we couldn't see beyond our pain.

Georgia O'Keeffe's paintings illuminate the incredible diversity of life. Her pictures compel us to notice the beauty in the tiniest details of the world around us. In fact, these works of art have the potential to draw us into their beauty, filling us with awe and wonder.

In recovery we are learning to slow down. We are learning to look beyond ourselves and our pain. We are discovering that the important things in life—coming to value ourselves, being proud of who we are, building honest friendships—take time.

Today I will make time to pause and experience the joys of nature and friendship.

November 18

Nothing cures like time and love. —LAURA NYRO

Years ago I was in an automobile accident. Traffic had been moving along just fine, but as I reached the peak of the bridge I could see it was bumper-to-bumper ahead. I screeched to a halt, but the four cars behind me couldn't stop in time. The worst part was looking in my rearview mirror, knowing I was about to be hit, and then seeing it all happen. For months afterward, whenever I saw a flash of something in my rearview mirror, it was as if the accident were occurring all over again.

Traumatic events and situations have that kind of impact on us. The images, sounds, and feelings imprint themselves on our brains. And often something that is only remotely like the traumatic event can trigger all the associated fears and anxiety. For many of us, learning to move beyond the effects of various traumatic events is an important part of our recovery process. It may be a personal illness or injury, the loss of someone close to us, a breakup with a lover, or experiences of abuse.

Recovery takes time. In the beginning, I jumped almost every time I looked in the rearview mirror. A little while later, it was just the occasional panic. Eventually my fear subsided and I no longer overreacted, even when something real was happening around me on the road.

Today I will be gentle with myself, recognizing that all change takes time.

November 19

You cannot love people who refuse to help themselves.
—OPRAH WINFREY

All of us know people who refuse to help themselves: family members who continue abusing drugs and alcohol despite the ways it is destroying their lives; friends who remain in abusive relationships year after year; relatives who refuse to follow medical advice despite their failing health. We offer to take them to twelve-step meetings; we listen to the pain they feel about their lovers; we drive them back and forth to doctors. We do everything we can possibly do to help them get their life together, but their problems remain.

At some point we are forced to grapple with the truth of Oprah Winfrey's observation. We cannot fix someone else's life for them. Our love cannot set them free from their addiction. Our compassion cannot force them to leave an abusive lover. Our willingness to care for them cannot replace their need to care for themselves. At some point, we must accept the limitations of our love and allow others to assume responsibility for themselves. We cannot help them if they refuse to help themselves.

Today I will remember that while I can offer support to those I love, I cannot fix their lives for them.

November 20

We must prevail over the times we are living in with the help of our ancestors. —RIGOBERTA MENCHU

Twelve-step programs teach the importance of listening to the wisdom and experience of others. Many of us have sponsors who share their stories as a way of nurturing our growth and survival.

As sober lesbians in a homophobic, racist, and sexist society, we must draw upon the strength of those who have gone before us. Our "ancestors" may be sober friends and lovers. They may be family members, biological or adopted, that we love and trust. They may be extended family whose life experiences and wisdom strengthen us. Our ancestors may emerge from folktales, from ethnic stories of survival, from the whispered lives of historical women who challenged the status quo, or from the silenced voices of thousands of women who loved other women.

These women can empower our survival and nurture our recovery. These women can enable us to prevail over the times in which we live.

Whose story and strength can I draw upon to nurture my survival and sobriety?

November 21

We learn best to listen to our own voices if we are listening at the same time to other women—whose stories, for all our differences, turn out, if we listen well, to be our stories also. —BARBARA DEMING

We cannot recover and grow in isolation. We need one another for support, feedback, affirmation, and strength. Sharing our stories breaks down the walls of isolation and helps us become clearer about our own story. Learning to listen is an essential skill for ongoing recovery.

Listening means that I pay attention to both your speech and your silence. Listening to you means that I take in your words and your body language. Listening to you means that I focus on you, as opposed to figuring out what I want to say next. Listening to you means that I suspend my assumptions and judgments, so that you can fully tell your story.

Few of us grew up with a consistent experience of being listened to. Later on we were often so wrapped up in our addiction, we were incapable of truly listening to anyone else. Learning to listen to one another in recovery is a skill that takes practice.

When others speak to me today, I will value our journeys by offering my full attention.

November 22

Momentary euphoria . . . will never quell the inner emptiness that comes from forgetting how to love, how to live in community, and how to care for one another. —CHARLOTTE DAVIS KASL

When we were still in our addictions, euphoria was our goal. We wanted to feel good. We would settle for almost anything that would take us out of ourselves. We didn't care if it was only a quick fix or a short-term solution. We just wanted out.

Today we still sometimes wish for an easy way to make things feel better, but we now know that quick fixes rarely last. We've learned that while they may make us feel better for the moment, they don't really address the emptiness inside us.

Learning to care for ourselves and respond to our inner yearnings is a lifelong process. These yearnings are spiritual. They are about our disconnectedness from ourselves and those around us. Filling this kind of emptiness means we need to learn to love ourselves, and then discover how to care for, and love, one another. Only then will the emptiness inside become full.

Today I will remember that momentary euphoria is an illusion; the emptiness I feel inside is filled through my connectedness with myself and others.

November 23

If you're going to hold someone down you're going to have to hold onto the other end of the chain. You are confined by your own repression. —TONI MORRISON

At some point in our lives, most of us have felt held down by others. As lesbians, the expectations and rules of others have prevented us from becoming ourselves and achieving the things we wanted to accomplish. We know the feeling of their "foot on our neck," and we know the damage that accompanies this oppression. Their envy, their repression of us, their refusal to let us change and develop hurt us and stunted our growth.

Envy and repression are also damaging to the perpetrator. When I envy your qualities or achievements, my own self-esteem suffers. When I refuse to let you change and mature, my own growth is aborted. When I hold you back, my progress is limited. As Toni Morrison writes, when I attempt to chain you down or chain you to me, I inevitably find myself tangled up in the same chains. Our movement forward is inextricably interdependent.

Am I limiting my own recovery by holding on to someone else and preventing their growth? Am I envying another's achievements?

November 24

There are hurts so deep that one cannot reach them or heal them with words. —KATE SEREDY

Sometimes we come to a place of pain too deep for words. Try as we may, we are unable to understand or express our feelings fully. It may be the pain of reexperiencing childhood abuse. It may be grief for pushing ourselves aside in order to be what others expected. It may be the cumulative effect of years of believing that there was something wrong with us, of being told that loving women was perverted. Whatever its source, the weight of our pain isolates us. Our inability to express it separates us, even from the ones we love most.

At these moments, we need to go gently on our journey. We need to search out even the smallest things that comfort us. We need to find new ways to nurture ourselves so that we can begin to heal our pain. When words fail us, it may be that we can find some comfort in music or dance or just sitting quietly with ourselves or a good friend.

Alone as we feel in these moments, we can remind ourselves that others have traveled this road before us. Letting others in, to share the silence of our pain, may feel awkward and uncomfortable, but learning how to do this is a part of our healing.

Today I will remember that healing can occur, even when I cannot fully understand or articulate my pain.

November 25

Striving for excellence motivates you; striving for perfection is demoralizing. —HARRIET BRAIKER

Many of us have difficulty differentiating between what Harriet Braiker calls excellence and perfection. We are plagued by our compulsive drive for perfection. Nothing is ever good enough. No matter how hard we try, we have not done enough. No matter how satisfied others may be, our own inner critic tells us we failed, that we came up short of what we could have done.

This drive for perfection robs us of the joys of recovery. We can never appreciate our own changes and growth because we are never satisfied. This kind of compulsive drive toward perfection reflects our continuing struggles with self-esteem. It is not that what we do isn't good enough. In reality, we still do not believe that we are good enough.

In order to move beyond this drive toward perfection, we need to learn that sometimes "good enough" is enough. We need to recognize that our inherent worth and value as lesbians is not contingent on what we do; it rests on who we are. Constantly driving ourselves to be perfect will eventually exhaust us. Celebrating who we are is a far better motivator in the long run.

Am I driven by my desire for perfection? How can I begin to value myself for who I am, rather than for how much I accomplish?

November 26

I have lost friends, some by death . . . others through sheer inability to cross the street. —VIRGINIA WOOLF

Virginia Woolf's comment conjures up an image of two friends who have been estranged. One day they see each other on opposite sides of the street and neither wants to cross the street first. Sure of their own rightness and convinced that they are owed an apology, they wait for the other to make the first move.

All of us have experienced these situations: waiting for friends to call and apologize; refusing to speak to our lover because we don't want to be the first to make up; shutting out our families because we know we are in the right. Holding off and waiting for the other person to cross the street often feels good. We like the sense of self-righteousness it brings. But after a while, the newness wears off. If we persist in our stubbornness, we run the risk of losing the person completely.

There are some relationships we have no choice about losing. Lovers move on, friends die of AIDS and breast cancer, family members age and die. But we do have a choice about crossing the street. What does it matter if we are the first to say, "I'm sorry. I don't want to lose you. Your friendship is important to me." Perhaps being willing to speak first will keep us from losing someone we value.

Are there people with whom I have been unwilling to cross the street? What steps can I take toward reconciliation?

November 27

The only thing they have to look forward to is hope ... hope for a better world, hope for a better tomorrow ... And you, and you, and you, you have to give people hope.
—HARVEY MILK

As a San Francisco city supervisor in the late 1970s, Harvey Milk was this country's first openly gay elected city official. His visibility as a gay man elected to a public office was a sign of hope for lesbian and gay people everywhere.

One of the most profound gifts we have received in recovery is hope—hope for a way out of despair, hope for sanity and sobriety, hope for freedom from obsession and isolation, hope for health and wholeness in recovery.

As sober lesbians, we are responsible for offering hope to those around us. When another lesbian, still suffering from the pain of addiction, reaches out for help, will we be there to offer hope? When another lesbian, trapped in the isolation of self-hatred and despair, reaches out for help, will we be there to offer hope?

◊

How can I offer hope to those around me today?

November 28

Power comes from living in the present moment, where you can take action and create the future.
—SANAYA ROMAN

During our addictions, we lost much of our power by dwelling in the past or trying to project ourselves into the future. We were consumed with regret for what we had or hadn't done, overwhelmed by guilt and shame, and constantly reliving yesterday's failures. At the same time, we were relentlessly worried about the things to come. We imagined all kinds of potential disasters, fretting about whether we were truly prepared, or could ever be prepared, to face what might occur tomorrow.

In recovery we are learning that we are empowered when we choose to live in the present moment. From a practical point of view, today is all we have. Yesterday's mistakes and accomplishments are finished, and tomorrow's possibilities cannot be predicted with any certainty. The only real choices we can make lie within this day. Our power is in the present tense. Yesterday and tomorrow offer only memories or projections. Today we can take actions.

For today, I will try to stay in and live in the moment, recognizing that my power comes from taking actions in the present.

November 29

There is no such thing as security . . . Security is when everything is settled; when nothing can happen to you; security is the denial of life. —GERMAINE GREER

Many of us struggle against this truth. We try desperately to create the illusion of security, doing whatever we can to make ourselves feel safe, even when we are not. We linger in relationships long after they need to end rather than risking being alone. We stay in jobs that long ago ceased to fulfill us rather than risking something new. We hang on to old patterns of behavior because they are familiar and help us maintain our illusions of being in control.

Letting go of these illusions is essential to our serenity and growth in recovery. Life is a series of risks. Every day we are faced with a new set of choices and left without the ability to fully predict their outcomes. We are frequently called upon to take actions without being able to foresee all of their consequences for ourselves and others. All of these choices involve risks. We cannot live in this world and have complete security.

My serenity increases as I am willing to relinquish the illusion of security and accept the many choices I face in recovery.

November 30

As I communicate something of God to my lover thru my work, play and lovemaking, so she reveals something of God's nature to me. This communication, this revelation, is both emotional and physical.
—LORNA HOCHSTEIN

These words from an essay entitled "Mirroring God" challenge us to look deeper into how we encounter the divine in one another. From Hochstein's perspective, all our interactions—work, play, love, and sex—can be moments for revelation; all our encounters hold the potential for teaching us something new about the divine.

This idea may be surprising. Most of us grew up believing God had nothing to do with sex, especially lesbian sex. Given these beliefs, the God of our childhood may be the last thing we want to encounter while in bed with our lovers!

In reality, we are all created with something of the divine within us. This means that as we allow ourselves to encounter one another, we may encounter God. The messages we received growing up were wrong. Our sexuality—including our lesbian sexuality—is a gift from God, to be affirmed and celebrated. God wants us to enjoy and appreciate God's creation.

Today I will focus on celebrating my sexuality as a gift, in anticipation of encountering the divine within myself and others.

December 1

Over and over . . . not just a lover dead, but friends and friends of friends, dozens of them, until it seems that AIDS is all there is and all there will ever be.
—JANE GROSS

AIDS has had, and continues to have, an incredible impact on our communities. Few of us, if any, have been left untouched. Most of us have times of despair, of feeling completely overwhelmed by the repeated losses we have experienced. We are frazzled by news of yet another friend testing positive, exhausted by the ongoing hospital visits, worn out by memorial services and funerals. There are moments when it seems that AIDS is all there is. It dominates the "queer agenda," often subsuming everything else, including other lesbian health concerns.

In the midst of this demanding epidemic, it is critical that we remember to take care of ourselves. Despite the needs around us, our recovery must be an ongoing priority. Forcing ourselves to focus on our sobriety is one way of ensuring that we do not get lost in the overwhelming emotions of living with AIDS. We cannot ignore the events of our lives—we must face the reality of AIDS, our fears about ourselves and our lovers, our love and concern for friends, our losses and ongoing grief. But we must also focus on caring for ourselves and continuing in our recovery.

Today I will try to balance caring for myself while caring for others.

December 2

She was someone who could not be rushed. This seems a small thing. But it is actually a very amazing quality.
—ALICE WALKER

Most of us spend our lives being rushed. We run here and there, filling our lives with people and places and commitments and pleasures. We find it difficult to pace ourselves and easily get irritated at those around us who suggest that perhaps we should relax a little and slow down.

I once worked with a woman who fit Alice Walker's description. It seemed to me that she did everything in slow motion. Regardless of the pressure surrounding her, she completed her tasks in her own time. She refused to allow the anxiety of others to make her frantic. It sometimes seemed to me that she would never finish a project. Yet she was not a lazy woman, and the necessary tasks were always accomplished in sufficient time.

Over the years, I have come to respect her ability to set her own agenda, to do things according to her schedule. In particular, I appreciate the ways she was able to maintain a sense of calm even when surrounded by the anxiety of others. This was indeed an amazing quality and one that offers valuable lessons in our own process of learning to care for ourselves.

Today I will give myself permission to slow down and not be rushed by those around me.

December 3

A change of heart is the essence of all other change and it is brought about by a reeducation of the mind.
—EMMELINE PETHICK-LAWRENCE

Our willingness to be visible can have a powerful impact on societal attitudes and beliefs. Public surveys consistently demonstrate that straight people who know and interact with us are more open and accepting than those who are unaware of knowing lesbian and gay people. Our willingness to openly interact with those around us is the most significant tool for social justice and change.

When we share our lives, other people learn new information about who we are, what we are like, and what is important to us. When we share our lives, they are confronted with the gaps between the myths and stereotypes they have internalized and the truth of our lives. When we share our lives, they are enabled to move beyond their prejudice and homophobic belief.

Accepting this task is not easy. Sometimes we get tired of educating others. Yet the reality is that it is our lives that can create the greatest changes in people's hearts and minds. Our visibility is our greatest tool for the reeducation of society.

How have I reeducated those around me? Are there individuals with whom I am willing to risk being more open?

December 4

Coming out means that we stake our ground, and we claim that territory for ourselves both as Latinas and as lesbians, whole persons who live and work in the context of a community. —MARIANA ROMO-CARMONA

In these words from the introduction to the anthology *Compañeras*, Mariana Romo-Carmona writes about the ways in which we as lesbians are often viewed through the lens of sex. She goes on to describe how this complicates our coming out process, how it makes it difficult for us to arrive at an integrated sense of ourselves. When heterosexual people look at us, sometimes all they see is "lesbians"; other aspects of our being fade into the background and go unacknowledged.

Recovery means doing the work that it takes to uncover all of who we are: our strengths and weaknesses, our varying ethnic and cultural backgrounds, our differing talents and abilities, our many life stories and experiences. Recovery means learning how to recover and integrate these varying facets of our lives. Recovery means discovering communities in which to live and work where we can find a sense of wholeness about ourselves. This is no easy task, but it is the essence of our coming out together.

Despite the limiting ways others may view me, I am slowly learning to stake my ground and claim the wholeness of my person.

December 5

Alcoholism isn't a spectator sport. Eventually the whole family gets to play. —JOYCE REBETA-BURDETT

Addiction is not something we experience in isolation. When one person becomes an addict, everyone close to them is affected by the progression of the disease. Everyone gets pulled into maintaining and managing the addiction.

In recovery we need to recognize the ways our active addiction impacted others. We are not the only ones who were hurt. Our lovers, family, and friends were affected by what we said and did. We need to acknowledge the ways we hurt them and make amends for these behaviors.

We also need to acknowledge the ways we have been affected by the addictions of others. Whether lovers, parents, other relatives, or friends, most of us know and love someone who is an addict. We too have been affected by their disease. Our recovery rests in part on our ability to identify how their addiction hurt us. How were we caught up in their illness? How did we enable them? How did we take responsibility for what belonged to them? How did we help them maintain their web of rationalization and denial?

Am I recognizing and addressing the full effects of addiction—both my own and that of others close to me?

December 6

At fifteen life had taught me undeniably that surrender, in its place, was as honorable as resistance, especially if one had no choice. —MAYA ANGELOU

Surrendering to our addictions was the first step in our recovery. We couldn't get sober as long as we resisted this basic fact. Fighting against it just prolonged our misery.

Many of us struggled with surrender. We didn't like the concept. It sounded like giving up or giving in, and we were too tough for that. We were afraid surrendering would leave us helpless and vulnerable.

In recovery we have learned surrender can mean other things as well, like it did when we first got sober. Surrendering to our addictions meant admitting we had a problem. It meant owning up to the reality of our lives. Surrendering meant acknowledging we could not get sober by ourselves. This meant learning to ask for help. When we got sober, surrendering was the first step toward a new life. It was our surrender that opened up the path to wholeness and recovery.

Are there times in my recovery when I am resisting the wisest choice: to let go and open myself to new alternatives?

December 7

The average, healthy, well-adjusted adult gets up at 7:30 in the morning feeling just plain terrible.

—JEAN KERR

If you are a "morning person," the above thought probably doesn't apply to you. However, for those of us who aren't morning people, Jean Kerr's comment is a welcome relief. It means that there's nothing wrong with the way we feel when we wake up. We are not crazy or sick. The way we feel when we wake up is normal!

Most of us have trouble recognizing what is normal in recovery. Our views are skewed and distorted by the messages we received growing up and by patterns established during our active addictions. We don't know what "normal" people think or how "normal" people are supposed to feel. We can't assess whether our feelings and conflicts fall within the realm of normalcy or if they mean we are crazy.

This struggle to define normalcy is a natural part of recovery. The truth is, average, well-adjusted adults sometimes wake up feeling lousy. Average, well-adjusted adults sometimes feel overwhelmed by their lives. Average, well-adjusted adults need others to help them sort through their feelings and make constructive choices.

Today I will try to value my thoughts and feelings as a necessary part of recovery, recognizing that "normal" is really about being human.

December 8

Before a secret is told, one can often feel the weight of it in the atmosphere. —SUSAN GRIFFIN

Telling our secrets is the first step in any recovery process. Those of us who have survived abuse, as children or adults, know that the healing journey begins when we break the silence and speak the truth about our lives. For those of us in recovery from addictions, the first step toward wholeness involves the willingness to name our experience—to say, "I am an addict."

As lesbians, many of us know the painful weight of secrets: the shame of hiding, the fear of being found out, the terror of our identity unintentionally slipping out. We grew up carrying the secret of our differentness deep within us. Our identity was such a secret that sometimes it was hidden for years, even from ourselves.

Today we are learning to find safe places to share our secrets, safe places to risk breaking the silence, safe places for coming out. Coming out—about our identity and our experiences—opens the door for healing.

What secrets do I continue to carry? Can I begin to free myself by breaking this silence?

December 9

When relationships are determined by manipulation, by the need for control, they may possess a dreary, bickering kind of drama, but they cease to be interesting.
—ADRIENNE RICH

Addicts are experts at manipulating and controlling their environments. We do whatever we need to do to manage our addictions and maintain our illusion of being in control.

We often carry this same approach into recovery. We continue to manipulate and control the world around us in an effort to get what we want. This is most detrimental in our relationships. Manipulating our lovers may get us what we want for the moment, but it ultimately robs us of honest love. Attempting to control our lover's feelings and reactions may make us feel better, but it will ultimately drive us crazy and probably drive her away.

Honest, sober relationships depend on our willingness to relinquish manipulation and allow our lovers to freely make their own choices and be themselves.

Are there ways in which I am attempting to gain love and acceptance by manipulating and controlling others?

December 10

> Imagination frames events unknown,
> In wild, fantastic shapes of hideous ruin,
> And what it fears creates.   —HANNAH MORE

The "What If's" can make us crazy: What if the woman I just started seeing doesn't like me? What if I fail the exam? What if my family never speaks to me again? What if my lover gets involved with someone else? In our anxiety, our imaginations sometimes take off and we envision all kinds of horrible possibilities. Never mind how likely they are; in the midst of our fears and worries, they are already a "done deal."

Managing anxiety about the unknown is essential to our serenity. We need to learn to slow down and take things one step at a time. We need to put a halt to the "what if" syndrome before it swings into full gear. Maybe we won't get the job, or maybe we will. Maybe our lover will break up with us, or maybe our relationship will last a lifetime. Either way, worrying about what might happen isn't likely to change things.

In early recovery we learned that sharing our obsessions eased them. In the same way, sharing our fears with another sober lesbian often lessens their power over us.

What fears am I harboring about the future? How can I share them before they rule my mind and emotions?

December 11

I believe we are compelled, and empowered, to risk whatever we must risk to create with God a climate in which all people can be who they are.
—CARTER HEYWARD

Twelve-step programs teach us that we can only keep our recovery by giving it away. Sharing our experience, strength, and hope with those around us is how we move forward in our own healing journey. In early recovery the focus is largely on ourselves. It has to be. Getting sober, whatever the addiction, is hard work. It requires our full attention.

As we recover, we begin to heal. We regain our self-esteem. We learn to see ourselves in new ways. We move beyond our sense of powerlessness. We practice giving up our identities as victims and discover the power of surviving. We begin to find a sense of purpose and fulfillment. We learn to celebrate our newfound freedom as proud sober dykes.

And we begin to look for ways to pass this on to others who are still struggling. In discovering our own power, we are empowered to reach out to other lesbians, young and old, who are still afraid to claim their own inherent goodness. Celebrating our recovery compels us to tell our stories and pass on our experience, so others can risk becoming their true selves.

Today I will look for an opportunity to give back what I have gained in my recovery.

December 12

Sometimes it's worse to win a fight than to lose.
—BILLIE HOLIDAY

It is easy for us to get caught up in winning an argument. We are convinced that we are right, and we are determined to prove that to the world, or at least to those with whom we are arguing. In the heat of the moment, everything else pales. Everything else that is important to us suddenly seems insignificant; winning becomes paramount.

Billie Holiday reminds us that winning isn't everything. Sometimes winning an argument can mean losing a friendship. Winning an argument can create an estrangement between ourselves and family. Winning an argument can lead to our girlfriend refusing to speak to us for the rest of the evening.

Allowing winning to overshadow everything else places our need to be right above our relationships. It places our need to justify ourselves above our commitment to others. Having to be right means winning the fight may turn out to cost more than we bargained for.

Today I will try to allow my relationships with others to be more important than winning or losing an argument.

December 13

Hope is the feeling you have that the feeling you have isn't permanent.
                                                    —JEAN KERR

One of the most amazing revelations I had early on in recovery came in the form of the saying "This too shall pass." I can remember depressed days, thinking I would feel this way forever, wondering how I could ever get through this without a drink.

And then something would happen—I'd go to a meeting, talk with a friend, or get involved in a task—and at some point, I would realize that I wasn't so depressed anymore. Sometimes I didn't even really do anything to make my feelings change, but they shifted anyway. I was absolutely astonished to discover that feelings weren't permanent.

This principle continues to be an important part of my recovery. Regardless of what I am feeling in the moment, I find hope by reminding myself that it will not last forever. If I stay sober, the feeling will change. It may not always get better immediately, but it will change.

Regardless of what I encounter today, I will remember that my feelings aren't permanent and "this too shall pass."

December 14

Connections are made slowly, sometimes they grow underground. You cannot tell always by looking at what is happening. More than half a tree is spread out in the soil under your feet. —MARGE PIERCY

Building healthy relationships takes time. The skills needed to repair old friendships, as well as those necessary for establishing new ones, cannot be gained immediately. Even once we have the skills, the very building of a relationship takes time—time coming to know each other, time trading stories and sharing experiences, time listening to each other's joy and sorrow.

As addicts, we sometimes become impatient with this process. Marge Piercy reminds us that establishing a sense of connection with ourselves and others happens slowly. We cannot rush friendship. When we feel impatient, we must remind ourselves that we cannot see the whole picture from our vantage point. Our friendships may be further along than we think they are. Our relationships may be more stable than is apparent to us. If we are doing the work necessary to building the relationship, if we are risking and trusting and giving of ourselves, then we need to step back and allow the growth to take its own course.

◇

Today I will remember that making friends and finding lovers takes time. I need to trust my growth as I utilize the new skills I am gaining in recovery.

December 15

> I'm totally out with my family, but at her house I'm just "the friend." I'm always talking nonstop there because I'm afraid if things get quiet, I'll just lose it and yell, "We're lesbians!" —SUZANNE WESTENHOEFER

Dealing with our own and each other's families can make us feel like screaming. Many times they "know" we are lesbians, but refuse to acknowledge or discuss this aspect of our lives. Our identity as lesbians is invisible when we are with them.

Their inability to deal with who we are is sometimes quite overt: refusing to invite our lover for family dinners, expecting us to spend the holidays with them as if we were single, leaving our lovers out of family pictures that include all the other spouses, never asking about our lover when they call. Other times we experience a marginal acceptance—tolerating our lover's physical presence at family gatherings but ignoring her in the conversation, failing to acknowledge our anniversaries in the same way that they celebrate our siblings' marriages, or just avoiding all mention of the "L word" or lesbian issues.

Sorting this out requires honesty and patience. We have to acknowledge our frustrations and find constructive ways to deal with the feelings generated by our interactions with families. And we need to recognize that dealing assertively with our families is a process that happens step by step. It cannot be accomplished overnight.

◊

Today I will be patient with myself as I learn to deal assertively and openly with my family.

December 16

> **i found god in myself and I loved her
> i loved her fiercely.** —NTOZAKE SHANGE

During our addictions, there was little that made us feel good about ourselves. In addition, many of us had painful childhood experiences that contributed to poor self-esteem. Consequently, self-acceptance poses one of the most difficult challenges of our recovery. Ntozake Shange's words point out one path along the way. Recognizing the divine within us is part of the movement toward self-acceptance.

Recognizing the divine within us means acknowledging that the child we once were was good and valuable. Recognizing the divine within us means acknowledging all that is inherently trusting and trustworthy about us. Recognizing the divine within us means acknowledging that we are created in the image of the divine and, as such, have purpose and meaning simply by being alive. Recognizing the divine within us means celebrating our survival as proof of the existence of the divine.

Today I will look for god within myself, and allow myself to grow by loving her fiercely.

December 17

I hear and I forget. I see and I remember. I do and I understand. —CHINESE PROVERB

We all need to hear others describe their experiences in recovery and watch the changes that occur in their lives. However, applying the truths of recovery to our own lives requires action. It is not enough to listen and observe; most of us learn best by doing.

When was the last time you bought something that needed to be put together before you could use it? Hearing someone else tell you how to put it together may be helpful; reading the directions and looking at the pictures provides more information. But the real learning happens when you do it yourself.

Other lesbians can tell us how they worked through their internalized homophobia. They can share their strategies for getting through anxiety-producing situations or surviving a breakup with their lover. But real learning happens only when we try out the wisdom of others, and in the process make it ours.

Today I will remember that while seeing and hearing may be important, real changes occur only when I take action to internalize the principles of recovery.

December 18

In the act of loving each woman I have learned a new lesson; I have learned to love myself. —PAT PARKER

One of the slogans bantered about in twelve-step groups is "Let us love you till you learn to love yourself." Most of us have difficulty loving ourselves when we first get sober. Over the course of our active addictions, we lose our sense of accomplishment and competence. Our self-respect and self-esteem plummet. By the time we enter recovery, there doesn't seem to be much left to love.

Since recovery is about being good to ourselves, we need to learn to love ourselves in order to maintain our sobriety. Most of us begin learning this lesson through the love of those around us. We continue it through loving others. Each time we open ourselves up to another woman, each time we allow ourselves to see her fully, each time we experience loving her completely, with her strengths and weaknesses, we are learning to value ourselves. We are learning to accept our own strengths and weaknesses. We are learning to love ourselves.

Today I will celebrate the ways loving other women has enabled me to begin valuing and loving myself.

December 19

The truth remains a secret to the rest of the family and friends, and I must decide whether to continue to sew this cloth of denial or break free.
—MAKEDA SILVERA

This line occurs in an essay about family life. Like Silvera, each of us faces an ongoing struggle with the truth of our lives. There are no right or wrong answers. No one else can tell us when to speak the truth, when to be silent, or whether to speak the whole truth. Only we can decide to what extent, with whom, and when we will share the essence of our lives. Only we can determine the real risks and benefits of self-disclosure. We make these choices based on where we are in our recovery, where we are in our process of self-acceptance, which risks we feel we can afford to take, and which risks are simply too much for the moment.

Owning this choice, owning responsibility for speaking our truth on our timetable, is an important part of our recovery. We cannot give this responsibility away. It is ours and ours alone. We are the ones who must decide.

Today I will reflect on my choices and choose to speak the truth when and where it seems appropriate to me.

December 20

In all proper relationships there is no sacrifice of anyone to anyone.
—AYN RAND

Years ago I dated a woman who liked herbal tea. She served it whenever we spent time at her place. It took me six months to tell her I hated herbal tea. In retrospect, this story has become a rather harmless, though humorous, illustration of how we sometimes sacrifice ourselves for others.

Many of us struggle with being honest about who we are in relationships. We hedge about our likes and dislikes and hold back on what is really important to us, attempting to avoid offending the other person. In a sometimes desperate effort to not make waves, we dance around the truth time and time again.

In healthy, sober relationships, none of us need to sacrifice ourselves for others. Of course, there are times when we choose to make sacrifices—to stay home when our girlfriend feels sick, to go out of our way for a friend in trouble, to make an unplanned trip home to surprise someone. These occasional choices are different from becoming a sacrifice. A continual pattern of denying and sacrificing ourselves only ensures that eventually there will be no one left.

Are there ways in which I have been denying myself or sacrificing myself for someone else?

December 21

Our sexuality is such a deep, spontaneous, and powerful part of our core identity that the conscious need to falsify it is a little death. —GLORIA STEINEM

Addiction represents a slow but steady death. It separates us from ourselves. It builds walls around us so no one can touch us or love us. It buries our feelings and saps our strength. Slowly, but surely, it cuts us off from the very life source within us.

Denying our sexuality works in the same way, cutting us off from our feelings, violating our sense of connectedness with those around us, eventually leaving us profoundly alienated from ourselves and our world. Each time we deny our sexuality, we deny ourselves. Each time we deny our sexuality, we deny that place of joy, spontaneity, and creativity within us. Each time we deny our sexuality, we deny our need and ability to love and be loved in return. Slowly, but surely, denying our sexuality cuts us off from the very life source within us. Reclaiming our power demands that we recover our sexuality in all its fullness and beauty.

Today I am recognizing the ways in which acknowledging my sexuality affirms the new life within me.

December 22

The road was new to me, as roads always are, going back.
—SARAH ORNE JEWETT

Sometimes we underestimate the power the past has in our lives. We visit with old friends who shared our addiction, unprepared for the impact they will have on us. We go home for the holidays and wonder why we are so out of sorts while we're there. We travel through a neighborhood where we used to live with an ex-lover and only later recognize the confused feelings that were triggered.

Going back—to old places, former friends, or family—is always different. It is never quite the same as we remembered it. Sometimes places and people have changed. More often, we have changed. And our changes make our interactions new. The road may seem familiar, but it is also new and different.

When we go back to old places, we need to think through what this experience may bring. We need to reflect on how it may affect us, emotionally and spiritually. We may need to carry the phone number of someone we trust, so we can touch base and get a "reality check" once in a while.

When I need to revisit former friends and places, I will recall that my recovery may make the experience different than I remember it.

December 23

You need only claim the events of your life to make yourself yours. When you truly possess all you have been and done, which may take some time, you are fierce with reality. —FLORIDA SCOTT-MAXWELL

All too often we tend to minimize ourselves and the experiences of our lives. We write off what we have survived as "no big deal," or at least nothing to brag about. We fail to truly appreciate and internalize our accomplishments. In Florida Scott-Maxwell's words, we fail to possess all that we have been and done.

Claiming the events of our lives means applauding ourselves for having defined and identified ourselves in a society that continually attempts to silence and destroy us. Claiming the events of our lives means congratulating ourselves for the ability to find love in the midst of a society that believes our love is perverted and abnormal. Claiming the events of our lives means celebrating our attainment of sobriety in a society that would just as soon see us drink ourselves to death.

If we truly claim the events and experiences of our lives, no one can hold us back. We will know our strength and our power. We will be, as Scott-Maxwell says, fierce with reality.

How can I allow my survival to empower and embolden me?

December 24

Any ritual is an opportunity for transformation.
—STARHAWK

Rituals play an important part in our recovery. Rituals mark and help us make changes. They offer opportunities for healing and moving on. They provide a means for celebration and affirmation. Rituals bring people together and build community.

As lesbians, we are excluded from many traditional societal rituals: adolescent dating rituals, engagement parties, wedding showers, marriage ceremonies, and baby showers. Consequently, it is essential that we create and celebrate our own rituals with lovers, friends, and supportive family members.

Rituals can be big events, like birthday parties, housewarmings, or memorial services. Rituals can involve liturgies we create to celebrate our commitments with lovers, mark an anniversary, or grieve the loss of a good friend. Rituals can also be smaller events: vacationing at the same beach house each year, going out for dinner with friends to celebrate a promotion, sending a sober anniversary card to a friend in recovery, or even something as small as kissing our lover every time we're in an elevator alone. Rituals, both big and little, can be markers, reminders of our love and joy, celebrations of community and affirmation.

What rituals are important to me? Are there new ones I would like to create and celebrate?

December 25

> I must acknowledge the miracles in my life . . . wonders and marvels and astonishing accidents, fortunate juxtapositions and happy encounters, some resulting from work and luck but others unexplained and unexplainable.
> —DOROTHY ALLISON

In an essay entitled "Survival Is the Least of My Desires," lesbian writer Dorothy Allison talks about the miracles of her life: surviving her childhood; graduating high school and going to college; realizing through feminism that she did not have to be ashamed of herself; discovering her sexuality; and "women and men met at the right time . . . soon enough to save me from giving up or doing myself more damage than I could survive."

We too have survived—our childhoods, our choices and those of others, our coming out, and our addictions. We have survived and we are sober. We too have women and men who appeared in our lives at just the right time, people who somehow loved us through our pain, people who taught us what we needed to survive. Acknowledging the miracles in our lives keeps our gratitude for recovery alive and growing.

◇

Today I will remember and celebrate the miracles of my recovery and survival.

December 26

Nothing great was ever done without much enduring.
—ST. CATHERINE OF SIENA

Some days sobriety is exciting. We are full of gratitude for the ways our obsession to drink and drug has been lifted; we can see the changes happening in our relationships; we feel good about our ability to navigate each day sober; we are excited about the ways we have begun to experience the promises of recovery.

However, not every day is like this. While there are lots of exciting moments, much of recovery is about ordinary persistence. Sometimes ongoing recovery is like the old story of the tortoise and the hare. It was the slow and steady persistence of the tortoise, not the flashy excitement of the hare, that won the race.

Staying sober requires willingness to keep plugging away day after day. It means putting in the day-to-day, painstaking efforts that are essential to reaping the long-term promises of sobriety. It means remembering that our everyday efforts are just as important as our flashy successes.

Today I will remind myself that patient persistence is important; all my successes result from a series of day-to-day efforts.

December 27

Re-vision—the act of looking back, of seeing with fresh eyes, of entering an old text from a new critical direction—is for women more than a chapter in cultural history; it is an act of survival. —ADRIENNE RICH

Adrienne Rich's comment challenges us to look back over our collective and personal pasts with fresh perspective. She encourages us to rethink our experiences, examining them critically for their present lessons. This re-visioning, as she states, is how we survive as lesbians and women.

As this calendar year draws to a close, what lessons have we learned? What experiences do we need to re-vision? Is there a situation we earlier viewed as failure that can now be valued as a time of learning? Was there a closed door that can now be viewed as an opening to a new path? Are there messages we once internalized that we now recognize as mistruths or lies? Were there situations that appeared hopeless but now hold the possibility of change?

May the goddess/god/spirit of truth give us fresh eyes for the re-visioning of our past and future journeys.

December 28

It would have made all the difference for me had I grown up knowing that the reason I didn't fit in was because they hadn't told me there were more categories to fit into. —MICHELLE SHOCKED

Ignorance kept many of us in the closet. We sensed we were not like others, but didn't have a name for that difference. We knew we had feelings for other women, but no one told us you could build a relationship out of loving another woman. Michelle Shocked is right: they didn't give us the whole picture; they left out the information we needed most.

Things are slowly beginning to change. Today there are children growing up who know that some women love men and other women love women. Today there are children who see the varied ways people love each other.

We need to let the children in our lives know that lesbians exist. We need to let them know that being lesbian is one of the "categories." We need to let them see that being a lesbian is good and right. The visibility of our lives may make a difference in their self-acceptance and growth.

How can I allow my visibility to make a difference in the life of someone else?

December 29

Understand that any rift among you means power to those who want to do you in. —ADRIENNE RICH

The first tradition for all twelve-step groups is "Our common welfare comes first; personal recovery depends on our unity." This principle was arrived at through the wisdom that Alcoholics Anonymous, the first twelve-step group, would not survive unless the unity of the group came first. And the survival of the group was essential if suffering alcoholics were to continue to have safe space in which to recover.

Surrounded by a society that is heterosexist and homophobic, we, as lesbians, need to find ways to bridge the gaps that sometimes exist between us. We cannot afford to allow those who would silence us to use our differences to pit us against one another. Our survival depends on our ability to stand and work together despite our differences. Our survival depends on our ability to make space for each of our stories, to celebrate our uniqueness, perhaps even to creatively utilize our differences in the work for peace and justice.

Are there ways that I am allowing my "differentness" to become a barrier between me and someone else?

December 30

> it will be hard to let go
> of what i said to myself
> about myself
> when i was sixteen and
> twentysix and thirtysix
> even thirtysix but
> i am running into a new year
> and i beg what i love and
> i leave to forgive me. —LUCILLE CLIFTON

Over time in recovery our image of ourselves shifts. Our self-perception when we first get sober is radically different from how we see ourselves at two, five, ten, or twenty years into recovery. Indeed, we change.

Allowing these changes to inform and empower us requires letting go of old images. As we change and grow, we need to let go of what we said to ourselves and the things we believed about ourselves. If we continue to hang on to them, they will hold us back and stifle our growth.

It is time to move on. It is time to let go of those ideas and beliefs about ourselves that are no longer valid. It is time to reach beyond those images of ourselves that hold us back. It is time for new ideas, new messages, and new growth.

As the coming year approaches, what changes do I want to make in how I see myself? What old ideas and beliefs need to be relinquished?

December 31

Go well, knowing that hard as the recovery process is, it's easier than walking the death spiral of continuing to drink. And it does get better, better than you can remember and better than you have any ability to hope for just now. —BEVERLY WILDUNG HARRISON

These words were a gift to me in early recovery. They offered hope at a time when hope seemed impossible. When I could not imagine life without alcohol, these words offered new life. They acknowledged the pain of getting sober, yet held out the promise that things would get better. Years later, I remain grateful for the ability to trust these words.

As this year draws to a close, we can journey forward trusting the wisdom and experience of other sober lesbians. Regardless of what we are feeling in the moment, we can allow their hope to empower and sustain us.

As I enter the new year, I will trust the wisdom of other sober lesbians, remembering that my future in recovery holds more than I can imagine or hope for today.

Topical Index

ABUSE: February 9, July 10
ACCEPTANCE: January 13, March 1, June 6, July 28, September 22, November 19
ACTION: February 10, May 2
ADDICTION: January 14, May 3, September 17, December 5
ADDICTIVE RELATIONSHIPS: March 25, July 26, October 2
AGE: February 11, June 7, October 3
AIDS: May 4, December 1
ALIENATION: March 3, July 27
AMBIVALENCE: May 5
AMENDS: April 3, July 14, November 16
ANGER: February 13, May 6, September 20
ANTICIPATION: January 12
APPROVAL: February 8
ASSERTIVENESS: March 8, July 29, November 13
AWARENESS: January 15, June 30, November 17
BALANCE: April 10, July 12, October 12
BELONGING: February 16, June 9, October 1
BODY IMAGE: February 7
BREAKING UP: May 7, November 14

CARRYING THE MESSAGE: April 4
CHALLENGES: May 8, October 5
CHANGE: January 16, March 10, May 28, September 27
CHARACTER DEFECTS: June 5
CHILDREN: June 2, October 7
CHOICES: February 17, March 6, August 4, September 6
CIVIL RIGHTS: February 18, October 13
COMING OUT: January 17, April 6, May 12, June 8, July 7, September 1, October 11
COMMITMENT: March 5, November 7
COMMUNICATION: January 11
COMMUNITY: February 22, June 18, October 9
COMPASSION: August 27
COMPLACENCY: January 10
CONFLICT: July 2, December 12
COURAGE: February 19, March 4, May 10, August 5
CREATIVITY: January 1, July 3
CRITICISM: February 6, April 27, October 4
DEFENSES: August 28
DENIAL: January 18, June 11, September 7, November 15
DEPRESSION: November 8
DISCOURAGEMENT: February 5
DIVERSITY: January 9
DREAMS: February 1, July 5
EMPTINESS: April 7, August 7, November 22
EXPECTATIONS: January 20, August 13, October 15
FAILURE: March 9, June 12, October 10
FAITH: January 19, April 15, July 9, September 8, November 1
FAMILY: April 9, May 9, September 9, December 15

FEAR: January 21, April 8, June 13, August 8,
October 14
FEELINGS: February 20, March 7, April 11, May 16,
August 9, September 14, December 13
FORGIVENESS: March 11, August 23,
September 10
FREEDOM: March 31, May 1, September 11
FRIENDSHIP: April 14, July 11
FUTURE: January 2, January 4, June 14
GRATITUDE: March 12, August 10, October 16
GRIEF: June 3
GROWTH: January 22, June 15, October 17
HEALING: April 12, July 15, November 18
HEALTH: April 2, September 5
HELP: May 11, October 18
HERSTORY: March 29, June 16, November 20
HIGHER POWER: March 23, May 22, July 16,
September 12, December 16
HOMOPHOBIA: January 7, April 13, May 20,
September 13
HONESTY: April 5
HOPE: April 22, November 27, December 31
HUMANNESS: June 24
HUMILITY: January 23, May 15, October 20
HUMOR: May 24, September 15
IMPOSTOR SYNDROME: March 27
INDIFFERENCE: August 25
INSANITY: August 12, September 16
INSECURITY: March 30
INTIMACY: May 18, September 18
INVENTORY: March 24, December 27
JOY: February 29, June 17, October 21
JUDGING OTHERS: January 25, July 17
LEARNING: March 17, July 13, December 17

LESBIAN IDENTITY: April 16, May 17, October 23, November 9
LETTING GO: April 17, July 18, December 30
LISTENING: May 19, November 21
LONELINESS: January 8
LOSS: April 18, July 1, August 14
LOVE: February 14, September 4
MANIPULATION: December 9
MIRACLES: December 25
MISTAKES: February 25, July 19
MONEY: March 14, October 24
NEGATIVE THINKING: January 27, August 15
NEW SKILLS: June 20, September 19
NORMALCY: December 7
OBSTACLES: November 12
OPENNESS: April 19, October 25
OPPRESSION: August 3, August 16, November 23
PAIN: March 13, April 20, July 22, November 24
PARENTS: September 21
PASSING: March 15, August 17
PAST: February 21, May 14, August 11, October 19, December 22
PATIENCE: April 21, September 2
PERFECTIONISM: January 24, March 19, July 24, November 25
PERSISTENCE: February 26, May 21, September 23, December 26
POLITICAL ACTION: June 22
POWER: January 28, May 23, August 18, November 28
POWERLESSNESS: September 24
PRAYER: April 23
PRIDE: June 1, October 31
PROCRASTINATION: November 11

PURPOSE: January 6
RATIONALIZING: April 24, October 26
REACHING OUT: August 2
REACTING: November 4
RECONCILIATION: November 26
RECOVERY: January 29, March 22, April 25, May 27, August 19, September 25
REGRETS: March 21, September 26
RELATIONSHIPS: February 27, May 25, July 20, August 26, August 31, December 14
RESENTMENT: January 5
RESPONSIBILITY: April 26, October 27, December 11
RISK: January 26, August 20, November 29
RITUALS: December 24
ROLE MODELS: August 29
SACRED: February 24, June 4, October 28
SECRETS: December 8
SECURITY: November 6
SELF-ACCEPTANCE: April 1, May 26, July 21, August 6, December 18
SELF-CARE: February 28, June 10, September 3, December 2
SELF-DISCLOSURE: March 18, August 21, December 19
SELF-DISCOVERY: April 28, November 2
SELF-ESTEEM: January 30, July 4, July 23
SELF-PITY: June 25
SELF-SABOTAGE: February 15, June 21, September 28
SELF-SACRIFICE: April 29, July 6, December 20
SELF-WORTH: March 26, September 29
SEXUALITY: March 16, May 29, August 22, October 30, December 21
SEXUALITY AND SPIRITUALITY: January 31, May 13, September 30, November 30

SHAME: July 30
SHOWING UP: June 26
SINGLENESS: February 12
SOCIETAL CHANGE: January 3, July 25, December 3
SOLITUDE: March 28
SPIRITUALITY: March 2, June 23, August 24, October 6
SPLITTING OFF: November 5
STARTING OVER: February 2
STONEWALL: June 28
STRENGTH: June 27
SUFFERING: November 3
SURRENDER: December 6
SURVIVAL: April 30, July 8, December 23
TOLERANCE: June 19, October 22
TRUST: February 4
TRUTH: August 30
TURNING IT OVER: March 20, October 29
UNIQUENESS: August 1, November 10
UNITY: December 29
VALUES: May 30, October 8
VISIBILITY: June 29, December 28
VULNERABILITY: July 31
WHOLENESS: December 4
WORK: February 3
WORRY: February 23, May 31, December 10

ABOUT THE AUTHOR

ELEANOR C. NEALY is an ordained clergyperson with the Universal Fellowship of Metropolitan Community Churches (UFMCC). She is currently employed as the director of Project Connect, the alcohol and other drug prevention and intervention program of the Lesbian and Gay Community Services Center of New York City.